FROM REDLINING TO REINVESTMENT

Conflicts in Urban and Regional Development, a series edited by John R. Logan and Todd Swanstrom

FROM REDLINING TO REINVESTMENT

Community Responses to Urban Disinvestment

edited by Gregory D. Squires

TEMPLE UNIVERSITY PRESS
Philadelphia

Temple University Press, Philadelphia 19122
Copyright © 1992 by Temple University. All rights reserved
Published 1992
Printed in the United States of America

Library of Congress Cataloging-in-Publication Data

From redlining to reinvestment : community responses to urban
disinvestment / edited by Gregory D. Squires.
    p. cm. — (Conflicts in urban and regional development)
    Includes bibliographical references and index.
    ISBN 0-87722-984-8
    1. Bank loans—United States. 2. Discrimination in mortgage
loans—United States. 3. Community development—United States.
I. Squires, Gregory D. II. Series.
HG1642.U5F76 1992
332.1'753'0973—dc20   92-7421

Contents

COMMUNITY REINVESTMENT
IS GOOD FOR CITIES, GOOD
FOR LENDERS

REINVESTMENT and the federal Community Reinvestment Act are good for the residents of our cities and for businesses operating in cities, including lenders. It is true that some of my colleagues have been brought to the table kicking and screaming, and still others have not yet decided to participate. Yet a growing and significant number of lenders today see both the future of their cities and the self interest of their institutions as inseparable from increased community reinvestment.

This book offers several chapters in what is a most important story. While there are important distinctions in the precise manner with which Community Reinvestment Act initiatives have been launched and carried out in different communities, this book describes what has emerged as a vital national social movement; and while community reinvestment is still evolving and continuously being reinvented in many creative ways, this book unlocks many of the keys to successful reinvestment in urban America.

No single institution or industry can solve the many problems facing most depressed neighborhoods in our cities, but lenders obviously can play an important role. More are doing so everyday. Despite the persistence of many social problems, most notably the heightened racial tensions in cities, there is reason for hope. Growing awareness among lenders of opportunities and responsibilities for community reinvestment as well as lenders' successful collaboration with neighborhood organizations around the country constitute major reasons for that hope.

My bank, Norwest Bank, has learned much and profited substantially from its working relationships with community groups around the country. We are still learning. This book offers many lessons for my industry, community organizations and constituencies, their elected officials, scholars and students of the city, and anyone concerned with the future of our metropolitan areas. Perhaps the most important lesson it offers is that community reinvestment is good for our cities, for all institutions operating in cities, and for everyone who lives, works, and plays in our nation's cities.

EDWARD MCDONALD
Community Relations Officer
Norwest Bank, Wisconsin N.A.

FROM REDLINING TO REINVESTMENT

COMMUNITY REINVESTMENT: AN EMERGING SOCIAL MOVEMENT

If a neighborhood is to retain stability, it is necessary that properties shall continue to be occupied by the same social and racial classes.
    Federal Housing Administration, 1938 (Berry 1979: 9)

Well, I'm not a statistician, but when blacks are getting their loan applications rejected twice as often as whites and, in some cities, it's three and four times as often, I conclude that discrimination is part of the problem.
    Sen. Alan J. Dixon, Chairman of the U.S. Senate
    Subcommittee on Consumer and Regulatory Affairs
    (Subcommittee on Consumer and Regulatory Affairs 1990: 1)

Community based organizations helped us understand how to market ourselves better and understand the market and programs that might have to be developed to meet the needs in the inner city.
    Timothy Elverman, Vice President of Government Relations,
    Bank One, Milwaukee, Wisconsin (Weier 1990)

A COMMUNITY REINVESTMENT SOCIAL MOVEMENT has emerged in urban America in recent years. After watching their neighborhoods deteriorate from the gradual but persistent loss of public services and private goods, angry residents in cities throughout the United States have joined together in community organizations to fight back. Often with the assistance of local public officials, sympathetic academics, reporters, and other community activists, successful campaigns have been launched by a variety of individuals to save their neighborhoods. The problem, in a word, is redlining. The solution is reinvestment.

While there is no explicit starting point for this social movement, it has its roots in the civil rights movement of the 1950s, the antipoverty campaigns of the 1960s, and a range of populist struggles of the 1970s and 1980s. Specific targets have included declining public services ranging from education and training to garbage collection and road repairs. Discriminatory tax assessment policies have been the focus of some efforts. Unavailability of automobile and homeowners' insurance have generated organizing drives (Boyte, Booth, and Max 1986; Perry 1987). The most persistent redlining battle has been over the lending policies and practices of banks and savings and loans, with the most volatile confrontations being over the racially discriminatory consequences of mortgage lending behavior. The most successful campaigns have been those in which community organizations have targeted lending institutions. According to one count, approximately $18 billion in urban reinvestment commitments have been negotiated with lenders by over three hundred groups in more than seventy cities throughout the United States (Bradford 1992).

Redlining is a process by which goods or services are made unavailable, or are available only on less than favorable terms, to people because of where they live regardless of their relevant objective characteristics. Given the essential nature of financial services for home ownership, business development, and neighborhood revitalization generally, disinvestment by financial institutions has been particularly problematic. When lenders refuse to lend or do so only on more stringent terms in designated neighborhoods, regardless of the expected yield or loss in those areas, the personal costs to those families become social costs to the broader metropolitan area as entire neighborhoods are threatened. These problems are compounded when the principal issue is race.

This book tells the stories of residents who have successfully begun turning the process of disinvestment into a process of reinvestment. Organizing drives in six cities and one statewide effort are examined by those most intricately involved in these campaigns and in key national initiatives to counter redlining by lending institutions. Each case reviews the history of the problems within the respective communities, the central actors who made the case for and negotiated the terms of local reinvestment agreements, the tools they used (e.g. statutes and court cases, social science research, media reports, civil disobedience), the specific elements of the agreements, and the impact of the organizing drive and subsequent lending commitments.

There are important commonalities among these reinvestment campaigns as well as critically unique features in each one. Much has been learned in terms of the strengths and weaknesses of each campaign, offering valuable lessons for future reinvestment initiatives. The implications for the future of this social movement are discussed in the concluding chapter. However, in order to comprehend the social, political, and economic context framing current efforts, and no doubt shaping future developments as well, it is important to understand the history of racially discriminatory lending practices; a history that continues into the present.

MORTGAGE LENDING AND RACE

Race is a factor that has long been explicitly identified and overtly utilized in all aspects of the housing industry and in public sector regulation of that industry. While current local, state, and federal statutes today require equal opportunity in virtually all aspects of housing, the post– World War II development of U.S. cities has been directly shaped by public policies (in conformance with private practice) that were intentionally racially discriminatory. The defining outcomes for metropolitan areas have been booming, predominantly white suburbs and declining, increasingly minority central cities. These patterns are not the outcomes of natural ecological processes or the results of neutral market forces. Rather, they are the outcomes of choices that leaders in private industry and government have made consciously. People do adapt to their environments and market forces are quite real, but the decisions of individuals and the direction of market forces are shaped by policy decisions made by public and private sector actors.

Two developments in the area of home ownership, both dealing with the financing of housing, led the way to both the expansion of home ownership by American families and the racially exclusionary practices and housing patterns. One was the development of the long-term mortgage and the other was the creation of federal insurance for mortgage loans. The first made housing more affordable to a much broader segment of the population. The second reduced the risk for lenders, thus

Gregory D. Squires

providing a major incentive to make home loans available which, in turn, stimulated housing construction. At each step, racial exclusion was a given.

The long-term, self-amortizing mortgage with uniform payments spread over the life of the loan was developed by the Home Owners Loan Corporation (HOLC), a federal agency created in 1933 with the intention of serving various urban housing and economic needs that had been exacerbated by the Great Depression (Jackson 1985: 195–203). While HOLC did provide financial assistance that enabled many city residents to retain or purchase homes, its appraisal practices may well have been the beginning of redlining in the United States (Jackson 1985: 197). The HOLC appraisers collected detailed information on urban real estate and developed a rating system that undervalued dense, mixed, or aging neighborhoods. Four categories were identified and titled First, Second, Third, and Fourth with corresponding code letters of A, B, C, and D and color-coded green, blue, yellow, and red. Racial homogeneity was explicitly identified as a criterion for evaluating properties; but it was clear that not all homogeneous neighborhoods were equally valued. The appraisal of one St. Louis County neighborhood concluded that houses had "little or no value today, having suffered a tremendous decline in values due to the colored element now controlling the district" (Jackson 1985: 200).

At the time, HOLC appraisers simply reflected what their counterparts in the real estate industry were doing. From 1924 until 1950 the National Association of Real Estate Boards included the following statement in its national code of ethics, "A realtor should never be instrumental in introducing into a neighborhood a character of property or occupancy, members of any race or nationality, or any individual whose presence will clearly be detrimental to property values in the neighborhood" (Judd 1984: 284).

This is one area of public life where sociology exercised significant impact on policy. University of Chicago sociologist Ernest Burgess argued in 1928 that "the entrance of the Negro into a white community results in an immediate apparent depreciation in land values. . . . At present the fact stands out that Negro occupancy is an unmistakable symptom of depreciation—an indication that the value of property has fallen to their economic level as well as an aid to depreciation in its last stages" (Burgess 1928: 113–114). Burgess' university colleague, Homer

4

Hoyt, exercised even more influence through his work with realtors and government housing agencies. In a 1933 report for the Federal Housing Administration (FHA), Hoyt ranked fifteen racial and ethnic groups in terms of the impact of their presence on property values. Those having the most favorable impact were English, Germans, Scotch, Irish, and Scandinavians. Those having the most detrimental impact were Negroes and Mexicans (Hoyt 1933: 315–16). Appraisal, underwriting, lending, real estate sales, and other housing industry practices have long reflected these beliefs. To this day black and Hispanic homeseekers experience discrimination in over half their encounters with real estate sales and rental agents (Turner, Struyk, and Yinger 1991: vi, 37).

The second major innovation in home financing was mortgage insurance provided by the federal government—FHA since 1934 and the Veterans Administration (VA) since 1944. The FHA was created in 1934 by the National Housing Act to stimulate private sector housing construction as part of a broader effort to reduce unemployment (Jackson 1985: 203–18; Hays 1985: 79–89). By insuring mortgages, the federal government eliminated much of the risk of such lending. More buyers could enter the market and more money would be available for housing construction. Continuing the traditional practices of HOLC, racial composition was a major concern of FHA underwriters. In its 1938 *Underwriting Manual* the FHA advised:

> Areas surrounding a location are to be investigated to determine whether incompatible racial and social groups are present, for the purpose of making a prediction regarding the probability of the location being invaded by such groups. If a neighborhood is to retain stability, it is necessary that properties shall continue to be occupied by the same social and racial classes. A change in social or racial occupancy generally contributes to instability and a decline in values.
>
> (U.S. Federal Housing Administration 1938: par. 937)

Consistent with this philosophy, the FHA also endorsed racially restrictive covenants that prohibited property from being sold to racial minorities, until the U.S. Supreme Court declared in the 1948 cases of *Shelly v. Kraemer* that federal courts were prohibited from enforcing such covenants.

The FHA has played a major role in stimulating home ownership in the United States. From its inception until 1959 the FHA financed 60 percent of home purchases. From the mid-1940s through the mid-1950s less than 2 percent of FHA-insured loans went to blacks. The vast majority of FHA as well as VA loans went to white suburbanites during the early postwar years. The explicit racially discriminatory language was removed from FHA underwriting manuals by the 1960s but the influence lingered on as the training manuals of private appraisal associations continued to include such language through the 1970s (Lief and Goering 1987: 228–31). As late as the 1977 edition of *The Appraisal of Real Estate*, published by the American Institute of Real Estate Appraisers which is a division of the National Association of Realtors, the institute cited one of the factors to be included for neighborhood analysis as "prevailing nationalities, infiltration." Training materials used by the institute included the following example in its illustration of neighborhood analysis: "The neighborhood is entirely Caucasian. It appears that there is no adverse effect by minority groups" (Greene 1980: 9).

The FHA provided major public subsidies for various sectors of the private housing industry. During its first three decades it virtually required racial segregation in its underwriting practices, and then only serviced white neighborhoods, particularly those in the suburbs. The agency could have operated according to different standards. As Columbia University urban planning professor Charles Abrams stated, the FHA could have made other choices: "A government offering such bounty to builders and lenders could have required compliance with a non-discrimination policy. . . . Instead, FHA adopted a racial policy that could well have been culled from the Nuremberg laws. From its inception FHA set itself up as the protector of the all white neighborhood" (Jackson 1985: 214).

In the mid-1960s the FHA did a sudden turnabout and began making insured mortgages available in the nation's central cities. The manner in which these services were provided, however, made fair housing an even more distant dream. Unscrupulous real estate sales representatives and developers coaxed unwary first-time (often minority) home-buyers to purchase homes they could not afford to maintain, frequently resulting in foreclosure of the loan and loss of the home. With the mortgage insured and closing costs paid up-front, the financial interests of real estate sales representatives and lenders were protected. Indeed many profited handsomely by turning properties over several times, with the only losers being the families who lost their savings through unwise housing investments. Coupled with blockbusting and other scare tactics, the FHA became a central cog in a real estate machine that was quickly turning white city neighborhoods into black neighborhoods and expediting white flight to the suburbs (Bradford 1984, 1979; Jackson 1985; Helper 1969; Pearce 1983).

These two housing innovations—the long-term mortgage and federal mortgage insurance—reflected and reinforced other trends in the housing industry and government policy that nurtured the uneven development of metropolitan areas. Home ownership has long been subsidized by the federal tax deductions associated with mortgage interest and property tax payments. Federally subsidized construction of the nation's highway system facilitated the flight to the suburbs. As indicated above, blockbusting along with more subtle forms of racial steering by real estate agents has nurtured the segregated nature of the nation's housing patterns. Racially discriminatory appraisal practices and redlining by property insurers reinforce the effects of redlining by lending institutions. A variety of institutional actors have contributed to the decline of central cities, the rise of the suburbs, and the racial exclusivity of both in America. Lending institutions, and governmental regulatory agencies that oversee lending practices, have clearly been at the center of these developments.

FROM DUAL HOUSING TO FAIR HOUSING AND COMMUNITY REINVESTMENT

Residents of the nation's cities have not been blind to these processes. A racially discriminatory dual housing market has been entrenched in the United States, but efforts have also been made in recent years to dismantle it, and some with success. During the 1960s the federal government took several initiatives to alter its posture from one of a "protector of the all white neighborhood" to, at least according to the letter of the law, an advocate of fair housing. A number of forces accounted for this reversal. The civil rights movement itself brought fair housing issues to the forefront throughout the decade (Metcalf 1988; Weisbrot 1990). Antipoverty movements, the officially declared war on poverty, and Lyndon Johnson's Great Society programs provided further reinforcement (Piven

and Cloward 1977). Moreover, the beginnings of the community reinvestment movement by residents who wanted to combat the evident redlining of their communities made lending a central urban development
and civil rights issue (National Commission on Neighborhoods 1979).

Several significant legislative changes occurred at the federal level
beginning in the 1960s that directly pertained to housing and housing
finance (Dane 1989; M. Sloane 1983: 137–140; Lief and Goering 1987:
231–39). In the 1960s and 1970s a patchwork quilt of federal rules and
regulations was enacted. Under these provisions different agencies super-
vise different housing actors with at least four federal financial regulatory
agencies directly overseeing distinct groups of lenders. Types of discriminatory behavior that are prohibited and groups that are protected vary.
Some rules require disclosure of information only, while others require
provision of specific services, and still others simply ban certain activities. Collectively, however, these rules have significantly altered the
legal environment and practices of those providing housing and housing
related services.

The first significant legal step occurred in 1962 when President
John F. Kennedy signed Executive Order no. 11063 into law prohibiting
discrimination in all housing that received federal financial support.
Congress strengthened this prohibition in Title VI of the Civil Rights
Act of 1964, which banned discrimination in any program or activity
receiving federal financial assistance, including public housing.

The landmark Federal Fair Housing Act, Title VIII of the Civil
Rights Act of 1968, provided sweeping prohibitions against discrimination on the basis of race, color, religion, sex, national origin, or (with
the 1988 amendments to the act) age, disability, and presence of children in the family. Discrimination is prohibited in the sale or rental of
housing units, terms and conditions of housing transactions, advertising,
and other practices related to the availability of housing. Specifically
prohibited practices include racial steering, blockbusting, and "discrimination in the financing of housing." Subsequent court decisions inter-
preting the Federal Fair Housing Act have added discriminatory appraisal
practices (*United States v. American Institute of Real Estate Appraisers*),
discriminatory land use and zoning practices (*United States v. City of
Parma*), and refusal to make home loans available or to make them available on terms less favorable than in other areas due to the racial compo-

sition of the neighborhood (*Laufman v. Oakley Building and Loan Company*) to the list of prohibited acts (Gelber, Hopp, and Canan 1983).

Other developments included the promulgation by the U.S. Department of Housing and Urban Development (HUD) in 1972 of regulations requiring affirmative fair housing marketing in HUD housing projects. The Equal Credit Opportunity Act as enacted and subsequently amended in the 1970s prohibits lending discrimination, including mortgage lending, on the basis of race, color, national origin, age, sex, marital status, religion, receipt of public assistance, or exercise of rights granted by consumer protection statutes.

Each of these executive orders, statutes, and court decisions embody limitations in coverage and enforcement. Yet they have yielded many benefits, financial and others, for immediate plaintiffs and they have altered the direction of public policy. Most important, the legal initiatives beginning in the 1960s began the process by which the letter of federal law shifted from being a mechanism for enforcing racial segregation to being a tool available for use by advocates of fair housing.

The legal linchpin of the community reinvestment movement is represented by two subsequent federal laws; the Home Mortgage Disclosure Act of 1975 (HMDA) and the Community Reinvestment Act of 1977 (CRA). In combination, these two statutes have provided teeth that were missing in the federal government's enforcement of its own rules pertaining to discriminatory mortgage lending practices.

In fact, it was the failure of the four major federal financial regulatory agencies to enforce nondiscriminatory lending requirements that led to HMDA and CRA. The fair housing law states that "all executive departments and agencies shall administer their programs and activities relating to housing and urban development in a manner affirmatively to further the purposes of this title" (G. Sloane 1983: 86). Such agencies include the federal financial regulatory agencies that oversee the practices of federally chartered banks and savings and loans; the Federal Reserve Board (FRB), the Federal Home Loan Bank Board (FHLBB)—now the Office of Thrift Supervision (OTS)—the Federal Deposit Insurance Corporation (FDIC), and the Office of the Comptroller of the Currency (OCC). Frustrated with the failure of these agencies to meet their fair lending obligations, in 1971 the Center for National Policy Review was retained by eleven civil rights organizations, including the National Association for the Advancement of Colored People (NAACP) and the National Urban League, to sue these four agencies to develop regulations and enforce the fair housing act as it pertained to their responsibilities.

A central concern was the lack of any systematic statistical data on racial lending patterns. Following a subsequent lawsuit in 1976, settlements were reached resulting in three federal agencies (OCC, FHLBB, and FDIC) agreeing to maintain records on the race of mortgage loan applicants. At the same time, the Metropolitan Area Housing Alliance in Chicago requested that the Federal Home Loan Bank Board office in that city provide data on the geographic location of loans made in Chicago by each bank under its jurisdiction to determine whether or not racially discriminatory lending practices were occurring, as the group suspected. The board agreed to provide aggregate data on the zip code location of selected loans made between 1971 and 1973 by these lenders. Subsequent analyses of that information revealed that indeed racially discriminatory mortgage lending was practiced in Chicago (Bradford, Rubinowitz, and Grothaus 1975; Listokin and Casey 1980; G. Sloane 1983; Feins and Grothaus 1975).

The value of nationwide disclosure data become apparent. The National People's Action (NPA), a nationwide coalition of community organizations, and the National Training and Information Center (NTIC), a technical assistance arm of NPA, worked with Sen. William Proxmire (D-Wis.) in writing and securing passage of HMDA. (The NPA and NTIC—both headed by Gale Cincotta—were instrumental in passage of the CRA two years later.)

The HMDA has required federally regulated banks, savings and loans, and credit unions to report annually the number and dollar amount of mortgage loans they make by census tract in all metropolitan areas since the law took effect. Data are broken out into several loan categories including conventional, FHA/Farmer's Home Administration (FMHA)/VA, home improvement, multifamily dwelling, and nonoccupant loans. Reporting institutions are required to make their HMDA reports available to the general public at the cost of reasonable duplicating fees. In each metropolitan area, a central depository is identified where reports for all institutions in that area are available. Beginning in 1990, as part of the savings and loan bailout plan (the Financial Institution Reform, Recovery, and Enforcement Act [FIRREA]) HMDA also applied to mortgage bankers who account for an increasing share of mortgage loans exceeding one quarter of the market in many cities. In addition, FIRREA requires all reporting institutions to disclose the race, gender, and income of all mortgage loan applicants along with the final disposition of each application. These data have proven useful to community groups around the country in tracking the flow of mortgage money by neighborhood throughout metropolitan areas. In conjunction with census data, much has been learned about the socioeconomic factors that are associated with the distribution of mortgage money. A major limitation of HMDA, particularly prior to the 1990 amendments, was the absence of any information on demand or the decisionmaking process within institutions that could explain reasons for investment patterns (Shlay 1989). In conjunction with the CRA, however, the information available through HMDA has proven useful in generating reinvestment activity.

The Community Reinvestment Act states that federally regulated financial institutions "have a continuing and affirmative obligation to help meet the credit needs of the local communities in which they are chartered . . . consistent with safe and sound operation of such institutions." Such institutions are required to prepare a CRA statement in which they delineate their service areas (a map explicitly identifying the service area must be included), identify the credit needs of those communities including low and moderate income areas, and indicate how they are meeting those needs. They must also maintain and make available to the public a file containing any comments received from the public regarding their CRA performance. Federal regulatory agencies are obligated to assess the CRA record of lenders under their jurisdiction and to take that record into account in evaluating applications from those lenders for a charter for a national bank or savings and loan association, deposit insurance, establishment of a branch office, merger or acquisition involving a regulated financial institution, or other related business transactions.

In fact, federal regulatory agencies have rarely initiated any action on the basis of a CRA evaluation. In February of 1989, the Federal Reserve Board denied an application from Continental Bank of Chicago for an acquisition because of an inadequate CRA rating; the first time it had made an adverse decision because of CRA (Guskind 1989). The CRA does permit third parties to file challenges to applications based on poor CRA performance, and challenges can and do delay consideration of applications. Delays in approving applications can be quite costly. That cost provides community groups leverage in negotiating with lenders. Rather than engage in extended litigation regarding the merits of CRA challenges, lenders generally enter into negotiations with the organization filing the challenge in order to have them withdraw that challenge, thus eliminating expensive delays. Armed with investment patterns identified from HMDA data and the leverage of a CRA challenge, community groups have successfully negotiated reinvestment agreements with lenders: As indicated above $18 billion in reinvestment commitments have been negotiated in over 70 cities around the country.

The CRA regulations have been strengthened in recent years. For instance, FIRREA requires regulators to make public the CRA ratings that they assign to each institution. Evaluations begun after July 1, 1990, culminate in each institution being rated in one of the four following categories: (1) outstanding record of meeting community credit needs, (2) satisfactory record of meeting community credit needs, (3) needs to improve record in meeting community credit needs, and (4) substantial noncompliance in meeting community credit needs. In conducting the review regulators assess performance in five different areas: (1) ascertainment of community needs, (2) marketing and types of credit extended, (3) geographic distribution and record of opening and closing offices, (4) discrimination and other illegal credit practices, and (5) community development.

Specific assessment factors are identified within each of these categories. For example, in the area of discrimination regulators look for the presence of practices that discourage applications for loans, including whether or not advertisements are disseminated throughout all parts of the service area, whether or not training programs have been implemented to prevent illegal discouragement or prescreening of applicants, and adequacy of reporting and reviewing mechanisms to assure non-discrimination (Office of Thrift Supervision 1990). At least preliminary steps have been taken to encourage a more thorough CRA compliance review by federal financial regulatory agencies.

Despite these actions, racial discrimination and redlining have not disappeared from the nation's mortgage lending markets. Throughout the 1980s and into the early 1990s blacks continued to be rejected for mortgages twice as often as whites even among applicants with comparable incomes (Dedman 1989; Nash 1990; Canner 1991). Recent studies of mortgage lending in several cities have documented the persistence of racial disparities even after taking into consideration family income and wealth, age and condition of housing, residential turnover, and other factors related to the credit worthiness of residents and security of property—factors that affect the risk presented by mortgage applicants and presumably serve as the basis for underwriting decisions. (The academic research supporting this basic finding is substantial. The following items and several citations in their references are illustrative: Shlay 1989; Bradbury, Case, and Dunham 1989; Squires and Velez 1987.) A limitation of many studies is their focus on the volume of lending by geographic area rather than on the decision to lend, due to the scarcity of information on demand for mortgage loans. The individual application data that HMDA began requiring in 1990 is only beginning to be analyzed. Those studies where measures of demand are included, however, yield similar findings: incorporating demand as measured by mortgage applications (Schafer and Ladd 1981), number of housing units for sale (Pol, Guy, and Bush 1982), or proportions of applications received and loans granted to home sales (Taggart and Smith 1981) does not eliminate the effects of race.

Researchers with the Federal Reserve Board and several lenders note that many studies documenting the persistence of racial discrimination fail to take into consideration factors such as the credit records and indebtedness of individual applicants, and conditions of specific properties (Canner 1982; Canner and Smith 1991; Galster 1991). Yet anecdotal testing evidence demonstrates that blacks and whites with identical qualifications are treated differently. For example, blacks are often steered to FHA loans and mortgage banking corporations where whites are offered conventional financing. In other cases blacks are told the process of qualifying for a loan is quite lengthy while whites are advised it will take just a few minutes. Where applicants do not quite meet standard debt to equity ratios, whites are often advised on how they can overcome such deficiencies in order to present an approvable application whereas blacks receive no such counseling and are simply rejected. In some cases blacks are told they do not qualify because their ratios are just over the limit whereas whites with similar debt to equity ratios are approved (Center for Community Change 1989). While the severity of racial disparity varies, a consistent finding across the vast majority of research on mortgage lending and race demonstrates significant racial disparities in access to loans; disparities that do not disappear when relevant socioeconomic factors are taken into consideration.

There are several reasons for the persistence of these racial disparities. First, a decision to accept or reject a mortgage application is only one link in a chain of events that precedes a formal loan application as part of the home buying process. Several other institutional actors are involved before a mortgage application is even submitted. As indicated above, real estate sales agents continue to practice racial steering, sometimes discouraging families from buying a home altogether. Discriminatory appraisal practices further limit the ability of minority homeseekers to buy. Where the appraisal is below the agreed-upon purchase price, a loan application may be denied or the size of the down payment may increase to the point where the home becomes unaffordable. Even if the deal still goes through, discriminatory appraisals can reduce the value of the home which depresses the equity the buyers subsequently accumulate, thus limiting what they could pay for their next home if they chose to move. Redlining by property insurers also restricts the ability to buy. Insurance is essential if a credible mortgage loan application is to be made. If insurance is available, but at a higher cost due to discrimination, home ownership itself becomes more costly and, in some cases, unaffordable. A history of discrimination by any or all of these institutions may discourage some potential homeowners from even considering such a purchase. Whether that discouragement is nurtured by lending institutions or other actors, the result is to reduce the number of mortgage applications (Schafer and Ladd 1981).

A second factor is a dilution of law enforcement efforts in the past decade in civil rights generally and fair housing in particular. While the Federal Fair Housing Act was enacted in 1968, interpretive regulations were not proposed by HUD, the agency designated to enforce the law, until 1980. In 1981 the Reagan administration withdrew those regulations and it was not until after the law was amended in 1988 that HUD formally issued regulations. During these years, HUD relied increasingly on voluntary compliance and informal negotiations in responding to fair housing complaints. Rather than systematically monitoring sales, rental, financing, and other aspects of housing, and utilizing the sanctions that are available, voluntary compliance has been the focus of HUD enforcement efforts in recent years. At the same time, fair housing litigation by the Civil Rights Division of the U.S. Department of Justice has been curtailed (M. Sloane 1983: 140–41; Lief and Goering 1987: 24–57). In some cases, the Justice Department has officially intervened to block efforts to establish and maintain integrated housing. For example, in the controversy over the use of racial quotas to preserve the integrated character of Starrett City, a federally assisted housing project in New York, the Justice Department entered on behalf of the plaintiffs who contended that the quota violated the Federal Fair Housing Act on the grounds that it constituted a denial of housing opportunity because of race. The case, which was initially filed in 1979, was settled shortly after the Justice Department entered in 1984 (Yinger 1986: 304–5).

Inactivity appears to characterize fair lending enforcement by federal financial regulatory agencies (Dane 1989). Between January 1987 and August 1989 the OCC, which regulates national banks, received 37,000 written consumer complaints, 16 of which alleged racial discrimination. Subsequent investigation by OCC found no violations of law. Similarly, the Federal Deposit Insurance Corporation, which regulates state chartered banks, found only five acts of unlawful discrimination in mortgage lending over a three-year span in the late 1980s (Subcommittee on Consumer and Regulatory Affairs 1990: 40, 49). "Incredible" is the word that Senator Alan J. Dixon, Chairman of the Senate Subcommittee on Consumer and Regulatory Affairs, used to describe this record when it was presented at a 1989 subcommittee hearing on discrimination in mortgage lending. Dixon concluded, "I think it to be somewhat incredible that the substance of the testimony is mostly that you haven't found any violations when the evidence is pretty clear out there that a lot of violations have to be taking place. . . . We have incredible testimony. . . . I'm not trying to pick on anybody, but I want to suggest that I find it pretty close to remarkable that we never find any violations (Subcommittee on Consumer and Regulatory Affairs 1990: 118).

Throughout the 1980s the push for integration and equal opportunity was resisted at the federal level. That resistance was fueled by a rekindling of a culture-of-poverty ideology that once again blamed the victim. The federal government was armed with a justification for its reduction in civil rights law enforcement and other social programs by an ideological commitment to the belief that poverty, and particularly that which pervaded minority communities throughout urban America, resulted from faulty values within the home and within the poor themselves, and that welfare and equal opportunity agencies served only to exacerbate these problems by nurturing dependence on government bureaucracies (Orfield 1988).

Gregory D. Squires

Among the problems that are inadequately addressed by this law enforcement posture is redlining. The Federal Fair Housing Act, Equal Credit Opportunity Act, the Community Reinvestment Act and other statutes provide various federal agencies with tools to combat redlining. Failure to take an aggressive stand on civil rights law enforcement certainly contributed to the perpetuation of redlining problems. To the extent that these legal remedies have been utilized, it has been primarily at the initiative of fair housing and other community organizations. One consequence is the uneven enforcement of these statutes.

A third factor contributing to racial disparities in mortgage lending is the widespread use of underwriting rules that have an adverse racial effect, even though no racial animosity may be intended and no violation of law may occur. The nexus between some of these practices and objective characteristics of credit worthiness are questionable, however, raising questions about the intent as well as effect of their utilization. Among the standards that rule out a higher proportion of minority than white applicants are the maximum age and minimum value limits of property. Since racial minorities are concentrated in older neighborhoods and in lower valued homes (in part because of discriminatory appraisal and steering practices) they are more likely to be rejected, or required to meet more stringent loan terms (e.g., higher points, mortgage insurance requirements, larger down payments, higher interest rates) (Greene 1980: 11). For example, in Milwaukee neighborhoods where minorities account for more than one-quarter of the population, almost half of the housing stock was built prior to 1940 compared to less than 35 percent of the housing units where the minority population is smaller. And while 21 percent of single-family dwellings in Milwaukee were valued at $35,000 or less in 1988, in those same minority communities over 78 percent of the homes were valued at that level (Squires, Velez, and Taeuber 1991). In addition, since most mortgages originated by lenders today are sold in the secondary mortgage market (primarily to federally related agencies including the Federal Home Loan Mortgage Corporation [FHLMC], the Federal National Mortgage Association [FNMA], and the Government National Mortgage Association [GNMA], the underwriting rules of these institutional investors, often more stringent than those of the originating institution, frequently restrict mortgage lending in minority communities. Similarly, lenders frequently require private mortgage insurance and private mortgage insurance firms also often utilize underwriting criteria that adversely affect applications from minority communities. The fact that minorities in general are less likely to have an established relationship with a lending institution, in part because of the relatively small number of businesses and other organizations owned or operated by minorities, also contributes to this pattern (ICF Incorporated 1991).

Even when the underwriting rules themselves are racially neutral, subjective biases can enter into the process by which applications are reviewed, with racially exclusionary effects. For example, lenders may require credit checks more frequently from minority applicants than from similarly situated nonminorities. Where an applicant has substantial cash for a down payment, questions are more likely to be raised about the possibility of the funds being derived from an unlawful source. Moreover, if the application contains information suggesting potential problems (e.g. higher debt to income ratio than is normally required), lenders are more likely to work with nonminority applicants to determine whether or not there are compensating factors that would qualify the loan (Peterson 1990). Absence of minority staff in lending institutions exacerbates these problems (ICF Incorporated 1991).

Finally, perpetuation of cultural stereotypes along with old fashioned intentional racial discrimination continues to exist within financial institutions, though no doubt on a lesser scale than in previous decades. In a series of focus group interviews with lenders in twelve cities across the nation lenders were asked what distinguished black and white neighborhoods. Several pointed to "pride of ownership" and "homeowner mentality" (ICF Incorporated 1991). The sales manager of a major property insurer recently advised several agents: "you write too many blacks. You gotta sell good, solid premium paying white people. . . . They own their homes, the white works. . . . Those are the people you want to go and see. Very honestly, black people will buy anything that looks good right now, but when it comes to pay for it next time, you're not going to get your money out of them" (*NAACP v. American Family Insurance* 1990).

UNCERTAIN PROGRESS: THE STRUGGLE CONTINUES

If there has been a step backward for every two taken forward, there has been significant, measurable progress toward combating redlining in recent years. The clearest victories have been the dramatic reversals in the

Gregory D. Squires

letter of the law, most concretely manifested in the lending agreements
that were negotiated. The HMDA and CRA were particularly valuable tools
in these efforts, but other resources have been nurtured and utilized, as
circumstances dictated. The following chapters tell the vital stories of
the community reinvestment movement in the United States.

In Boston, a $400 million reinvestment commitment by the city's
major banks was triggered by a study conducted for the Federal Reserve
Bank documenting substantial racial disparities in mortgage lending patterns during the mid-1980s. Accompanying this study was an effective
organizing campaign directed by a coalition of several community groups
with the aggressive support of a mayor committed to "share the prosperity" of that city's growth in the 1980s. This story is told in the next
chapter by University of Massachusetts economist James T. Campen,
who has closely monitored lending activities in that city.

In Chicago, organizers have experience campaigning around redlining issues that dates to the early 1970s. In 1984 a Chicago Reinvestment Alliance negotiated $173 million over five years in agreements
with three major banks for a range of housing and business loans. In
1988 and 1989 these agreements were extended by $200 million over an
additional five-year period. Two Chicago-based organizations, the National Training and Information Center and the Woodstock Institute,
have participated in over one hundred agreements nationwide and assisted in these efforts. Jean Pogge, vice president and manager of development of South Shore Bank in Chicago and former president of Woodstock, describes how this process evolved in Chicago.

The Pittsburgh Community Reinvestment Group (PCRG), a coalition of community development groups, negotiated a five year $109 mil-
lion lending agreement with one of that city's major banks. With support
from the city government, PCRG has negotiated additional agreements
with other lenders. John T. Metzger, who served as coordinator of the
PCRG, recounts and assesses the Pittsburgh experience.

"The Color of Money," a Pulitzer Prize–winning series of stories
written by Bill Dedman in 1988 when he was with the *Atlanta Journal/
Constitution*, was a major factor in negotiating support for Atlanta's $65
million reinvestment program. Stan Fitterman and Lynn Brazen of the
Atlanta Community Reinvestment Coalition, who helped prepare the
newspaper stories, join with Georgia Tech planning professor Larry Keating, who has been active in housing issues, to describe the events leading
up to those negotiations and the impact they have had on Atlanta.

Newspaper reports also played a key role in Detroit in securing the nation's largest group of CRA agreements, totalling $2.9 billion. Aggressive enforcement of a state community reinvestment act by the commissioner of the Michigan Financial Institutions Bureau and effective negotiations conducted by a coalition of housing groups, civil rights organizations, churches, labor unions, business leaders, and others were also key ingredients in the Detroit effort. *Detroit Free Press* reporter David Everett led that paper's investigation and relates the Detroit reinvestment experience.

A network of community organizations in Milwaukee negotiated a total of $50 million in five-year agreements with two area lenders in 1986 and 1989. Encouraged by these agreements and national press on continuing problems in that city, the mayor of Milwaukee and the governor of Wisconsin created a Fair Lending Action Committee in Milwaukee consisting of lenders, community organizers, public officials, and others to stimulate a broader attack on redlining. In turn, more lenders and neighborhood groups have collaborated voluntarily (again with the stick of CRA always in the background) on lending programs. Mike Glabere, one of the organizers of the campaigns leading up to the 1986 and 1989 agreements, examines these ongoing developments.

A series of statewide campaigns in California culminated in several reinvestment agreements, including a ten-year $8 billion commitment by three major banks. Supportive elected officials working closely with many community organizations have negotiated wide-ranging programs with lenders around the state. David Paul Rosen, who assisted in many of these negotiations, analyzes this statewide effort.

In the final chapter Gale Cincotta and Calvin Bradford, two central figures in the national efforts to obtain passage of HMDA and CRA and to organize community reinvestment movements, discuss the implications of these efforts for future reinvestment activities. Specific recommendations are suggested for future research and policy to build upon the victories of prior community reinvestment campaigns.

Several lessons from early CRA efforts have been learned and are reflected in current developments as reported in these case studies. One important lesson is the fact that redlining and disinvestment, and community responses to them, do not exist in a vacuum. Disinvestment and reinvestment struggles emerged from and constitute part of a broader struggle over an array of poverty, race, and urban development issues. Effective organization of diverse coalitions has been a central ingredient of almost every successful campaign. Such coalitions would not have been possible in the absence of the widely recognized variety of problems directly related to disinvestment. Community-based organizations, churches, civil rights groups, labor unions, sympathetic elected officials, reporters, and academics have worked together in the belief that the absence of credit creates many problems that reinvestment can help solve. When credit is unavailable, families cannot buy or improve homes. Businesses cannot start or expand, or they may have to shut down or leave, costing many jobs in the process. Revenues from property taxes and income taxes decline, further threatening already strapped budgets for schools, police, infrastructure, and other public services. Minority residents and neighborhoods are clearly the most adversely affected. Conversely, increasing the availability of credit is responsive to the interests of these various groups. More mortgage loans help more people to own and improve their homes. Increased availability of commercial credit enable businesses to expand and create more jobs. Tax revenues increase and public officials are able to deliver more and better public services. Throughout, local media and researchers have an interest in following these developments. Differences do emerge. Some groups and cities have been more inclined to utilize more aggressive direct action tactics. Boston and Chicago are notable examples while such tactics were not as significant in Milwaukee. There is always at least the potential of splits along racial lines as neighborhoods are selected for reinvestment targets, and such splits did emerge in Milwaukee. But what is more striking is the perception and reality of mutual interests and the effectiveness of coalition building around those interests.

A related lesson is understanding that this is both a national and local issue, with state level initiatives occasionally playing significant roles. The critical leverage is provided by federal statutes like the CRA but the issue is usually played out at the local level, as each of these cases demonstrates. The California organizing campaigns, the aggressive role of Michigan's Financial Institutions Bureau commissioner in the Detroit effort, and the role of two of Massachusetts' statewide coalitions in assisting the Boston initiative illustrate the importance of state action at least in selected cases. Nationwide efforts are particularly critical. In addition to federal legislation, several studies including those done by Bill Dedman in Atlanta have led directly to successful campaigns in Pittsburgh and Milwaukee and many other cities. Several nationwide coalitions, including the NTIC, the Center for Community Change (CCC), and the Association of Community Organizations for Reform Now (ACORN)—and nationally known experts like Calvin Bradford from Chicago and Charles Finn with the Hubert Humphrey Institute at the University of Minnesota—have provided assistance to dozens of local groups on a variety of fronts. The role of such expertise, described in some detail in each of these case studies, has had a significant impact on virtually all reinvestment efforts. These organizations and consultants helped draft the major legislation. They have educated community groups around the country about the lending industry, and they have trained organizers in many cities on the tactics and strategies of community reinvestment campaigns. At the same time, most CRA organizing is initiated by local activists at the local level. Successful reinvestment efforts depend on credible community groups knowing who the key local actors are (in terms of their adversaries and allies), understanding local lending patterns and problems, and determining the remedies for their particular problems. Frequently a campaign against a lender in one city provides leverage for a group challenging that lender in another city, as illustrated by the assistance Milwaukee organizers received from ACORN staff in Arizona in the Milwaukee campaign against a major bank that was operating nationwide. In the process, organizations across the country have learned much from each other. The details of reinvestment campaigns, however, are developed at the local level. Understanding the many levels of these issues, from the local neighborhood to the federal government, is vital to understanding the dynamics of reinvestment.

A third lesson is the importance of distinguishing between gentrification and reinvestment that assists low- and moderate-income residents and communities. The potential for gentrification may be greater in larger, more cosmopolitan communities like Boston or Chicago than in smaller ones like Pittsburgh or Milwaukee. Yet, as the Pittsburgh case suggests, even in the smaller areas, avoiding gentrification requires conscious planning. The new disclosure requirements established by FIRREA as of 1990 reflect the degree to which this lesson has in fact been learned. Knowing the income and race of applicants and borrowers, in addition to knowing the geographic distribution of loans, will enable all observers to determine precisely who is getting loans and who is getting rejected. With the new data, it can be determined, for example, how many loans in a neighborhood went to wealthy white investors, low-income black homeowners, or borrowers who have any combination of race, gender, and income characteristics. This legislation and the subsequent disclosure of vital information would not have occurred in the absence of strong lobbying by neighborhood organizations and support of public officials, like Rep. Joseph Kennedy from Massachusetts, who sponsored the key bills. Again, as the Boston case illustrates, the linkages between local community groups and supportive elected officials are vital to successful reinvestment activity, with efforts at the local and national levels reinforcing each other.

A fourth lesson is the importance of accountability. The existence of local, state, and particularly federal laws requiring lenders to be responsive to the credit needs of their entire service area, including low- and moderate-income neighborhoods, is critical. The availability of disclosure data to document lending practices is equally important. Without the leverage provided by such legal mandates few, if any, of these developments would have taken place. Law enforcement alone—in the absence of organizing, media attention, direct action, and other tactics—would, of course, be insufficient. Some reinvestment efforts may occur voluntarily but the existence of legal requirements pertaining to lending practices and disclosure provide a context that encourages voluntary initiatives and assures other efforts that simply would not otherwise occur. As Tim Elverman, vice-president of government relations for Bank One, says in the Milwaukee case, "without the law, the bank would never have done these things on its own" (Elverman 1990).

Perhaps the most significant lesson that has been learned is the fact that real changes can be made in the policies and practices of lending institutions and that such changes do materially affect the lives of people in distressed communities. A corollary is that while diverse institutional allies provide valuable assistance, the key to reinvestment, past and future, is solid community-based organization in which those residents most affected by disinvestment have central roles in the reinvestment effort. Because of these community-based efforts, millions of dollars have been committed to low- and moderate-income neighborhoods by many lenders, well above and beyond the amount they had made available to those communities in previous years. As these cases document, many of these dollars are now going to targeted areas. It is difficult to define precisely the number of loans and dollar volume of loans that have been made as a direct result of pressure from local community groups or federal regulators and to what extent reinvestment agreements reflect loans that would have been made anyway by lenders in the normal course of events. As each of these case studies illustrates, however, it is apparent that substantial dollars have been invested in areas where loans would have not been made in the absence of the reinvestment movement. It appears that at least some lenders have experienced a genuine change in their attitudes toward older urban communities and minority borrowers. Clearly most lenders who have made serious reinvestment agreements view their participation as both good business and good politics. Again, as Bank One's Tim Elverman observed, "it's good business, you don't lose money doing CRA, it's the right thing to do" (Elverman 1990). Though some lenders are acting primarily out of political expediency, the loans they ultimately make are entirely consistent with safe and sound lending practice, since most of these new loans are proving to be good business. In Pittsburgh, for example, no residential loans made by Union National Bank under its lending agreement had defaulted as the program entered its third year. Understanding lenders' motivation is important, particularly for developing strategies for future efforts. The motives of lenders may have been mixed in the past, but their attitudes and practices have changed enough in at least some cases to benefit low- and moderate-income residents and their communities.

The victories described in the following chapters are significant. They have concretely improved many people's lives and the neighborhoods in which they live. Yet the continuing uneven development of metropolitan areas and the persistence of the dual housing market (Massey and Denton 1987, 1989) suggest that the community reinvestment movement cannot yet declare victory. Valuable lessons have been learned, but emerging issues will have to be confronted if redlining is to become part of the nation's history rather than a contemporary social reality.

OBSTACLES TO REINVESTMENT IN THE 1990s

Deindustrialization and Uneven Urban Development

The decline of central cities and the growth of the suburbs, combined with race-based exclusion in metropolitan housing markets, is a story that has unfolded and been told many times. This reality is driven home by the often quoted passage from the Kerner Report: "To continue present policies is to make permanent the division of our country into two

23

societies; one, largely Negro and poor, located in the central cities; the other, predominantly white and affluent, located in the suburbs and in outlying areas" (*Report of the National Advisory Commission on Civil Disorders* 1968: 22).

What has been recognized only in recent years is how this pattern of uneven development also has been shaped and strengthened by structural changes in the national and international economy, the integration of the United States into a global economy, and the politics surrounding these developments. After World War II the United States emerged as the leading economic force in the world. Beginning in the mid-1960s, growing international competition from such industrialized countries as Japan and West Germany, and in selected industries from many Third World nations as well, began to erode the dominance of the United States. Particularly problematic for U.S. cities was the subsequent decline of manufacturing industries like automobile and steel production.

The political response to these global realities exacerbated the economic and related social problems that emerged. Rather than responding with a set of policies to improve the productivity of American firms and the human capital of their workers by investing in manufacturing plants along with research and development, the United States engaged in what Robert Reich labeled "paper entrepreneurialism" (Reich 1983: 140–72). Capital was expended on corporate mergers and acquisitions, speculative real estate ventures, and other financial investments in which "some money will change hands, and no new wealth will be created" (Reich 1983: 157). In the stated interest of unleashing America's entrepreneurial spirit, other components of this effort to stimulate a profit-led recovery for American corporations include reducing labor costs, cutting expenditures on public services, and reducing government regulations (Bluestone and Harrison 1982, 1988; Bowles, Gordon, and Weisskopf 1983). Consequently, many factory jobs have been lost, the social safety net has been shred, and the U.S. economy has become more concentrated yet less competitive. Public policy has reinforced private decisions that encouraged the postwar restructuring of the U.S. economy and the emerging social costs for the nation's cities.

The globalization and concentration of the national economy have had dramatic effects on the spatial development of cities and associated social problems in urban neighborhoods. As blue collar, industrialized neighborhoods have been devastated by the loss of a manufacturing base, service industries have thrived in the downtown central business districts (Smith and Feagin 1987). Professionals attracted to those relatively high-paid professional service jobs needed housing, and usually that meant more demand for suburban homes (Levine 1987). Following the lead of the federal government, local redevelopment policy has focused on providing a "good business climate" as city and state officials compete with their neighbors in attracting private capital. Again, this has meant incentives (e.g., tax abatements, subsidized loans, enterprise zones) to private capital and reductions in public services (Barnekov, Boyle, and Rich 1989).

The racial effects of these developments are evident. Racial minorities are concentrated in those manufacturing industries, blue-collar occupations, and central city communities that have been most adversely affected by capital mobility and economic restructuring. They are underrepresented in the service industries, professional occupations, and suburban communities that have prospered (Wilson 1987). The racial effects are not entirely fortuitous. There is evidence that racial composition of communities is a factor that at least some corporations explicitly examine in selecting sites for new plants (Cole and Deskins 1989). If the overt use of race in public policy and private practice has eroded in recent years, the economic and political forces shaping the uneven development of metropolitan areas and racial separation in urban America may be stronger today than ever.

Globalization and Deregulation of Financial Industries

While much attention has been focused in recent years on changes within the nation's manufacturing industries, globalization and deregulation of financial institutions have been equally dramatic and perhaps even more problematic for older urban communities. Deregulation and homogenization across the nation's financial industries have led to increasing concentration, de-emphasis on housing, and an even less stable market for mortgage loans and urban development initiatives generally.

Like many other industries, U.S. financial institutions faced increasing competition and declining profitability as the decade of the sixties was coming to a close. Foreign banks began to control increasing shares of the U.S. market (Florida 1986). Traditional domestic investments in declining manufacturing industries were proving less profitable, placing additional pressures on U.S. banks (Feldman and Florida 1990).

Rising inflation and interest rates squeezed savings and loans, whose profitability had long been tied to attracting low-cost savings deposits that were reinvested in local housing markets as mortgage loans (Meyerson 1986). Large banks and thrifts, in particular, demanded that the federal government respond to these financial difficulties with deregulation.

Under the regulatory structure that had been established during the New Deal in response to the Great Depression, specific financial activities were delineated for various segments of the industry and restrictions were established to maintain a separation of functions. For example, commercial banks were permitted to offer checking accounts but were prohibited from interstate operations. Banks were also prohibited from offering insurance or trading in securities. Investment bankers and securities dealers were permitted to cross state lines, but they could not accept deposits or make loans. Savings and loans were also prohibited from operating across state lines, offering checking accounts, or making commercial loans. Rather, they were required to invest in housing; but they were provided tax benefits to do so and they were permitted to pay higher interest rates on savings accounts than banks as an inducement to attract capital for mortgages (Florida 1986). This basic regulatory structure held for four decades, but was effectively challenged by the early 1980s.

The central stated assumption behind the push for deregulation was that the resulting free competition would allow capital to be used more efficiently. Banks needed to operate on an interstate basis in order to compete with their foreign competition. With money market funds attracting dollars that previously had been deposited in savings accounts at banks and savings and loans, interest rate ceilings also had to be lifted to attract capital. Thrifts wanted to diversify out of housing, and banks wanted to invest in real estate. Arguing that the United States invested too much money in housing while the nation needed to reindustrialize, there was explicit pressure from several sources to redirect capital from housing to other economic sectors.

Congress enacted several laws in the early 1980s to reduce federal regulations and provide the requested flexibility. Pressure continues to be exerted by lenders, along with federal regulators themselves, for even more deregulation and greater flexibility (Pizzo, Fricker, and Muolo 1989; Labaton 1990; Tolchin 1990). Early in 1991 the Bush administration proposed the most sweeping changes in the regulatory structure of financial institutions since the depression. The proposal would permit industrial companies to own banks, eliminate divisions between banking, insurance, and securities industries, lift restrictions on interstate banking, limit federal insurance for depositors to one $100,000 account per institution, and generally further deregulate banking (Labaton 1991). While these specific legislative proposals were not enacted in 1991, the current direction of industry and regulatory restructuring is clear. One consequence has been a substantial concentration within these industry as merger and acquisition rules were lessened. Stronger institutions took over weaker ones, with the savings and loan bailout and its fallout representing just one dimension of this phenomenon. The homogenization and concentration of the financial industries reduces the tie between any particular segment and the nation's needs for housing finance.

To illustrate, the percentage of thrift investments in residential mortgages declined from 80 percent in 1978, to 64 percent in 1983, and to 54 percent in 1988 (*Savings Institutions Sourcebook* 1990: 30). Thrifts' share of all mortgage originations declined from nearly 75 percent in the mid-1970s to 33 percent in 1980, 29 percent in 1989, and 19 percent for the first quarter of 1990. Much of the slack has been picked up by mortgage bankers and commercial banks. In addition thrifts are selling an increasing proportion of the loans they do originate to investors in the secondary mortgage market. Two federal agencies—FNMA and FHLMC—now purchase a majority of loans originated by thrifts. In the mid-1970s only one-third of these mortgages were so traded (Florida 1986: 221–25; Office of Financial Management 1990). These developments by no means assure an adequate supply of capital for mortgage loans and housing finance, particularly in older urban communities.

As a result of these structural changes in U.S. financial industries, availability of housing credit depends less and less over time on the supply and demand specifically for mortgage loans and increasingly on the supply and demand for credit in international markets generally. Deregulation, and the concomitant concentration, homogenization, and globalization, means that housing consumers in American cities may have to compete with Brazilian coffee producers and Japanese computer manufacturers as well as U.S. real estate developers and tobacco growers for credit. While this might result in a more efficient market from the perspective of the profitability of lenders and other investors, the outcomes may not be so sanguine for the housing needs of the nation. In their essay, Bradford and Cincotta describe how specific banking products and practices are being altered by these developments in ways that undercut reinvestment efforts. While most industrialized nations have public policies allocating credit to assure an adequate flow into housing, the United States has moved in the opposite direction, making housing credit availability increasingly dependent on its attraction to private investors relative to other investment opportunities that are available on a worldwide basis.

In this environment, the Community Reinvestment Act takes on even greater significance. There can be little doubt that the increased pace of mergers and acquisitions in the 1980s facilitated CRA agreements as lenders moved expeditiously to remove any challenges to such applications. Foreseeable trends for at least the next decade portend even more mergers, acquisitions, and other forms of restructuring, thus indicating an increasingly critical role for the CRA. Given the frequency of such activity and the large size of institutions involved, challenges could prove to be even more expensive to lenders. (For example, Bank America and Security Pacific—until recently the nation's third and sixth largest bank holding companies—merged in 1992 to become the second largest bank company in the United States (Thomas 1991; Pollack 1992). In turn, however, such developments may strengthen the resolve of some lenders to "reform" the CRA. In 1991 and 1992 attempts were made to dilute the CRA by limiting its coverage to a handful of larger lenders, and among them only those who received less than a satisfactory CRA rating. Of those institutions examined since the new rules were passed requiring public disclosure of the CRA rating, only 10 percent have been rated less than satisfactory (Quint 1991). While these efforts were defeated, it is reasonable to assume that future efforts will be made to revise the Community Reinvestment Act.

Commodification of Housing: The Next Challenge to Reinvestment?

These structural changes in the political economy of home finance raise an even more fundamental challenge to the community reinvestment movement; the centrality of private profitability in lending. In the current financial environment, conceivably all racial barriers in the mortgage market (and other market impediments associated with geographic location that bear no objective nexus with risk) could be eliminated and

28

the supply of funds available would still be inadequate for the need. Even though race and other characteristics of older urban communities have a significant marginal effect on the allocation of mortgage loans, the vast majority of lending decisions and the overall pattern of where loans are made are still accounted for by objective factors like ratios of requested loan amount to income and property value (Schafer and Ladd 1981: 280–81). Given the adverse conditions that exist in selected neighborhoods in most cities, rational, market-based, profit-seeking behavior by lenders will discourage mortgage and related business loans in the most depressed communities. As David Harvey observed:

> The banks naturally have good rational business reasons
> for not financing mortgages in inner city areas. . . .
> Given the drive to maximize profits, this decision cannot
> be regarded as unethical. In fact, it is a general charac-
> teristic of ghetto housing that if we accept the mores of
> normal, ethical entrepreneurial behavior, there is no way
> in which we can blame anyone for the objective social
> conditions which all are willing to characterize as appall-
> ing and wasteful of potential housing resources. . . .
> Consequently, it seems impossible to find a policy within
> the existing economic and institutional framework which
> is capable of rectifying these conditions.
> (Harvey 1973: 140)

It would be a mistake, in other words, to assume that purely objective, market-based allocation of mortgage loans via the private sector would necessarily be the most direct avenue to meeting the social need for housing finance. Maximum efficiency from the perspective of housing finance providers is not necessarily equivalent to maximum effectiveness in meeting human need.

In fact, a report of the Institute for Policy Studies Working Group on Housing (1987) argues persuasively that it is precisely the treatment of housing and housing-related services as commodities, coupled with reliance on the profit-maximizing private sector, as the primary housing provider that accounts for the array of housing problems confronting the nation today. The large private profits that are associated with all aspects of housing (e.g., construction, sales, insurance, appraisal, and finance,

coupled with the withdrawal of support for low-income housing by the
federal government, are the principal causes for the increasing unavailability and unaffordability of housing in recent years, according to the
working group report. The appropriate response to such commodification
of housing, the report argues, is to move toward social ownership and
control of all aspects of housing so that housing is treated as a public
need and entitlement rather than as a private good to be obtained via
the market. In the area of home finance, specific recommendations include differential taxes and reserve requirements to reward lenders doing
socially preferred lending, specific set-asides for the amount of loans to
be directed to designated housing objectives, requirements for a specific
number of loans to be made at below-market rates resulting in low-income borrowers being subsidized by others, capitalization of nonprofit
housing developers to assure long-term financing of socially owned housing, and direct capital financing by government agencies.

Such an approach clearly contradicts strong ideological beliefs
that have shaped public policy generally and housing policy in particular
throughout U.S. history. As R. Allen Hays observed in his history of the
ideology shaping federal housing policy, that policy has been guided by
three central tenets: (1) the chief driving force behind human productivity is the individual desire to enhance material well-being, and such
acquisitiveness must be rewarded in order to maximize societal material
well-being; (2) the free market is the most efficient and least coercive
allocator of goods and services; and (3) government should play a role
that supplements the private market's in regulating human interaction
(Hays 1985: 17–18). Any policy that runs contrary to these assumptions
and, more important, to the interests of powerful groups who benefit
from policies consistent with the dominant ideology, will encounter
strong resistance from those groups.

Where can the challenge to commodification come from? How
can financial institutions be coaxed into lending when "banks naturally
have good rational business reasons for not financing mortgages?" Hays
argues that the state should play a stronger role that would involve more
aggressive regulation and, where necessary, provision of essential services
to those unable to purchase them through the private market (Hays
1985: 17–18). Yet given current economic institutional arrangements
and the prevailing free market ideology, public officials are under pres-

sure to maintain a business climate that is attractive to private capital. Even the most sympathetic black elected officials often find that they must adopt strategies that subordinate the interests of their own black constituency to private developers, because of the dependence of the public sector and the community generally on private sector investment decision making (Reed 1988). In this environment, the tools available to public officials in dealing with lenders are limited. Yet, the failure to address the urgent human needs of their communities will lead to a loss of legitimacy among a majority of constituents and to the loss of the next election. Clearly, the state has a delicate balancing act to perform if it is to serve the functions Hays assigns to it.

The community reinvestment movement straddles this ideological dilemma. On the one hand, reinvestment efforts that begin with a commitment to programs which are "consistent with the safe and sound operation of such institutions" (i.e., those which are predicated on maximum private profitability for lenders) would fall safely within the category of mainstream, market-based lending practice and risk embodying all the limitations of commodification. On the other hand, many CRA agreements simply call for increased numbers of loans or dollar volume of lending in designated areas and, therefore, amount to a form of credit allocation based on identified human needs in those areas. Such efforts do not require the making of bad loans, but they recognize the need to balance public and private interests (as well as the private interests of high- and low-income families), if necessary through the creation of alternative forms of lending institutions. Which direction this movement takes in the near future not only may determine the next stage of the reinvestment effort, but may also have profound implications for American politics generally. In their essay, Calvin Bradford and Gale Cincotta conclude that the lending community's responsiveness to current CRA rules may be decisive in determining whether or not pressure will be mounted for more direct public control over the allocation of credit, not just for home loans but for commercial and business investment as well.

It has been a difficult political struggle to begin to eliminate racial barriers to the home finance marketplace, but it will be even more difficult to overcome the barriers represented by the commodification of lending. If this is the next stage in the struggle, however, the community reinvestment movement may be the key vehicle for such social change.

In mortgage lending, as in so many aspects of urban development, it is becoming increasingly difficult to disentangle and effectively respond to the effects of race and class.

These broader historical and ideological forces also raise questions about the current status of the reinvestment movement and the utility of those tactics it has used most effectively. Elected officials at all levels of government have been critical allies in the past. For the reasons noted earlier, and because many rely on financial institutions and the business community for campaign funds, the support of elected officials for the reinvestment movement as it expands may be sporadic at best. Given the relationship between elected officials and those directing enforcement agencies, and given the future career aspirations of many regulators, enforcement efforts may become less, rather than more, aggressive.

The media also have been important sources of support for reinvestment initiatives. Individual reporters personally benefit by exposing the racially discriminatory practices of powerful institutions. Yet in general the media, along with financial institutions, other local businesses, cultural institutions, and public officials, constitute key components of local growth machines that mutually benefit by maintaining a healthy business climate. A widely shared belief among the leaders of these institutions is that providing financial incentives to private capital is essential for maintaining that climate (Logan and Molotch 1987). Support for reinvestment initiatives from the media—particularly those that expressly challenge the commodification of lending—may therefore be tenuous at best.

The role of professional research also poses questions for future reinvestment campaigns. One irony of the community reinvestment movement is that the most effective research, in terms of generating agreements, is not necessarily the best from a scientific perspective. For example, a 1989 article in an Atlanta newspaper reporting that the racial disparity in mortgage loan rejection rates was highest in Milwaukee among the fifty cities included generated an immediate response as the mayor of Milwaukee and the governor of Wisconsin created the Fair Lending Action Committee, which led to several lending initiatives. A study published two years earlier in an academic journal that utilized regression equations to document a racial effect in mortgage lending, independent of income, age and condition of housing, and other neighborhood characteristics, was briefly noted in the local press with no subsequent action taken. Despite many common interests, the publication demands on university faculty do not always lend themselves to the kinds of research that community groups can most effectively utilize.

A related but more significant research question that will receive increasing attention in the future asks what the numbers of loans and dollar volume of the loans in reinvestment agreements actually mean. Precise numbers on how lending patterns have been affected by community reinvestment coalitions, regulators, or voluntary lender initiatives often are not available. As time goes by and more agreements are negotiated, the demand for more comprehensive evaluation will increase. Community organizations and lenders share an interest in casting the agreements and their implementation in the most positive light. Rigorous research may, however, undermine some of their claims.

These, then, are some of the challenges that face the reinvestment movement. The bedrock of that movement, as Bradford and Cincotta demonstrate, lies in the power of effectively organized local communities. "People power," they observe, is what started the movement and it will be critical to maintaining the movement. Despite the many limitations and barriers, it is reasonable to assume that the community reinvestment movement will grow in the near future. Though precise estimates are unavailable, it is clear that significantly more money is being invested in central cities than would otherwise be the case, and that those investments make a difference to the residents as well as to the communities generally. Some lenders have genuinely changed their perspectives and practices regarding urban lending markets. These changes have occurred because of conscious political activity and strategic planning by community-based organizations utilizing an array of resources. Securing reinvestment agreements is a contentious political process. As with the decline of cities, the growth of suburbs, and the concommitant racial concentration in urban housing markets, reinvestment is not an ecological inevitability or natural outcome of market forces. Just as the FHA made conscious choices in its early years to protect white neighborhoods, other choices for other ends are being made by key actors today. The community reinvestment movement has met with much success and learned from that success. At the same time, it continues to encounter substantial barriers to further progress. If its future direction is somewhat cloudy, one conclusion appears certain: the community reinvestment movement is here to stay, at least for awhile.

33

REFERENCES

Barnekov, Timothy, Robin Boyle, and Daniel Rich. 1989. *Privatism and Urban Policy in Britain and the United States.* New York: Oxford University Press.

Berry, Brian J. L. 1979. *The Open Housing Question: Race and Housing in Chicago, 1966– 1976.* Cambridge, Mass.: Ballinger.

Bluestone, Barry, and Bennett Harrison. 1988. *The Great U-Turn: Corporate Restructuring and the Polarizing of America.* New York: Basic Books.

———. 1982. *The Deindustrialization of America: Plant Closings, Community Abandonment, and the Dismantling of Basic Industry.* New York: Basic Books.

Bowles, Samuel, David M. Gordon, and Thomas E. Weisskopf. 1983. *Beyond the Waste Land: A Democratic Alternative to Economic Decline.* Garden City, N.Y.: Anchor Press/ Doubleday.

Boyte, Harry C., Heather Booth, and Steve Max. 1986. *Citizen Action and the New American Populism.* Philadelphia: Temple University Press.

Bradbury, Katharine , L., Karl E. Case, and Constance R. Dunham. 1989. "Geographic Patterns of Mortgage Lending in Boston, 1982–1987." *New England Economic Review* (Sept./Oct.), 3–30.

Bradford, Calvin. 1992. *Community Reinvestment Agreement Library.* Des Plaines, Ill.: Community Reinvestment Associates.

———. 1989. "Reinvestment: The Quiet Revolution." *Neighborhood Works* 12 (4):1, 22– 26.

———. 1984. "Report on the Role of the Veterans Administration in Causing Rapid and Massive Racial Resegregation." Submitted to the Court by the plaintiffs in the case of *Jorman et al. v. Veterans Administration et al.* C.A. No. 77 C 581: Northern District of Illinois (May 18).

———. 1979. "Financing Home Ownership—The Federal Role in Neighborhood Decline." *Urban Affairs Quarterly* 14 (3): 313–35.

Bradford, Calvin, Leonard Rubinowitz and Darel Grothaus, eds. 1975. *The Role of Mortgage Lending Practices in Older Urban Neighborhoods: Institutional Lenders, Regulatory Agencies, and Their Community Impacts.* Evanston, Ill.: Center for Urban Affairs, Northwestern University.

Burgess, Ernest W. 1928. "Residential Segregation in American Cities." *The Annals of the American Academy of Political and Social Science* 140 (Nov.): 105–15.

Canner, Glenn B. 1982. "Redlining: Research and Federal Legislative Response." Washington, D.C.: Board of Governors of the Federal Reserve System.

Canner, Glenn B., and Dolores S. Smith. 1991. "Home Mortgage Disclosure Act: Expanded Data on Residential Lending." *Federal Reserve Bulletin* 77 (11): 859–81.

Center for Community Change. 1989. *Mortgage Lending Discrimination Testing Project.* Washington, D.C.: Center for Community Change and U.S. Department of Housing and Urban Development.

Cole, Robert E., and Donald R. Deskins, Jr. 1989. "Racial Factors in Site Location and Employment Patterns of Japanese Auto Firms." *California Management Review* 31 (1): 9– 22.

Dane, Stephen M. 1989. "Federal Enforcement of the Fair Lending, Equal Credit Opportunity, and Community Reinvestment Laws in the 1980s." In *One Nation, Indivisible: The Civil Rights Challenge for the 1980s,* ed. Reginald C. Goyan and William L. Taylor Washington, D.C.: Citizen's Commission on Civil Rights.

Dedman, Bill. 1989. "Blacks Turned Down for Home Loans from S & Ls Twice as Often as Whites." *Atlanta Journal/Constitution,* Jan. 22.

———. 1988. "The Color of Money." *Atlanta Journal/Constitution,* May 1–4.

Elverman, Tim. 1990. Interviewed by Sally O'Connor, Sept. 14.

Feins, Judith, and Darel Grothaus. 1975. "An Analysis of the Federal Home Loan Bank of Chicago Survey of Urban Lending and Savings Patterns by Cook County Insured Associations." In *The Role of Mortgage Lending Practices in Older Urban Neighborhoods: Institutional Lenders, Regulatory Agencies and Their Community Impacts,* ed. Calvin Bradford,

Leonard Rubinowitz, and Darel Grothaus. Evanston: Center for Urban Affairs, Northwestern University.

Feldman, Marshall M.A., and Richard L. Florida. 1990. "Economic Restructuring and the Changing Role of the State in U.S. Housing." In *Government and Housing: Development in Seven Countries*, ed. William van Vliet and Jan van Weesep. Newbury Park, Calif.: Sage Publications.

Florida, Richard L. 1986. "The Political Economy of Financial Deregulation and the Reorganization of Housing Finance in the United States." *International Journal of Urban and Regional Research* 10 (2):207–32.

Galster, George. 1991. "Statistical Proof of Discrimination in Home Mortgage Lending." *Banking and Financial Services* 7 (20):187–97.

Gelber, Bruce S., Rachel Hopp, and Stacy Canan. 1983. "Recent Developments in Housing Discrimination Law." *Clearinghouse Review* 16 (8): 806–14.

Greene, Zina G. 1980. *Lender's Guide to Fair Mortgage Policies*. Washington, D.C.: Potomac Institute.

Guskind, Robert. 1989. "Thin Red Line." *National Journal* 21 (43): 2639–43.

Harvey, David. 1973. *Social Justice and the City*. Baltimore: Johns Hopkins University Press.

Hays, R. Allen. 1985. *The Federal Government and Urban Housing*. Albany, N.Y.: State University of New York Press.

Helper, Rose. 1969. *Racial Policies and Practices of Real Estate Brokers*. Minneapolis: University of Minnesota Press.

Hoyt, Homer. 1933. *One Hundred Years of Land Values in Chicago*. Chicago: University of Chicago Press.

ICF Incorporated. 1991. "The Secondary Market and Community Lending through Lenders' Eyes." Fairfax, Va: ICF Incorporated/Federal Home Loan Mortgage Corporation.

Institute for Policy Studies Working Group on Housing. 1987. "A Progressive Housing Program for America." Washington, D.C.: Institute for Policy Studies.

Jackson, Kenneth T. 1985. *Crabgrass Frontier: The Suburbanization of the United States*. New York: Oxford University Press.

Judd, Dennis R. 1984. *The Politics of American Cities: Private Power and Public Policy*. Boston: Little, Brown.

Labaton, Stephen. 1991. "Administration Presents Its Plan for Broad Overhaul of Banking." *New York Times*, Feb. 6.

———. 1990. "Bank Law Overhaul Proposed." *New York Times*, Sept. 26.

Levine, Marc V. 1987. "Downtown Redevelopment as an Urban Growth Strategy: A Critical Appraisal of the Baltimore Renaissance." *Journal of Urban Affairs* 9 (2): 103–23.

Lief, Beth J., and Susan Goering. 1987. "The Implementation of the Federal Mandate for Fair Housing." In *Divided Neighborhoods: Changing Patterns of Racial Segregation*, ed. Gary A. Tobin. Newbury Park: Sage Publications.

Listokin, David, and Stephen Casey. 1980. *Mortgage Lending and Race*. New Brunswick, N.J.: Center for Urban Policy Research.

Logan, John R., and Harvey L. Molotch. 1987. *Urban Fortunes: The Political Economy of Place*. Berkeley: University of California Press.

Massey, Douglas S., and Nancy A. Denton. 1989. "Hypersegregation in U.S. Metropolitan Areas: Black and Hispanic Segregation along Five Dimensions." *Demography* 26 (3): 373–91.

———. 1987. "Trends in the Residential Segregation of Blacks, Hispanics, and Asians." *American Sociological Review* 52 (6): 802–25.

Metcalf, George R. 1988. *Fair Housing Comes of Age*. Westport, Conn.: Greenwood Press.

Meyerson, Ann. 1986. "Deregulation and the Restructuring of the Housing Finance System." In *Critical Perspectives on Housing*, ed. Rachel G. Bratt, Chester Hartman, and Ann Meyerson. Philadelphia: Temple University Press.

Nash, Nathaniel C. 1990. "Panel Is Told of Racial Bias in Lending." *New York Times*, May 17.

NAACP v. American Family Insurance. 1990. Complaint 90-C-0750 (July 27), U.S. District Court for the Eastern District of Wisconsin.

National Commission on Neighborhoods. 1979. *People Building Neighborhoods: Final Report to the President and the Congress of the United States.* Washington, D.C.: U.S. Government Printing Office.

Office of Financial Management. 1990. Unpublished data on annual gross flows of long-term mortgage loans by eleven major lending groups. Washington, D.C.: Office of Financial Management, U.S. Department of Housing and Urban Development.

Office of Thrift Supervision. 1990. "OTS Approves CRA Evaluation Revisions." In *News*, June 5. Washington, D.C.: Office of Thrift Supervision.

Orfield, Gary. 1988. "Race and the Liberal Agenda: The Loss of the Integrationist Dream, 1965–1974." In *The Politics of Social Policy in the United States.* ed. Margaret Weir, Ann Shola Orloff, and Theda Skocpol. Princeton, N.J.: Princeton University Press.

Pearce, Diana. 1983. "A Sheltered Crisis: The State of Fair Housing Opportunity in the Eighties." In U.S. Commission on Civil Rights, *A Sheltered Crisis: The State of Fair Housing in the Eighties.* Washington, D.C.: U.S. Government Printing Office.

Perry, Stewart E. 1987. *Communities on the Way: Rebuilding Local Economies in the United States and Canada.* Albany: State University of New York Press.

Peterson, Margaret, 1990. Loan officer with Repbulic Capital Mortgage Corporation. Interviewed by Sally O'Connor. Milwaukee, Wis. Nov. 12.

Piven, Frances Fox and Richard A. Cloward. 1977. *Poor People's Movements: Why They Succeed, How They Fail.* New York: Vintage Books.

Pizzo, Stephen, Mary Fricker, and Paul Muolo. 1989. *Inside Job: The Looting of America's Savings and Loans.* New York: McGraw-Hill.

Pol, Louis G., Rebecca F. Guy, and Andrew J. Bush. 1982. "Discrimination in the Home Lending Market: A Macro Perspective." *Social Science Quarterly* 63 (4): 716–28.

Pollack, Andrew. 1992. "Fed Approves Merger of Big California Banks." *New York Times,* March 24.

Quint, Michael. 1991. "Racial Gap Found on Mortgages." *New York Times,* Oct. 22.

Reed, Adolph, Jr. 1988. "The Black Urban Regime: Structural Origins and Constraints." *Comparative Urban and Community Research* 1: 138–89.

Reich, Robert B. 1983. *The Next American Frontier.* New York: Times Books.

Report of the National Advisory Commission on Civil Disorders. 1968. New York: Bantam Books.

Savings Institutions Sourcebook. 1990. New York: U.S. League of Savings Institutions.

Schafer, Robert, and Helen F. Ladd. 1981. *Discrimination in Mortgage Lending.* Cambridge: MIT Press.

Shlay, Anne B. 1989. "Financing Community: Methods for Assessing Residential Credit Disparities, Market Barriers, and Institutional Reinvestment Performance in the Metropolis." *Journal of Urban Affairs* 11 (3): 201–23.

Sloane, Glenda G. 1983. "Discrimination in Home Mortgage Financing." In U.S. Commission on Civil Rights, *A Sheltered Crisis: The State of Fair Housing in the Eighties.* Washington, D.C.: U.S. Government Printing Office.

Sloane, Martin E. 1983. "Federal Housing Policy and Equal Opportunity." In U.S. Commission on Civil Rights, *A Sheltered Crisis: The State of Fair Housing in the Eighties.* Washington, D.C.: U.S. Government Printing Office.

Smith, Michael Peter, and Joe R. Feagin. 1987. *The Capitalist City.* New York: Basil Blackwell.

Squires, Gregory D., and William Velez. 1987. "Neighborhood Racial Composition and Mortgage Lending: City and Suburban Differences." *Journal of Urban Affairs* 9 (3): 217–32.

Squires, Gregory D., William Velez, and Karl E. Taeuber. 1991. "Insurance Redlining, Agency Location, and the Process of Urban Disinvestment." *Urban Affairs Quarterly* 26 (4): 567–88.

Subcommittee on Consumer and Regulatory Affairs. 1990. *Discrimination in Home Mortgage Lending.* Hearing before the Subcommittee on Consumer and Regulatory Affairs of the Committee on Banking, Housing, and Urban Affairs, U.S. Senate. Washington, D.C.: U.S. Government Printing Office.

Taggart, Harriett Tee, and Kevin W. Smith. 1981. "Redlining: An Assessment of the Evidence of Disinvestment in Metropolitan Boston." *Urban Affairs Quarterly* 17 (1): 91–107.

Thomas, Paulette. 1991. "Mortgage Rejection Rate for Minorities Is Quadruple That of Whites, Study Finds." *Wall Street Journal*, Oct. 21.

Tolchin, Martin. 1990. "Regan on S & L's: Too Many Curbs." *New York Times*, Oct. 2.

Turner, Margery Austin, Raymond J. Struyk, and John Yinger. 1991. *Housing Discrimination Study*. Washington, D.C.: Urban Institute.

U.S. Federal Housing Administration. 1938. *Underwriting Manual*. Washington, D.C.: U.S. Government Printing Office.

Weier, Anita. 1990. "First Financial Tops Inner-city Mortgage Lender List." *Business Journal*, April 23–29.

Weisbrot, Robert. 1990. *Freedom Bound: A History of America's Civil Rights Movement*. New York: W.W. Norton.

Wilson, William J. 1987. *The Truly Disadvantaged: The Inner City, the Underclass, and Public Policy*. Chicago: University of Chicago Press.

Yinger, John. 1986. "On the Possibility of Achieving Racial Integration through Subsidized Housing." In *Housing Desegregation and Federal Policy*, ed. John M. Goering. Chapel Hill: University of North Carolina Press.

James T. Campen   Chapter 2

THE STRUGGLE FOR COMMUNITY
INVESTMENT IN BOSTON,
1989–1991

"INEQUITIES ARE CITED IN HUB MORTGAGES: Preliminary Fed finding is 'racial bias.'"[1] On January 11, 1989, with this front page headline, the *Boston Globe* trumpeted the conclusions of an unpublished study by the prestigious Federal Reserve Bank of Boston. An accompanying diagram dramatized the finding that mortgage loans in the predominantly black neighborhoods of Roxbury and Mattapan would have been more than 100 percent greater "if race was not a factor." The second paragraph of the story on the leaked report quoted its damning finding that "this racial bias is both statistically and economically significant."

Almost exactly one year later, on January 10, 1990, the heads of the city's leading banks emerged from a meeting with Boston's Mayor Raymond Flynn to announce that they had agreed on a $400 million dollar program to help meet the need for affordable housing, adequate banking services, and economic development finance in the city's poor and minority neighborhoods. (When the Massachusetts Bankers Association's statewide "Community Investment Program" was unveiled at a Martin Luther King Day breakfast five days later, it was characterized as a $1 billion, five-year effort.)[2]

In the year between these two dates, Boston experienced a protracted set of struggles over community reinvestment that was unprecedented in the range of participants who were intensely involved and in the breadth of issues addressed. This chapter offers an account of those struggles, their antecedents, and their consequences. We begin by setting

38

the stage with a description of the circumstances in which the Fed's study was first undertaken, then set aside, and subsequently leaked. The second section surveys the major participants in the community investment struggles. The third section provides an account of the main events during the remarkable year that followed the leak of the Boston Fed study. The next two sections summarize the bankers' programs and present a critical review of what was accomplished in the eighteen months following their announcement. The last two sections evaluate the success of the struggle for community investment in Boston and identify some lessons from the Boston experience that may have more general relevance.

SETTING THE STAGE

One of the primary legacies of "the Massachusetts Miracle"—the boom years for the state's economy that came to an end in 1988 almost as abruptly as the presidential campaign of Governor Michael Dukakis that it had made possible—was an acute problem of housing affordability. By 1987, the Boston area had the largest gap between earnings and house prices of any of the nation's fifty largest metropolitan areas: the average Boston-area wage of about $25,000, although 10 percent above the U.S. average, was less than half the $60,000 family income needed to afford the median-priced Boston-area home—which, at $181,200, was approximately double the national average (Dreier, Greiner, and Schwartz 1988).

As housing prices soared, and federal housing funds plummeted, it became increasingly difficult for anyone, except those at the top of the income distribution, to purchase a home. The problem was exacerbated as the banks' conformance with standard secondary-market criteria to determine eligibility for mortgage lending unreasonably excluded many potential home buyers in all parts of the city. For example, banks continued to require that monthly mortgage and related payments not exceed 25–28 percent of income at a time when almost a third of Boston renters were paying over 40 percent of their incomes on housing costs.

Other bank practices, however, gave a distinctly racial dimension to Boston's housing affordability problem:[3] in low- and moderate-income white neighborhoods, readily available bank credit fueled the speculative frenzy of gentrification and condominium conversion that reduced the ability of long-time residents to afford to continue living in their own neighborhoods. Minority areas largely escaped this problem, but the banks' diminishing presence in, and general unfamiliarity with, minority neighborhoods made bank mortgages hard to come by there. Between 1978 and 1988, banks closed 40 percent of their branch offices in the predominantly minority areas of Roxbury, Mattapan, and Dorchester while increasing the number of branches in mainly white East Boston, Hyde Park, and West Roxbury by over 30 percent (Community Investment Coalition 1989: 5). A survey in early 1989 found that "Boston's twelve largest lending institutions have five times more offices in white areas than in areas [with the same total population] that are predominantly black or Hispanic" (Hanafin 1989).

Although Boston had been one of the major centers of the community reinvestment movement from the mid-1970s through the early 1980s (see Greenwald 1980: chaps. 5–6), the movement had been largely inactive for several years. Instead, various cooperative efforts to address the problem of housing affordability in Boston—involving banks, government agencies, nonprofit developers, and community groups—had been underway at least since the establishment of the Boston Housing Partnership in 1983. Bankers were also participating in the Task Force on Financing Affordable Housing led by the state's association of community development corporations (CDCs), with support from the Boston Fed and the Federal Home Loan Bank of Boston, that began meeting in mid-1987. Participants on all sides of the subsequent struggles over community investment told me that the personal relationships established during these earlier efforts were significant in facilitating a constructive dialogue when the struggle over community investment intensified in 1989.

One of the responses to the affordable housing problem involved city-aided efforts to develop mixed- and low-income housing projects, often on vacant parcels of land donated by the city. By late 1988, both minority developers and city housing officials perceived that banks were discriminating against projects in Roxbury, Boston's major black neighborhood. Meetings of bankers, city officials, and developers were held. The *Boston Globe* began to publicize the controversy. In this context—and well aware of the studies of mortgage lending discrimination in Atlanta, Detroit, and elsewhere—Boston Redevelopment Authority (BRA) Director Stephen Coyle and Director of Housing Peter Dreier proposed sponsoring a major study of lending patterns in Boston. They tentatively arranged for the study to be undertaken by Charles Finn, a U:'.versity of Minnesota economist who had played an important role in redlining studies in Detroit, Atlanta, and other cities. However, in late December the BRA's board of directors surprised observers by voting against going ahead with the study.

It was probably no coincidence that the politically explosive findings of the Boston Fed's draft study—cited at the beginning of this chapter—appeared on the front page of the *Globe* soon thereafter. With the disclosure of this study, the issue of community reinvestment in Boston irrevocably became a major local issue. What mattered even more than the study's findings—after all, racial disparities in lending patterns could hardly have been major news to anyone at all familiar with the situation—was its sponsorship. This was the first study by any of the four federal bank regulatory agencies that had contained such conclusions. The fact that the study was done at the Fed gave it and its findings a respectability and credibility that no study sponsored by community advocates or the media could hope to achieve. Furthermore, the Boston Fed, in its capacity as a regulator, could hardly refrain from following up on the findings of its own research department.

Ironically, the draft study, by researcher Constance Dunham and community affairs officer William Spring, considered patterns of mortgage lending by race almost incidentally (only three of the thirty-two pages of the draft manuscript's text were devoted to the topic) in the course of a more general exploration, using Boston as a case study, of how the Community Reinvestment Act (CRA) could be used more effectively to promote the creation of affordable housing. Noting that one motive behind passage of the CRA was "the hope of eliminating geographical discrimination in credit" and that "studies of lending in Boston in the 1970s showed that uneven patterns in housing finance did exist, and that these were related to the racial composition of neighborhoods," the authors undertook an econometric analysis of mortgage lending data for the city's sixteen major neighborhoods from 1981–85. They found, in brief, that Boston "continues as a city with significant racial lending bias" (Dunham and Spring 1988: 3, 6–8).

The Boston Fed's initial reaction to the leak was to claim that its failure to publish the study was due to concern with methodological problems and data reliability, and it resisted numerous calls by community advocates and public officials for the study's release. (Indeed, the draft study has to this day not been made public by the Fed.) Instead, the Fed promised, on the same day that the story appeared in the *Globe*, that a rigorous and methodologically sound study would be completed and released within the next few months. The next day, prodded by an open letter from Mayor Flynn, the BRA board reversed itself and approved the hiring of Charles Finn to undertake a study of Boston lending patterns.

Thus, the initial response to the leaking of the draft study guaranteed that the issue of racial discrimination by banks would not quietly fade away. Even if some bankers could hope that the revised Fed study would somehow exonerate them (Robert Sheridan, president of the Massachusetts Bankers Association, bravely stated that "the record of the industry is impeccable. . . . A thorough, complete analysis will show no bias" [*Boston Globe*, Jan. 12, 1989]), they were convinced that Finn's findings would be highly critical. Knowledge that these two reports would be forthcoming conditioned everything that followed.

The press coverage given to the leak was influential in a second way, as well. While Dunham and Spring were motivated primarily by the general issue of housing affordability, it was the issue of racial disparities that dominated press coverage. Although all parties to the events that followed recognized the importance of both issues, everyone also remained aware that it was the racial aspect of the situation that would dominate the publicity and the politics, and that would ultimately be the main factor in providing pressure on the bankers to improve their performance.

Introducing the Actors

Perhaps the most striking feature of the struggles over community investment in Boston is the very large number of participants who played significant roles. The three central roles can be characterized as those of "the community," "the banks," and "the city." But none of the "actors" who played these principal roles was a single entity; each had its own constituent groups, internal structure, tensions, and disagreements. In addition, many other actors made important contributions to the events of 1989 and after.

The Community

On the community side, the major actor was the Community Investment Coalition (CIC), an alliance of six member groups formed in early 1989 specifically to carry out a campaign for increased bank investment in

Boston's minority community. The Massachusetts Affordable Housing Alliance (MAHA) is itself a statewide coalition of over one hundred groups working to increase public and private funding for affordable housing; MAHA's Home Buyers Union is a group of low- and moderate-income tenants, primarily black women, organized to create opportunities for becoming first-time home buyers. The Greater Roxbury Neighborhood Authority is a community organization advocating on behalf of Boston's minority community. The Dudley Street Neighborhood Initiative is a cross between a neighborhood organization and a community development corporation, working to empower residents while physically and economically redeveloping the Dudley Street area of Roxbury. Hotel and Restaurant Workers Union, Local 26, is noted for its progressive social activism, including its recent first-in-the-nation successful contract negotiation for a housing trust fund for the union's members.

The CIC began with these four members, but by the summer had expanded to include two CDCs that build affordable rental and ownership housing in Boston's minority neighborhoods: Nuestra Communidad and Urban Edge. The members of the CIC united behind a comprehensive set of proposals including banking services, provision of affordable mortgages to low-income home buyers, and financing of affordable housing development. Nevertheless, the different emphases of the groups—some more concerned with affordable mortgages and others with development of additional affordable housing units—contained the potential for emergence of tensions later in the year.

Two statewide groups also played significant roles on the community side. The Massachusetts Association of Community Development Corporations represents more than forty CDCs statewide, most involved primarily in the development of affordable housing. The Massachusetts Community Action Program Directors Association (MASSCAP) represents twenty-five community action (antipoverty) agencies throughout the state. It had independently initiated a CRA campaign in early 1988 and maintained a single-minded focus on basic banking services.

The Banks

The major Boston-based banks responded to the situation collectively as well as individually. Their collective response was organized by the president and other top staff of the Massachusetts Bankers Association (MBA), the trade group whose membership included virtually all of the state's approximately two hundred fifty commercial and savings banks. To help

formulate and coordinate this response, the MBA hired community reinvestment consultant Jim Carras, one of the principal leaders of the local
community reinvestment movement during its heyday a decade earlier.

Boston's five largest banks played prominent individual roles in
addition to the roles that their executives played in shaping the collective MBA response. Bank of Boston, long the region's preeminent bank,
had recently found itself challenged by rivals whose growth was fueled by
mergers during the 1980s. By the end of 1988, both Bank of New England and Shawmut National Corporation (which had dual headquarters
in Hartford and Boston) were also in the nation's top twenty-five banking companies, ranked by total assets. Taken together, these three banks
held 30 percent of all deposits in Massachusetts banks and thrifts.

The other two Boston banks in the nation's top one hundred
(each ranked about sixtieth) were only about a third as large, with total
assets of approximately $10 billion apiece, and each was something of an
anomaly. Although Boston provided the corporate headquarters for the
statewide chain of banks operated by BayBanks, Inc., BayBank Boston
itself was relatively small, with assets of approximately $0.6 billion. State
Street Bank had retreated almost totally from retail banking during the
1980s, closing all but six branch offices and concentrating on providing
custodial, trust, and related financial services to mutual funds and other
institutional clients.

In addition, the Boston Bank of Commerce, in spite of its relatively tiny size (total deposits of $60 million), was able to play a signifi-
cant role by virtue of its status as Boston's only black-owned and black-
managed bank.

The City

At various points, the City of Boston was represented personally by
Mayor Raymond Flynn, perhaps the most populist/progressive of the nation's big-city mayors. However, the city's day-to-day involvement was
through two units of the city bureaucracy that often had conflicting
agendas. The BRA placed particular emphasis on the availability of affordable mortgages for low-income residents in all of the city's neighborhoods. The city's Public Facilities Department, in contrast, gave almost
exclusive emphasis to the formation and implementation of successful
partnerships for financing the development of additional affordable housing. Members of the Boston City Council, an entity with limited power

but substantial visibility, also spoke out, introduced local ordinances, and otherwise brought pressure to bear on the banks.

Other Actors

Although the other banking regulators maintained a fairly low profile, the Federal Reserve Bank of Boston under its new president, Richard Syron, chose to play an active role in the community reinvestment arena. Indeed, Syron expressed his intention of placing the Boston Fed "at the front of the pack" among the country's twelve regional Federal Reserve Banks (*Boston Herald*, June 16, 1989). Congressman Joe Kennedy, a member of the House Banking Committee whose district includes parts of Boston—and who had established his political credentials in this area by being largely responsible for the inclusion of amendments strengthening the federal CRA and the Home Mortgage Disclosure Act in the final version of the S & L bailout bill in August 1989—also intervened in the local struggles on a number of occasions. In addition, the Reverend Charles Stith, head of the national Organization for a New Equality (ONE), was an articulate spokesman for the needs of the minority community, even in the absence of a substantial local constituency. The excellent working relationships that he established with the presidents of the Boston Fed and the MBA enabled him periodically to play a mediating role.

Although there were no major research or investigative reporting initiatives (as in Atlanta or Detroit) by either of the Boston dailies, the *Globe* and the *Herald* both gave prominent attention to the ongoing struggles over community investment issues. Beginning even before the leak of the draft Fed study, one of the major dynamics throughout the community investment struggles was that one party would leak a story to the *Globe* or the *Herald*, and thus other parties were forced to react. There can be little doubt that much less would have been achieved in the absence of the unrelenting publicity provided by the local papers.

THE COMMUNITY INVESTMENT CAMPAIGN OF 1989

During the first few months of 1989, both the Community Investment Coalition and the Massachusetts Bankers Association were occupied primarily with internal matters, preparing themselves for the campaign ahead. Although initial talks toward forming the CIC began in January, the coalition only officially announced its existence in June with a letter to major banks that identified primary concerns and promised delivery of a comprehensive community investment proposal during the summer. MAHA proposed that the residents of black neighborhoods suffering from redlining make common cause against the banks with the residents of white neighborhoods hit by gentrification, but the CIC decided to focus its efforts on Boston's minority neighborhoods.

The Massachusetts Association of CDCs (MACDC) took part in the CIC's early discussions but ultimately decided to participate in the process independently, rather than as part of the coalition. The CIC's focus was almost exclusively on Boston, whereas MACDC wanted to push for a state-wide response to the problems of affordable housing development and community-based economic development that were facing its member CDCs throughout the state.

Meanwhile, the major banks (most of which operated throughout the state) and the MBA were debating among themselves over the nature of their response. The ultimate decision—that the response should not only be collective in nature but also involve an approach that was both comprehensive in program elements and statewide in scope—was not reached easily. Not the least of the difficulties, and a continuing source of tension as the year progressed, was the centrifugal force generated by the fact that the bankers were accustomed to competing intensely with each other rather than working together. Tensions among the big Boston-based commercial banks were, moreover, accompanied by long-standing rivalries between big and small banks, between Boston-based banks and banks based elsewhere in the state, and between commercial and savings banks.

Nevertheless, after some initial attempts to discredit the study being undertaken by Charles Finn for the BRA and to urge a lower-profile approach on the Boston Fed, the bankers agreed to adopt a constructive and cooperative approach, rather than a defensive and confrontational one. One factor pushing them in this direction was the "Joint Statement" on the CRA, released in March by the four federal bank regulatory agencies. This pronouncement clearly indicated that the regulators would henceforth be taking banks' responsibilities toward their local communities much more seriously (*Federal Register*, April 5, 1989: 13743–47). In any case, following the advice urged on them by the MBA executive staff and their consultant, Jim Carras, the major banks assumed a basic stance that amounted to saying "we want to do much better in these areas than we have in the past, and we welcome input from all parties into *our process* of deciding just what we ought to do and how we ought to do it."

One preview of controversies to come was provided by the Bank of Boston's May announcement of a first-time home buyers' program that targeted $5 million of below-market-rate mortgages for houses in Boston. The program was aimed at making mortgages affordable to purchasers with family incomes between $35,000 and $45,000. The CIC response criticized the program as a public relations gimmick that did not really address the needs of most residents of Boston's minority neighborhoods— where fully 80 percent of families had incomes below that level—and made clear that it was seeking mortgages that would be affordable to community residents with annual incomes between $15,000 and $35,000.

The process advanced to a new level in June and July, when the MBA, in cooperation with the Boston Fed, sponsored a series of three public forums. Audiences numbering in the hundreds heard representatives of community groups, nonprofit developers, city agencies, and banks discuss the entire range of issues that they thought the banks ought to be addressing in order to be more responsive to community needs. At the first forum, where a ten-member panel addressed the subject of affordable housing, a significant breakthrough came in the statement of Richard Driscoll, chairman of the Bank of New England:

> The problem of affordable housing . . . needs more in-
> volvement by everybody, certainly by banks, certainly by
> my own bank. Everybody involved needs to abandon old
> ideas about how this problem will be solved. Certainly
> banks have to stop saying "we've never done it this way
> before" or "our current policies prevent us from doing
> that" or "it's not my problem, let's give it to the govern-
> ment."
>
> (*Boston Globe*, June 23, 1989)

One of Boston's two black city councilors, Bruce Bolling, took the occasion to announce that he would be introducing an anti-redlining ordinance to prohibit the city from doing business with banks that practice discriminatory policies and to establish a city banking commission. This was the first step in a months-long series of city council actions, in which councilor David Scondras played the leading role, that added to the publicity and pressures confronting the bankers. One of these efforts was a task force established to devise and draft a linked deposit banking program for the city that would tie city deposits, and its other banking business, to bank performance in meeting community needs. Representatives from the CIC participated in this initiative.

On the day before the second forum, one focusing on bank products and services, community groups took the first of several direct actions. The CIC organized picketing and sit-ins at a Roxbury branch of the Bank of Boston to protest redlining of minority neighborhoods and the more limited hours and services at branches in minority areas than at other Bank of Boston branches; six people were arrested.

The third forum was on investing in community economic development, a topic placed on the agenda primarily as a result of an initiative by proponents within the banking community. They argued that neighborhood economic viability ultimately depended on successful locally based businesses that could generate the jobs and incomes necessary for residents to make mortgage or rental payments and to become profitable consumers of bank services. At the conclusion of this forum, MBA president Robert Sheridan committed his organization to coordinate further reviews by individual banks and by the MBA itself. He promised to convene a statewide bankers' meeting in early September to present the results of these efforts to formulate a comprehensive, programmatic response to the problems identified.

By this point it was clear that the banks were committed to adopting a program that would respond to the criticisms that they had not been meeting the needs of the minority community. It was also becoming clear to members of the CIC and the Flynn administration that while the bankers would solicit their input (as at the MBA/Fed forums), they wanted a banker-controlled process of review and decision-making. As Peter Dreier, the mayor's top housing adviser, told reporters after praising the process that allowed substantial community input at the forums: "This could be window dressing or it could be a window of opportunity" (*Boston Globe*, July 21, 1989). Much of what happened during the next six months needs to be understood as part of a protracted campaign by the CIC and the Flynn administration to prevent the banks from being able to proceed unilaterally.

Several developments during August put the bankers on notice that their control of the process was being contested. Early in the month, the Greater Roxbury Neighborhood Authority (GRNA) released the results of an independent study of mortgage lending patterns in Boston that it had commissioned in March (LaPrade and Nagle 1989). The study reinforced the conclusions of the draft Fed study leaked in January: prominent press coverage highlighted the comparisons of paired neighborhoods, with income and demographic characteristics similar except for racial composition, in which primarily black census tracts received only a fraction as many mortgage loans as primarily white census tracts.

On August 25, the CIC took the initiative by releasing its own "Community Investment Plan," an impressive twenty-nine page document that outlined problems of banking services and housing affordability and offered a detailed proposal for increased branches and improved services plus $2.1 billion ($210 million per year for ten years) to finance housing creation and preservation (Community Investment Coalition, 1989). The proposal was delivered directly, as well as indirectly via the front page of the *Boston Globe*, to over twenty leading Boston banks. The CIC requested prompt responses and invited the bankers to attend a community meeting in Roxbury on September 27 to discuss the proposal.

Three days later, the Massachusetts Association of CDCS (MACDC) unveiled its own community reinvestment proposal. This six-page plan, more comprehensive but less detailed than that of the CIC, was statewide in scope and emphasized the roles of CDCS in promoting small business development as well as in creating affordable housing. In MACDC's cover letter presenting this proposal to the MBA, the group pointedly noted the CIC's community investment proposal and indicated that it intended to work with "them and you."

Before anyone could work with anyone, however, the Boston Fed released its revised study of "Geographic Patterns of Mortgage Lending in Boston, 1982–1987" (Bradbury, Case, and Dunham 1989) on August 31. The study's methodology was much more sophisticated than that of the draft leaked almost eight months earlier, but the general conclusion reinforced the earlier findings:

> Housing and mortgage credit markets are functioning in a
> way that hurts black neighborhoods in the city of Bos-
> ton. . . . The ratio of mortgage loans to the potentially

> mortgagable housing stock is substantially lower in pre-
> dominantly black neighborhoods than in white neighbor-
> hoods. . . . Lower incomes, less wealth, lower-valued
> housing units, less housing development, and other fac-
> tors in black neighborhoods do not fully explain these
> persistent patterns by race. Adjustment for these neigh-
> borhood characteristics reduces the size of the discrep-
> ancy in mortgage lending . . . but a 24 percent difference
> remains. (p. 4)

Although the Fed's researchers were careful to point out that this state of
affairs might have had causes other than discrimination by the banks,
they also emphasized that "even if the disparities in mortgage activity
were not the fault of lenders, banks and thrifts would be expected to help
correct the situation," because of their obligations under the CRA (Bradbury, Case, and Dunham 1989: 4). The results of this careful study by the
Boston Fed again focused public attention on the community investment
struggles and highlighted their racial dimension. It further strengthened
the position within the MBA of those (already dominant) who argued for
a constructive response rather than stonewalling or denial.

The expectation had been that the Fed study and the Finn/BRA
study would be released at about the same time. Given the enormous
impact of the Fed study, however, BRA officials saw little advantage to be
gained from quick release of their study. They decided to withhold it
until it could have maximum impact on the ongoing process. Until that
moment, the Finn study would remain officially incomplete. In the
meantime, Mayor Flynn began to play a more active role in the process,
announcing that he had instructed the city's treasurer, the highest rank-
ing black member of his administration, to begin a round of talks with
local bankers.

The MBA's refusal to include CIC representatives among the community advocates invited to their industry-wide meeting, scheduled for
September 8 at a hotel twenty miles west of Boston, provided a dramatic
early example of the bankers' ongoing attempts to deal with those community advocates that they viewed as "moderate" or "pragmatic" while
excluding from the process those community representatives they regarded as more "militant" or "ideological." The *Boston Globe* (Aug. 29
and Sept. 1) reported a firm line by the MBA on this matter, but in the

face of threatened pickets—as well an important statement of solidarity by the MACDC, which said that it would not attend unless the CIC was also invited—the bankers changed their mind on the eve of the session.

That this particular attempted exclusion was symbolic rather than practical was apparent from the nature of the meeting, which consisted of a series of speeches by regulators, followed by presentations by the heads of four MBA special community-banking task forces, each of whom was a top official of one of the big Boston banks. These presentations, and an accompanying package of handouts, established the four-part structure that was eventually included in the programs announced four months later: bank products and services; mortgage lending; financing affordable housing; and minority economic development.

The bankers announced that the task forces in each of these areas would continue to meet and would be open to participation by all interested parties. Finally, MBA officials promised to unveil by mid-October, six weeks later, a community investment program, reflecting input by individual banks throughout the state, that would include specific dollar amounts along with program details. The next day's papers carried not only stories about the meeting and the promised programs but also accounts of demonstrations, organized by the GRNA, that included picketing at downtown Boston branches of the Bank of Boston and the Bank of New England.

Throughout the rest of September and October, the struggle over what sort of community investment program would ultimately emerge continued on many fronts. The MBA's four task forces each began to meet, a process that eventually involved more than two hundred regular participants in face-to-face discussions about the practical problems of putting together workable programs. Bankers and community advocates later agreed on the value of the task force experience not only in establishing personal relationships and lines of communication but also as a process of mutual education about the realities of the disparate worlds in which each worked.

On September 10, Mayor Flynn appropriated the city council's initiative by unilaterally announcing his intention to issue executive orders creating a linked deposit banking program and establishing the Community Banking Commission.

On September 12, MAHA submitted a formal CRA challenge to State Street Bank's application for approval from the state banking com-

missioner to open a branch office in Tokyo. In transforming itself into a
provider of financial services rather than a retail bank, State Street had
closed eleven Boston branches since 1983 and had a relatively poor record of providing credit to local low- and moderate-income neighborhoods. Two weeks after the mid-October public hearings on the challenged application, the bank invested $1.5 million in a limited equity
cooperative housing project in Roxbury, widely regarded as an investment that it would not otherwise have made.[4]

On September 13, action on another front was heightened when
the governor introduced legislation to promote bank investment in local
communities by, among other things, strengthening the state's CRA, already one of the strongest in the nation. The CIC and its allies introduced
several amendments.

On September 27, the CIC's community meeting in the auditorium of the Trotter elementary school in Roxbury drew a large and
enthusiastic crowd to hear community advocates articulate their needs
and concerns and summarize the content of the community investment
plan that the CIC had distributed to the banks a month before. Diana
Strother, cochair of both MAHA and its Home Buyers Union, pointedly
asked each bank's representative to respond "yes or no" to the question of
whether it would agree to negotiate with the CIC about this plan. Several
smaller banks said yes, but all of the major banks declined. Their general
position was essentially that they would be happy to talk with any community representatives, but that they wished to proceed on the basis of
their own program, not the CIC's.

On September 29, the U.S. House Banking Committee held a
day of hearings in Boston on local community reinvestment issues, its
first hearing outside of Washington, D.C., on a community credit issue.
State and local officials, bank regulators, and top banking executives all
testified to their commitment to respond effectively to the acknowledged
problems documented in the Boston Fed study. Committee chair Henry
Gonzalez was there, but it was Rep. Joe Kennedy's show, and he left
little doubt where he stood. In a press conference before the hearings
themselves, he endorsed the CIC's Community Investment Plan.

On October 20, the CIC filed a CRA challenge to the application
of BayBank Harvard Trust to open a new branch in the Allston/Brighton
area of Boston. The challenge was critical of the CRA record both of this
particular bank and of the entire BayBanks chain. Their very weak rec-

ord of mortgage lending in predominantly black census tracts was consistent with the fact that out of 230 branches statewide, none were in Boston's minority neighborhoods.

As October ended, the MBA had failed to meet its self-imposed mid-October deadline for announcing the final version of its plans with dollars attached; and the principal players—the CIC and the leading Boston bankers—still had not met in direct negotiations.

On November 8, for the first time, a top official from one of the major Boston banks agreed to negotiate directly with the CIC. Once again, the breakthrough initiative was taken by Richard Driscoll of the Bank of New England. The other major banks soon followed his lead, and the rest of the process involved numerous direct meetings among these parties.

Three days later, Mayor Flynn threw a third community investment plan into the arena. Calling for the commitment of $1 billion of bank funds over a five year period, the city's plan had the same basic elements as those of the CIC and the MBA. It differed in attempting to cast the issue more along class lines than racial ones, by including certain of the city's low- and moderate-income white neighborhoods among the targeted areas needing better treatment by the banks. Also in November, the Massachusetts CAP Directors Association (MASSCAP) released the results of a substantial survey of the need for and availability of basic banking services to low-income residents statewide. The survey report placed particular emphasis on the unwillingness of banks—particularly the "Boston Big 4 Banks"—to cash government welfare checks for individuals without accounts and on the lack of affordable basic bank accounts.

Frustrated by the process of forging a collective response, and seeking competitive advantage for themselves, two of the big banks announced initiatives of their own. On November 16, four days before the hearing on its challenged application, BayBanks announced its plan to open five new branches and twenty-five new automated teller machines (ATMs) in Boston's low- and moderate-income and minority neighborhoods within the next three years. The CIC responded with pickets both at the bank's busy Copley Square branch in downtown Boston and at the home of the BayBank Boston Chairman Richard Pollard (who was also serving as chairman of the MBA),[5] complaining that branches and ATMs were not enough and that the bank needed also to respond to the need for affordable housing construction and mortgages.[6] Two weeks later, in early December, the Bank of Boston announced its plan for improved service in the greater Roxbury area, including a new branch with an ATM, the upgrading of other branches, and the extension of banking hours.

Through mid-December the four MBA task forces continued to meet, and negotiations continued about the size and shape of the final program. General agreement was reached on most issues, but significant disagreements persisted. Most important, the bankers continued to resist the insistence of the mayor and some CIC members, particularly MAHA staffers Lou Finfer and Tom Callahan, that the final program include a substantial commitment for mortgages with below-market interest rates that would make homeownership possible for a significant number of first time homebuyers with incomes in the $15,000–$30,000 range. With this deadlock persisting, the bankers resolved to publicly unveil their program during the week before Christmas.

At this point, on December 20, the BRA created an uproar by releasing its long-overdue mortgage lending study (Finn 1989). Charles Finn's main quantitative finding was that banks made 2.9 times as many mortgage loans per thousand privately owned housing units in low-income white neighborhoods as in minority neighborhoods at the same income level (3.4 times as many if government-insured mortgages were excluded from the calculations.)[7] He reported individual white/minority lending ratios for each of the twenty largest banks in Boston; and the prose accompanying his quantitative results offered a much sharper indictment of bank performance than did the Boston Fed study.

The resulting publicity led the bankers to postpone announcing their program. Angry bankers and concerned editorialists offered numerous predictions that the entire initiative might unravel.[8] What happened instead was almost three weeks of intense negotiations, most around the issue of below-market-rate mortgages. The ongoing talks were punctuated by a number of high-profile compromise initiatives and mediating efforts. Mayor Flynn, whose clout was enhanced by growing speculation that he was about to announce his candidacy for governor (he would have been the instant front runner, had he decided to run), joined with the BRA in actively pushing for an agreement including below-market-rate mortgages, and he pledged city money to help fund part of the subsidized mortgage package. This position was opposed within city hall by the Public Facilities Department (PFD), which wanted to avoid jeopardizing the agreements already obtained from the banks for funding city-sponsored housing development projects. Similar stresses grew within the CIC: MAHA and its Home Buyers Union remained determined to hold out for the inclusion of below-market-rate mortgages in the final package, while another member group, Local 26 of the Hotel and Restaurant Workers Union, threatened a class action lawsuit against the banks, with the stated purpose of convincing the bankers to agree to provide subsidized mortgages. Yet Gus Newport, the black former mayor of Berkeley, California, who was now executive director of the Dudley Street Neighborhood Initiative—which wanted quick funding for the affordable housing projects on which it was cooperating with the PFD—allowed himself to be quoted in the press as being in favor of settling for what had already been agreed to. The bankers also disagreed among themselves on what was to be done.

In the midst of all this, the revelation that Charles Stuart was the prime suspect in the widely publicized (e.g., *Time* and *Newsweek* cover stories) murder of his pregnant wife Carol and near fatal wounding of himself the previous November raised racial tensions in Boston to the boiling point. Stuart, who jumped off a bridge to his death after learning of his imminent arrest, had cynically claimed that a black man had shot them both, and much of the city had succumbed to racial hysteria as police, press, and public all too readily accepted his story. Now Boston's blacks learned that the intense police harassment inflicted on residents of the neighborhood where the killing took place was the consequence of a cruel hoax perpetrated by a white man.

The desire of the city's white political and business leaders to calm the heightened racial tensions almost certainly was a factor in finally bringing the negotiators to agreement. On January 10, 1990, just six days after Charles Stuart's suicide, the city's leading bankers emerged from the mayor's office to announce a mutually acceptable community investment program.

The formal unveiling of the MBA's statewide "Community Investment Program" took place on January 15, at the annual Martin Luther King Day breakfast sponsored by Reverend Charles Stith. The MBA press release describing the program failed to give any special mention to the central roles played by the CIC and Mayor Flynn; it spoke instead in general terms of "elected officials and regulators and . . . more than 40 statewide and Boston-based community groups who were involved in the discussions that helped shape the package."

Two weeks later, the CIC sponsored a public meeting in the auditorium of the Dudley Square branch of the Boston Public Library. Willie Jones, GRNA board member, presided over a set of announcements by representatives of ten of the city's largest banks of the individual bank commitments for investment in Boston's minority neighborhoods that he and other CIC negotiators had obtained.

Only a highly abbreviated account of the community reinvestment struggles in Boston between January 1989 and January 1990 could be included here, and many significant events and influential actors had to be omitted. From what has been related, however, it should be clear that the Community Investment Coalition and its allies carried out a campaign that operated on many fronts. They effectively borrowed and built upon a variety of tactics developed in earlier efforts in Chicago and elsewhere, and subsequently employed in other cities. These included: (1) undertaking direct action (picketing and demonstrations); (2) sponsoring a research study on mortgage lending patterns; (3) preparing a comprehensive community investment plan; (4) holding community meetings, attended by bankers, in support of the plan; (5) making two CRA challenges to bank applications; (6) working in support of proposed state legislation, including some provisions that it had submitted; (7) supporting initiatives at the city level by progressive city councilors; (8) conducting direct negotiations with bankers; (9) submitting information to the local media on a regular basis; and (10) threatening a class action lawsuit.

WHAT WAS WON: THE BANKERS' PROMISED PROGRAMS

The statewide Community Investment Program announced by the Massachusetts Bankers Association in the middle of January 1990 contained dollar totals for various program elements, but no indication of amounts to be committed by individual banks. (This was probably because total individual bank commitments remained far below the announced totals; the MBA leadership had failed to elicit substantial participation in the program beyond that of the big Boston banks.) The Boston community investment initiatives announced by the CIC at the end of the month consisted of a compilation of individual bank commitments, some out-side of the MBA framework. Whereas the statewide program was in form clearly a unilateral program of the bankers, as opposed to an agreement with any community group or public agency, the Boston program took the form of commitments announced at a CIC-sponsored public meeting.

The MBA characterized its statewide initiative as a "$1 billion pro-gram" ($465 million of new bank funds, some in pools where dollars would be recycled two or three times during the five-year life of the program), whereas the CIC calculated the bank commitments to Boston over the next five years at $397 million, of which $206 million was part of the statewide MBA program. All such totals are suspect, and should be taken as providing no more than rough indications of the overall size of the envisioned programs. A better way to see what was involved is to review each of the four major program components.

Basic Banking Services

The banks agreed to provide nine new full-service branches and thirty-two new ATMs in Boston's minority neighborhoods over the next five years. An unspecified number of existing branches would expand their banking hours and range of services offered. An eighteen-member Massa-chusetts Community and Banking Council (MCBC)—with nine commu-nity representatives and nine banking representatives—would be es-tablished as a nonprofit corporation to oversee provision of banking services, sponsor consumer education about banking and credit issues, undertake community credit needs assessments, and provide a forum for continuing dialogue about community needs and bank performance in meeting these needs.

Affordable Housing Development

A second new nonprofit corporation, the Massachusetts Housing Invest-ment Corporation (MHIC), would be established to: assemble and admin-ister a $100 million loan pool for construction and rehabilitation of af-fordable housing; provide technical advice and assistance to facilitate $100 million of equity investments in low-income housing projects quali-fying for federal tax credits; and find sources for permanent (mortgage) financing of the affordable housing projects after completion of construc-tion.

Mortgage Lending

One element of the MBA program was referred to as the "FannieMae/GE" program, because the General Electric Capital Corporation agreed to provide up to $35 million of private mortgage insurance for the first 80 percent of mortgages to qualifying first-time homebuyers in targeted neighborhoods statewide, and FannieMae (the Federal National Mortgage Association) agreed to purchase the mortgages from the issuing banks in spite of their nonstandard terms. The terms were nonstandard in that the loans, made at market interest rates and perhaps with modest discounts from standard closing costs, would require just a 5 percent down payment and allow monthly housing payments of up to 33 percent of income (rather than the typical maximum ratio of 28 percent).

More important, in response to the final round of pressure applied by the Flynn administration and some CIC members, six banks committed themselves to provide a total of $30 million for mortgage loans in Boston's minority neighborhoods at one percent below the market interest rate. Part of the compromise agreement was that these subsidized loans would be outside of the MBA program itself. Pledges of up to $10 million in state and city government funds to subsidize interest and down payment costs promised to make homeownership possible at an income level below $20,000. With an average low-cost house priced at $75,000 (given Boston's inflated housing market), $30 million would make possible about four hundred mortgages. The details of the subsidized mortgage program were to be worked out over the next sixty days.

In addition, some individual banks announced commitments to lend a total of $150 million for home mortgages in minority areas over the next five years.

Minority Business Development

A third statewide corporation, the Massachusetts Minority Enterprise Investment Corporation (MEIC), would be established to provide equity capital, loans, technical assistance, and other support to minority businesses. The banks would supply the MEIC with $10 million capitalization and $50 million for lending.

WHAT WAS DELIVERED: THE FIRST EIGHTEEN MONTHS

Although the MBA program announcement included an explicit commitment to "development of an efficient mechanism, acceptable to all parties, to monitor the progress of the various program components and to assess their success in achieving their goals," implementation of such a monitoring mechanism had been only partially accomplished eighteen months later.

The CIC, the city, and the banks have continued to work on the development of a mutually acceptable framework for reporting on program progress. As of August 1991, the agreed-upon procedure involved quarterly submission of data by individual banks, compilation of these data by the CIC, and detailed review at a meeting of city, bank, and CIC representatives held one month after the end of each quarterly reporting period. The tables produced each three months covered only part of the overall community investment program: they provide information on new branches and ATMs and on the status of the four pools of money created by the MBA program (the MHIC pools for housing loans and equity investments and the MEIC pools for capitalization and for lines of credit.)[9] These detailed quarterly tables provide the principal source for this section's account of how bank performance through the first half of 1991 was related to the programs promised at the beginning of 1990.[10]

Basic Banking Services

The initial commitment to open nine new branches in Boston's minority neighborhoods had fallen to eight by mid-1991 (apparently because the reported commitment from one now-failed bank, First Mutual, was a typographical error), but two other branches were upgraded to full-service status. One of the eight branches was already open for business. Under the auspices of MCBC, a joint community-bank task force began meeting in January 1991 to consider collectively the merits of alternative locations for the remaining branches. Four high-priority sites were identified and by July individual banks had made specific commitments to locate branches at three of these four locations—Bank of Boston and Fleet Bank in the predominantly black neighborhoods of Grove Hall and Egleston Square,[11] respectively, and BayBank Boston in the low-income Hispanic neighborhood of Hyde Square. In addition, eighteen of the promised thirty-two new ATMs were already in operation.

The April 1990 implementation of a statewide government-check-cashing program—although not mentioned in the MBA's January 1990 announcement—has been justifiably heralded by the MBA as one of the program's great successes. Over two hundred banks, including all of the big ones, with over two-thousand branches statewide, were participating in the voluntary program, cashing government checks for non-account-holders with proper identification. (A maximum fee of fifty cents may be charged; most charge nothing.) Only those familiar with the stubborn resistance of bankers to such programs can appreciate the accomplishment that it represents; Massachusetts became the only state with such a program (voluntary or mandatory). Its adoption, the result of negotiations within the framework provided by MCBC, reflected primarily the efforts of MASSCAP, which focused its energy on accomplishing this specific goal.

The next item on the MASSCAP agenda was widespread availability of low-cost basic banking accounts for low-income people. In August 1991, MCBC was finalizing guidelines for a program whereby banks state-wide would voluntarily offer such accounts. Meanwhile, all of the major Boston banks had already introduced low-cost basic bank accounts that were much improved over what was available before the struggles over community investment began to intensify. The new basic checking accounts (savings accounts were also available) typically required no minimum balance, offered seven or eight checks and a similar number of ATM transactions per month, and cost about three dollars per month—less than the cost of cashing a single modest government check at a check-cashing store. In a closely related initiative, MCBC and the Massachusetts Department of Public Welfare jointly announced in July 1991 a new program allowing welfare recipients with accounts at participating banks to opt for direct deposit of their twice-monthly welfare checks; the great majority of the banks taking part in the check-cashing program chose to participate in the direct deposit program as well.

Affordable Housing Development

The Massachusetts Housing Investment Corporation began operations in July 1990. Bank commitments to MHIC's housing loan pool, originally targeted at $100 million, never grew beyond $55 million, and stood at $48 million in mid-1991. Of this, $35 million had actually been delivered to MHIC, which made its first loan in December, then made commitments through July on ten loans for a total of $7 million, and had numerous additional proposals pending in the pipeline.

Tax credit equity investments facilitated by MHIC in low-income housing projects were also targeted at $100 million. Bank commitments stood at $53 million in mid-1991, down slightly from the original level of

$55 million. Through June, equity investments of $11 million had been completed and $7 million more had been committed.

No progress toward MHIC's third objective, securing a regular source of permanent financing for the housing projects receiving its con-struction loans, had been made by mid-1991. Instead, project sponsors were forced to continue to seek such "take-out" financing on a case-by-case basis, although MHIC now offered assistance in this process.

Mortgage Lending

No reliable quantitative information on the mortgage lending portion of the banks' programs can be reported here because there was, as of mid-1991, no monitoring of this activity. However, representatives of the CIC and the major banks agreed in late July on a reporting format that will include, for each bank, the number of loans and the dollar amount in each special mortgage lending program (publicly subsidized below-market loans; FannieMae/GE mortgages; individual banks' special mortgage products), cross-tabulated by zip code, race of borrower, and income level. These reports are due semiannually, beginning in September 1991 for the period from program inception through June 1991.

Meanwhile, CIC representatives believed that the FannieMae/GE first-time homeowners program, highly touted by the bankers in January 1990, had been almost a total nonstarter in Boston and that the initial mortgage lending report would show that few loans had been made in the city under this program. In any case, the CIC from the beginning had made clear its view that the program offered little to make housing at Boston's inflated prices affordable to its primary constituency—the low-income residents of the city's minority neighborhoods.

In the area of mortgage lending, the major objective of the CIC and the Flynn administration was to create below-market-rate subsidized loans that would make homeownership possible for low-income residents. This was the issue on which they won bank concessions as a result of endgame pressure. The first such publicly subsidized, below-market-rate mortgage loan under the program was not completed until February 1991. As of mid-1991, it appeared that approximately two hundred of these loans—about half of the envisioned total—would be completed before available funding was exhausted sometime late in the year. It took a major struggle in the spring of 1990 for the CIC and the city to over-come the banks' announced intention of offering adjustable-rate rather than fixed-rate mortgages. The price of obtaining agreement on fixed-rate mortgages was making the interest rate one-half of a percentage point, rather than a full percentage point, below the market rate.

Another major struggle was over the state's and the city's promised contributions to the program. As a result of extraordinarily severe fiscal crises, the state's contribution was ultimately cut back from an initial promise of $8 million to $1 million and the city's contribution from $2 million (or more, in some public pledges) to $1 million. At times it appeared as if there might be no public money at all. The city finally agreed, in April 1991, to honor, even partially, its commitment to contribute only after being presented with a file folder full of press clippings that quoted the mayor vigorously denouncing the banks for failing to live up to their commitments in a timely manner. The program's ability to deliver mortgages affordable to low-income residents was also set back when the Bank of New England canceled its $5 million commitment (subsequently restored by Fleet in mid-1991) and when, after several months of waiting in vain to see public money, some other banks went ahead with offering below-market-rate loans without the public subsidies designed to accompany them.

Minority Business Development

The process of establishing the Massachusetts Minority Enterprise Investment Corporation (MEIC) was not complete until the very end of 1990, partly because of a several-month wait for the necessary regulatory approval of its innovative legal status as a community development corporation with a venture capital component, jointly owned by several banks. As of June 30, 1991, its capital stood at $3 million in hand, out of $4.1 million in current bank commitments (down from original commitments of $5 million, just half of the $10 million target announced in January 1990). In addition, $15 million in lines of credit had been committed by banks (out of the $50 million originally announced). In April 1991 MEIC began taking loan applications, and by the end of July it had approved three loans.

WHAT WAS ACCOMPLISHED: AN INTERIM ASSESSMENT

Given this account of what Boston banks promised in January 1990, and of what they delivered in the subsequent eighteen months, what can be concluded about the success of the Boston campaign for community investment? This section addresses this question in terms of the following three criteria: delivering loans and banking services to previously underserved neighborhoods; building institutions and creating relationships between banks and the community that contain the potential for bringing about and sustaining improved future performance; and changing the general political climate and awareness level concerning community investment issues.

This assessment is necessarily a preliminary one. Eighteen months is simply too short a period on which to base confidently a judgment of the programs' successes and failures. On the one hand, initiating innovative programs may require significant start-up time, so that it is inappropriate to expect one-third of the results in the first one-third of the five-year program period. On the other hand, early achievements may prove to be one-time phenomena and to be not sustained over a longer period of time. The most thorough and impressive evaluation of a community reinvestment program to date was completed a year after the conclusion of the first five-year period of the Neighborhood Lending Programs of three major Chicago banks (Bradford 1990); a similar timetable for reviewing the Boston community investment programs would result in a 1996 assessment.

Moreover, evaluating the accomplishments of the campaign for community investment in Boston involves a broader perspective than that required for assessing the accomplishments of the specific programs announced by the MBA and the Boston banks in January 1990. A number of positive developments outside of the framework of the announced programs can be reasonably attributed to the impact of the community investment campaign.

It must also be emphasized that the period immediately following the announcement of the bankers' program was an extremely difficult one for the local economy. The failure of the Bank of New England and the steadily deepening fiscal crises of the state and city governments were only the most visible results of the collapse of real estate markets and the onset of a severe regional recession. All of the big Boston banks (with the sole exception of State Street) not only suffered serious losses but also had their very survival called into question. This harsh economic environment helps to explain why the community investment campaign's greatest single success by mid-1991 was the government-check-cashing program (which costs the banks almost nothing), and its greatest disappointments were in the areas of lending for affordable housing development and minority business development (where viable projects were much more difficult to put together, especially in a period when fear of further loan losses was in the forefront of bankers' minds). Meanwhile, the immense pressures on state and local government budgets were primarily responsible for the slowing of the subsidized, below market-rate mortgage program and its shrinking to approximately half its intended size.

Delivery of Loans and Banking Services

In terms of actual loans and services, the latest CIC tables (based on bank data for the period ending June 30, 1991) indicate that out of a total of $260 million initially promised for the program's four pools (two each within MHIC and MEIC, just $18 million had actually been invested in projects during the first eighteen months of the five-year program. As of June 30, $48 million more had been turned over to the pools by the banks, and an additional $55 million of funds had been committed but not yet delivered. The overall total of these three sums, $121 million, stood at just 47 percent of the total announced in January 1990.

The shortfall in deliveries of loans and investments reflected the state of the economy and the banking industry as well as the lengthy start-up period for the nonprofit institutions. The shortfall in commitments also reflected the almost total failure of the MBA to meet its stated objective of obtaining widespread participation in its program by smaller banks in Boston and around the state. Indeed, the six biggest Boston banks (including the Boston Safe Deposit and Trust Company, a so-called nonbank bank) accounted for 90 percent of the total commitments to the program.

However, in the area of bank products and services, which are not reflected in these reported dollar totals, initial accomplishments more than lived up to promises: new branches and ATMs were being implemented at a pace that would meet the targeted number before five years was over, other branches were upgraded, the government-check-cashing program had been adopted by almost all MBA member banks, and the availability of low-cost basic bank accounts had been dramatically expanded.

Institutions and Relationships

By mid-1991 all three new statewide corporations were in active operation, under the leadership of full-time presidents well-respected by both bankers and community advocates. Both MHIC and MEIC clearly had the potential to contribute significantly to the development of affordable housing and minority businesses when economic conditions began to improve and MCBC, in particular, had successfully provided an ongoing forum for community representatives and banking leaders to deal with the entire range of community investment issues. The level of communication and mutual understanding between the various participants in the process of housing and small business development had expanded greatly beyond where it was when the community investment campaign began. All of these are very significant, although not easily quantified, accomplishments, with great potential to result in substantially improved delivery of credit and banking services in the years ahead. The mid-1990 selection of Richard Driscoll as the new president of the MBA was another promising development—as chairman of the local Bank of New England, Driscoll had made important contributions to moving the process ahead in 1989.

Outside of the framework provided by the new statewide corporations, a number of multibank loan pools and consortiums were created in different parts of the state—from Cape Cod in the east to Pittsfield in the west, Lawrence in the north, and New Bedford in the south, with Cambridge, Fitchburg, and other cities in between. Although the accomplishments of these new entities do not show up in any of the CIC's summary tables, their existence surely stems from the Boston-based struggles for community investment.

Public Consciousness of Community Investment Issues

The community investment campaign was enormously successful in raising general awareness of community investment issues among bankers, politicians, government officials, community residents, the press, and the public at large. The altered political climate concerning these issues was dramatically illustrated at least three times by mid-1991.

First, the attention focused on community investment issues enabled MAHA and its allies both inside and outside of the CIC to make a persuasive case for major state banking legislation aimed at furthering community investment. Among the numerous CRA-related provisions in the new law, enacted in July 1990, was one that coupled approval of nationwide reciprocal interstate banking with the requirement that any out-of-state bank acquiring a Massachusetts bank make available to the Massachusetts Housing Partnership (a state entity promoting affordable housing development) on favorable terms (at its average cost of funds) an amount equal to 0.9 percent of its new in-state assets.

Second, in the process that culminated in the Federal Deposit Insurance Corporation (FDIC) selection of Fleet/Norstar as purchaser of the failed Bank of New England, the press gave extensive coverage to demands by community groups and the Flynn administration that the FDIC give community reinvestment considerations significant weight when choosing among the competing banks. These demands were widely echoed, even by the state's new conservative governor, William Weld. In this climate, even though the FDIC had ruled that the state's July 1990 interstate banking law was not binding in the case of acquisition of a failed bank, Fleet chose nevertheless to announce that it would comply with the legislative provision. As a result, the April 1991 FDIC decision to award the Bank of New England to Fleet/Norstar led to the announcement by Fleet that it would provide the Massachusetts Housing Partnership with $63 million upon acquiring the $7 billion of assets from the Massachusetts component of the failed bank. In addition, Fleet proclaimed that it would honor or exceed all of the commitments, totaling at least $29 million, that the Bank of New England had made to the community investment programs announced in January 1990. In the midst of the state's fiscal and banking crises this was very good news, and it was news that almost surely would not have occurred in the absence of the struggles, beginning in January 1989, over community investment.

Third, the existence of scams in home improvement contracting and second mortgage lending emerged in May 1991 as a major public issue, and revelations about these scams can be traced directly to the community investment struggles of 1989. A detailed account of the behind-the-scenes maneuvering that preceded the saturation coverage of the issue by local television news (Channel 7) and the *Boston Globe* (where the story was given front page coverage on thirty-one out of the fifty-four days beginning on May 6) showed that news outlets originally discounted public interest in the scams. The fact that large numbers of poor, elderly black homeowners were actually losing their homes as a result of these scams was presented the previous summer to a rival TV station (Channel 5) and a rival newspaper (the *Herald*). These outlets considered the issue for months before deciding that it was not really "a story." Only when news personnel recognized that the areas in which the second mortgage scams were happening (Boston's black neighborhoods) were precisely the same areas that the 1989 mortgage lending studies showed were being underserved by banks did the media decide that they had a major story (Jurkowitz 1991). The story line was that banks were not just failing to serve black neighborhoods. They were actually profiting from the resulting conditions by supplying credit to unscrupulous second mortgage companies—companies that were exploiting vulnerable people with high interest rates and exorbitant fees before finally, in many cases, taking away their homes. It is still too early to tell what the consequences of the many-faceted struggles over this highly charged issue will be for the ongoing struggles over community investment in Boston. What is clear already is that it would not have become a major issue without the campaign that began in the aftermath of the leaked Boston Fed study in January 1989 (Dreier 1991).

Future Prospects

Throughout the campaign for increased community investment the MBA repeatedly emphasized that it was more important to establish the necessary foundation for long-lasting change than to provide a one-shot program or some "pots" of money. Community advocates generally agreed on the need for banking institutions to change so that serving the banking needs of low-income and minority neighborhoods would become a regular part of their business activities. At the same time, however, the advocates continually expressed their frustration at the slow pace of the process (especially as the bankers failed to meet their own self-imposed deadlines) and their worry that the bankers might be pursuing relationships and institutions not as a means for achieving the delivery of loans and banking services, but rather as a substitute for them. One of the merits of the current monitoring system, as partial and unsatisfactory as it may be, is that it reflects an agreement that relationships and institutions cannot persist without concrete accomplishments and that quantitative monitoring of actual performance is an important part of the joint process of delivering loans and services while continuing to build institutions and relationships. While future developments necessarily remain uncertain, the establishment of the three new statewide corporations and the considerable broadening and deepening of bank-community relationships have great potential for facilitating community investment in the years ahead.

CONCLUDING OBSERVATIONS

Boston's community investment campaign offers potentially useful lessons for other communities engaged in similar struggles. Five principles deserve particular emphasis.

An Inclusive, Constructive Approach

The Boston experience is notable for the broad range of participants. The primary community advocate, the CIC, was itself a coalition of six member groups representing a variety of different constituencies, and a number of other community advocates played major roles. Many banks were involved and they acted collectively, guided by the Massachusetts Bankers Association, as well as individually. Numerous government agencies played roles. Literally hundreds of people participated in task forces and meetings. Equally important, both the CIC and the bankers generally focused their energy on developing constructive programs rather than on a negative dynamic of criticism and defensiveness. The results showed that such a process can work. It produced a well-designed set of programmatic initiatives and new institutions dedicated to community investment and to expanded delivery of basic banking services. It also produced countless new human contacts and exchanges, with positive results ranging from new levels of understanding to productive working relationships.

The Necessity and Effectiveness of Militancy

At the same time, it is true that nothing significant would have been accomplished without intense pressure from the community groups and, at times, the city government. Every individual that I interviewed, on whatever side of the struggles, shared this perception. Even individuals involved in the bankers' efforts to exclude community militants from the process in favor of those perceived as more moderate acknowledged the effectiveness of militancy. Any particular militant action almost inevitably prompted bankers or editorial writers to respond by worrying that the militancy threatened to destroy the constructive process underway; in fact, militancy generally led instead to constructive dialogue and positive accomplishments. A corollary principle, also validated by the Boston experience, is that the announcement of an agreement or program, no matter how good, does not itself represent victory; it merely marks the end of one phase of struggle and the beginning of a new one. Careful monitoring, to provide the basis for renewed application of pressure when necessary, is an important part of this new phase.

The Primacy of Race

While the community reinvestment struggles of the 1970s tended to be framed in terms of inner-city neighborhoods versus the suburbs, those of the last few years have tended to be framed in terms of racial disparities in credit flows and banking services. Boston is no exception. The claim of racial disparities in lending patterns catapulted the Boston Fed's leaked draft study onto the front pages of the local papers and the confirmation of this finding in the revised Boston Fed study and then the BRA/ Finn study focused intense attention on community investment issues later in the year. In the media-dominated public and political arena, allegations of racial discrimination by banks can become a major issue. Furthermore, lack of media interest, combined with racial politics within the city, doomed the efforts by MAHA and the mayor to broaden the campaign. They had sought to frame the issue in class terms as well as racial terms by highlighting the need for improved bank performance in meeting the credit and affordable housing needs of lower-income white neighborhoods as well as those of lower-income minority neighborhoods.

Community Groups Need Allies

Although in Boston, as in most other places, the major push for improved community investment performance came from community groups, these groups are generally not strong enough to accomplish their goals entirely on their own. Significant gains usually require a set of political circumstances, reinforced by community group pressures, that lead the most important potential allies for community groups—government banking regulators and local politicians and government officials— to decide to temporarily support community group efforts. In Boston's community investment struggles, the mayor and the BRA allied themselves closely with the CIC in pressuring the banks. In addition, the Boston Fed played an important role both by sponsoring the initial and revised studies of mortgage lending patterns and by urging a constructive response to the banks from its position as a major bank regulator.

History Matters

Previous community reinvestment struggles, both locally and nationally, provided a foundation that made possible the accomplishments of the most recent community investment campaign in Boston. Locally, the earlier round of struggles provided experience, personal relationships, and state level legislation that was drawn upon in the most recent struggle. One example of this is provided by Jim Carras, a leading community reinvestment advocate during the decade-earlier period who now, serving as a community reinvestment consultant to the MBA, urged an avoidance of the mistakes of the past by emphasizing constructive approaches, community involvement in program design, and the need to build sustainable institutions. At the federal level, legislation won in the mid-1970s established the regulatory framework and goals which led to the draft Fed study that was eventually leaked. This legislation made available (through the Home Mortgage Disclosure Act) the data used in both the draft Fed study and the Finn/BRA study to document the existence of racial lending disparities. It also provided (through the Community Reinvestment Act) community groups and the Boston Fed with the basis for insisting that banks had an affirmative obligation to respond to the problems uncovered. Just as the participants in Boston's community investment campaign of 1989–91 built on the foundation laid down by previous struggles, it can be expected that their contributions will in turn help provide a basis for further accomplishments in future years.

NOTES

1. In preparing this chapter, I have benefited greatly from the generous assistance of numerous participants in the events described. I have assembled an extensive set of documents with the help of the Community Investment Coalition, the Massachusetts Bankers Association, and others. (For the most part, I have avoided cluttering the chapter with numerous citations to either newspaper articles or unpublished documents; I will be happy to furnish interested readers with information on the source for any statement or fact of particular interest.) My set of press clippings is much more complete than it would have been without access to the collections of Jim Carras and Peter Dreier. Many individuals shared their insights and recollections in interviews and provided helpful comments on previous drafts; these include Tom Callahan, Jim Carras, Jim Cuddy, Peter Dreier, Joe Feaster, Robert Fichter, Bonnie Huedorfer, Willie Jones, Tom Kennedy, Arthur MacEwan, Tom Schumpert, Ed Shea, Robert Sheridan, Bill Spring, Richard Thal, Kathy Tullberg, Ken Wade, and Marc Weiss. In addition, some of my knowledge is first-hand: I was an active member of the Task Force on Linked Deposit Banking formed in the summer of 1989 by City Councillor David Scondras. I also volunteered consulting services to Joseph McGrail, counsel to the city treasurer, as he worked during 1990–91 to implement Boston's Linked Deposit Banking Program, and attended a number of the public meetings mentioned in the text.

2. Although the following pages will show that there are important statewide dimensions of the reinvestment struggles discussed in this chapter, and of the resulting programs and institutions, I believe that it is correct to view what happened as primarily a Boston—rather than a Massachusetts—phenomenon.

3. In this chapter, the word "Boston" refers to the City of Boston itself, which contains only one-fifth of the Boston metropolitan area's population (563,000 out of 2.8 million in 1980). Blacks, who accounted for 22 percent of the city's population in 1980, were concentrated in just three of the Boston's sixteen planning districts: the contiguous neighborhoods of Roxbury, Mattapan, and Dorchester held over three-quarters of the city's blacks.

4. The banking commissioner approved State Street's application for the Tokyo branch on December 28.
5. One factor in BayBanks' decision to provide these new branches and ATMs was a personal experience that Chairman Pollard related later at public meetings. One day his illegally parked car was towed to a lot in Roxbury. When he went to claim it, he was informed that he needed to pay in cash. No problem, he thought, he would just go to a nearby BayBank branch or ATM. He was chagrinned to learn that the nearest one was miles away.
6. In January BayBanks withdrew its challenged application in the face of its almost certain rejection. In response, the commissioner communicated his negative assessment of the company's CRA performance by denying a different pending application by the parent corporation.
7. Finn's methodology was very different from that of the Boston Fed's researchers in several ways: he used Home Mortgage Disclosure Act (HMDA) data as reported by the banks rather than deed transfer data, he focused on neighborhoods that had at least 70 percent minority residents as opposed to those with at least 80 percent black residents, and his data covered a seven-year rather than a six-year period. Thus it was noteworthy that his finding of 66 percent fewer mortgage loans in minority neighborhoods than in white neighborhoods ($1/2.9 = 0.34$) was so close to the Fed's finding of 60 percent (Bradbury, Case, and Dunham 1989:21).
8. Although the precise timing of the study's release was clearly (and effectively) designed to advance the mayor's agenda at a crucial point in the process, the Finn report was, from the banks' point of view, a ticking time bomb that had to go off at some point. It was unrealistic to hope that the city could simply bury such a well-publicized study, even if it had wanted to do so. The situation was different from ten years earlier, when a city-sponsored study that found "pronounced racial redlining" by a number of large Boston banks was suppressed after the banks agreed to participate in the city's loan programs; in that case, the existence of the study was known to only a few, and the city's contract with the group that prepared the study prevented the researchers from releasing or discussing it (*Boston Globe*, January 29, 1989).
9. Although these sets of tables are informative for participants in the struggles over community investment in Boston, they are not public reports. The CIC intended to use them as a basis for preparing reports that would be released quarterly to its constituencies and to the media, beginning in October 1990, but it has not been successful in meeting this timetable. The CIC released its first report in December 1990. In mid-August 1991 it was anticipating the release of a second report in September and considering a more realistic goal of semiannual public reports.
10. I have also drawn upon an informative progress report issued by the MBA in January 1991 on the first anniversary of their program announcement, reports from the three statewide corporations created under the program, and personal interviews.
11. As discussed in the next section, Fleet Bank of Massachusetts became the successor bank to the failed Bank of New England in July 1991. Fleet agreed to honor the Bank of New England's original commitments to the community investment programs announced in January 1990, and even though these commitments were not finalized in time to be included in the CIC tables for the period ending June 31, they are counted in the totals given in this and the following section.

REFERENCES

Bradbury, Katharine L., Karl E. Case, and Constance R. Dunham. 1989. "Geographic Patterns of Mortgage Lending in Boston, 1982–1987." *New England Economic Review* (Sept./Oct.). 3–30.

James T. Campen

Bradford, Calvin. 1990. *Partnerships for Reinvestment: An Evaluation of the Chicago Neighborhood Lending Programs*. Chicago: National Training and Information Center.
Community Banking Commission, City of Boston. 1991. *Report to the Mayor: Linked Deposit Banking Program*. Boston: Community Banking Commission, June 6.
Community Investment Coalition. 1989. *Community Investment Plan: A Plan to Build and Preserve Affordable Housing and Improve Banking Services in North Dorchester, Roxbury, and Mattapan*. Boston: Community Investment Coalition.
Dreier, Peter. 1991. "Psst . . . Need a Loan? Bank Redlining Drives Second Mortgage Scams." *Dollars & Sense* (Oct.), 10–11, 21.
Dreier, Peter, Ann Greiner, and David Schwartz. 1988. "What Every Business Can Do about Housing." *Harvard Business Review* (Sept./Oct.), 52–61.
Dunham, Constance R., and William J. Spring. 1988. "Expanding the Potential of the Community Reinvestment Act: The Case of Affordable Housing in Boston." Unpublished paper. Boston: Federal Reserve Bank of Boston.
Finn, Charles. 1989. *Mortgage Lending in Boston's Neighborhoods, 1981–1987: A Study of Bank Credit and Boston's Housing*. Boston: Boston Redevelopment Authority.
Greenwald, Carol S. 1980. *Banks Are Dangerous to Your Wealth*. Englewood Cliffs, N.J.: Prentice-Hall.
Hanafin, Teresa M. 1989. "Bank Machines, Branch Offices Scarce in Boston Minority Neighborhoods." *Boston Globe*, Feb. 7.
Jurkowitz, Mark. 1991. "Anatomy of a Scoop: How the *Globe* and Channel 7 Broke the Best Local Story of the Year." *Boston Phoenix*, May 31.
LaPrade, Melvin W., and Andrea Nagle. 1989. *Roxbury—A Community at Risk: An Analysis of the Disparities in Mortgage Lending Patterns*. A report prepared for the Greater Roxbury Neighborhood Authority. Boston.

THE COMMUNITY REINVESTMENT ACT AND NEIGHBORHOOD REVITALIZATION IN PITTSBURGH

IN 1988, THE PITTSBURGH COMMUNITY REINVESTMENT GROUP (PCRG) negotiated a five-year, $109 million neighborhood lending agreement with Union National Bank of Pittsburgh, one of the largest agreements of its kind ever created with one bank, particularly in relation to the institution's asset size.[1] The PCRG is a citywide Community Reinvestment Act (CRA) coalition of nonprofit community-based organizations that represent homeowners, renters, small business owners, real estate developers and other property owners in Pittsburgh's low- and moderate-income and African-American neighborhoods. With funding support from its member organizations, the City of Pittsburgh, and local financial institutions, PCRG has continued to negotiate and monitor community lending initiatives with banks and savings and loans, and to increase local government leverage and support for CRA programs.

THE HISTORY OF PUBLIC–PRIVATE NEIGHBORHOOD REINVESTMENT IN PITTSBURGH

The emergence of PCRG followed three decades of neighborhood planning and revitalization that occurred amidst the turmoil of massive population loss, severe economic decline, and large-scale urban renewal. In the early twentieth century, Pittsburgh had established itself as a center for steel and electrical machinery production and financial services, becoming the headquarters for corporate giants such as the United States Steel Corporation (U.S. Steel, now USX), Westinghouse Electric Corporation, the

John T. Metzger

Aluminum Corporation of America (ALCOA), and Mellon Bank. The population of Pittsburgh virtually stopped growing during the 1930s, and after World War II the city embarked on an extensive urban renewal program under the mayoral leadership of New Deal Democratic machine boss David Lawrence. At the urging of the leading business executives and large downtown landowners, organized and represented through the Allegheny Conference on Community Development, Lawrence cleared sites in and adjacent to the central business district and remade the declining downtown area into the "Golden Triangle," preserving Pittsburgh's status as a corporate headquarters center. By the early 1960s, urban renewal had expanded outside of the "Golden Triangle" into the Hill District ghetto, the Oakland educational-institutional district, the East Liberty commercial zone, and the industrial and residential areas of the North Side. Thousands of low-income, minority families and small businesses were displaced by the redevelopment process, and the trends of population and job losses continued unabated (Lubove 1969; J. Lowe 1967; Weiss 1985; Stewman and Tarr 1982; Levitt 1987: 106–46; Weber 1988; Clark 1989; Frieden and Sagalyn 1989; Teaford 1990; also see Darden 1973; Hays 1989).

Pittsburgh's first public-private neighborhood reinvestment initiative during this era began in 1957 with the creation of the Allegheny Council to Improve Our Neighborhoods-Housing (ACTION-Housing). With the support of the Allegheny Conference on Community Development, ACTION-Housing mobilized resources from banks and local corporations to finance new and rehabilitated housing in Allegheny County for moderate-income rental and owner-occupancy. During the 1960s, ACTION-Housing attempted to mitigate the effects of displacement and relocation resulting from urban renewal by organizing neighborhood conservation and home improvement and rehabilitation programs (Lubove 1969; Cunningham 1965).

In 1968, ACTION-Housing and the Sarah Mellon Scaife Foundation joined forces with a group of minority and elderly residents on Pittsburgh's Central North Side to create the Neighborhood Housing Services (NHS) program. Fourteen years earlier, the city's urban renewal plan designated the area for slum clearance. Surrounded by the East Street highway construction, the Allegheny Center project, the new Three Rivers Stadium, and the Manchester urban renewal area, the Central North Side spiraled into decline during the 1960s. Financial institutions redlined the neighborhood and the physical condition of properties deteriorated. Citizens Against Slum Housing (CASH), led by North Side resident Dorothy Richardson, the Central North Side Neighborhood Council, and the North Side Civic Development Council worked with ACTION-Housing, the Scaife Foundation, Mayor Joseph Barr, the Pittsburgh History and Landmarks Foundation (PHLF)—a local historic preservation organization—and thirteen banks and savings institutions to establish NHS. Neighborhood Housing Services consisted of a "high-risk" below-market-rate revolving loan fund for low-income homeownership and home repairs, financial counseling and technical assistance, and a code enforcement program. The program succeeded in stabilizing the Central North Side as a mixed-income racially integrated community and, with PHLF, revitalizing the Mexican War Streets, a historic district within the neighborhood (Ahlbrandt and Brophy 1975a; 1975b; Ziegler, Adler, and Kidney 1975; Ziegler 1974). By the mid-1970s, NHS expanded to other cities and became a national program model endorsed by the Federal Home Loan Bank Board (FHLBB) and the U.S. Department of Housing and Urban Development (ACTION-Housing 1975). The national anti-redlining movement promoted NHS as a positive example of private "greenlining" of older urban neighborhoods. Gale Cincotta, the key figure and spokesperson in the movement, helped to start NHS in Chicago, and its success contributed to the passage of the Home Mortgage Disclosure Act in 1975 and the Community Reinvestment Act in 1977 (Metzger and Weiss 1988; Naparstek and Cincotta 1976).

During the late 1960s and early 1970s, community organizations emerged in the Manchester and Oakland neighborhoods in *opposition* to large-scale urban renewal plans. Manchester was a North Side residential neighborhood that became predominantly black during the 1960s, largely due to an influx of families displaced by the Lower Hill redevelopment project. Community activists and historic preservationists from PHLF were able to halt the demolition and building plans of the Urban Redevelopment Authority of Pittsburgh (URA), the city's urban renewal agency, and residents established a community development corporation, the Manchester Citizens Corporation (MCC), to guide the Manchester urban renewal program. Manchester and its Victorian homes were designated a historic district, and MCC worked with the URA and a local developer, Thomas Mistick and Sons, to implement several neighborhood rehabilitation and historic preservation projects without displacing the existing low- and moderate-income African-American residents (S. Lowe 1990).

In the Oakland educational and cultural district, the University of Pittsburgh's expansion plans were opposed by the working-class Italian, Greek, Irish, and African-American residents in the South, Central, and West Oakland neighborhoods. By the mid-1970s, Pitt's expansion program was slowed by the activism of People's Oakland, and a community planning organization, Oakland Directions Inc., was formed to engage in a long-range, joint, land use planning process with local educational, health care, and cultural institutions. By 1980, the new Oakland Plan had been adopted by the City of Pittsburgh, and a community development corporation, the Oakland Planning and Development Corporation (OPDC), was formed to revitalize the older residential and commercial areas (Weiss and Metzger 1987; Oakland Directions Inc., 1980).

Both MCC and OPDC represented a "new wave" of activist, nonprofit community development corporations (CDCs) in Pittsburgh that supplemented and eventually overshadowed the earlier activities of NHS and ACTION-Housing. These groups received financial support from the federal Community Development Block Grant (CDBG) program and local foundations, and were bolstered by the pro-neighborhood policies of Mayor Richard Caligiuri, who took office in 1977. Caligiuri performed a leadership role similar to Boston's Mayor Raymond Flynn in promoting community reinvestment (Ahlbrandt 1986; Lurcott and Downing 1987; Sbragia 1989; Jezierski 1990). In 1983, the Mellon Foundation, the Howard Heinz Endowment, and the Ford Foundation organized the Pittsburgh Partnership for Neighborhood Development (PPND), which pooled and centralized operating funds for five "core" CDCs: MCC, OPDC, North Side Civic Development Council, East Liberty Development Inc., and Homewood-Brushton Revitalization and Development Corporation. Other funders in PPND included Mellon Bank and the City of Pittsburgh through the CDBG program. The Allegheny Conference on Community Development sponsored the Local Initiatives Support Corporation to provide financial assistance for CDC real estate projects, and Pittsburgh National Bank and Equibank joined PPND during 1986–88. The PPND was one of the first instances in the country of banks providing direct grants for CDC operating budgets. By 1988, Hill Community Development Corporation and Bloomfield-Garfield Corporation joined the core group of PPND CDCs, while MCC, experiencing financial troubles, dropped out.[2]

Mellon Bank played an important role up through the mid-1980s in financing CDC real estate projects. Mellon financed many of the MCC–Thomas Mistick and Sons renovation projects in Manchester, and provided a construction loan for forty-six new moderate-income townhouses in South Oakland developed as a joint venture between OPDC and National Development Corporation, a private developer. Mellon formed a bank community development corporation in 1986 and helped to finance the Brewery Innovation Center, a high-tech small business incubator sponsored by the North Side Civic Development Council. The Mellon Bank CDC also assisted economic development projects in Homewood-Brushton and East Liberty.

The URA started to reorient its programs toward neighborhood rehabilitation and conservation beginning in the 1960s. In the late 1970s, the URA worked with community groups organized by the North Side Civic Development Council to implement a large-scale neighborhood-based redevelopment program on the North Side funded in part by a federal Urban Development Action Grant (Nenno and Brophy 1982: 73–79). The URA's mortgage revenue bond programs became an important source of housing finance in Pittsburgh's low- and moderate-income neighborhoods. Tax-exempt bond issues for home improvement, single-family homeownership, and multifamily rental housing financed the purchase, rehabilitation, or construction of 13,845 dwelling units during 1978–89, at a total cost of $190 million. The URA enters into contracts with local lenders to originate and service below-market rate single-family and home improvement loans insured by the Federal Housing Administration (FHA) and funded by the proceeds of bond sales (Urban Redevelopment Authority of Pittsburgh 1990).

The creation of PPND and the URA's expanding role helped to conceal that direct lending by Pittsburgh's financial institutions for neighborhood housing and real estate projects was diminishing. Table 3.1 shows the number and dollar amount of conventional and FHA-insured single-family purchase loans, home improvement loans, and multifamily loans made by Pittsburgh's four largest commercial banks in the city's low- and moderate-income census tracts during 1984–87. Mellon Bank, Equibank, and Union National Bank all reduced their home mortgage lending to these areas during the four-year period. The only bank to show any increase in lending was Pittsburgh National Bank, which until 1987 originated all of its mortgage loans through the Kissell Company, a

TABLE 3.1
NUMBER OF LOANS BY COMMERCIAL BANKS IN LOW- AND MODERATE-INCOME CENSUS TRACTS IN PITTSBURGH, 1984–1987

			LOAN TYPE			
	NUMBER	AMOUNT ($ THOUSAND)	FHA/ FmHA/ VA	Conventional	Home Improvement	Multi-Family
MELLON BANK						
1987	92	3,246	26	38	28	0
1986	179	4,074	0	69	110	0
1985	494	5,599	0	63	430	1
1984	320	3,619	0	50	266	4
Total	**1,085**	**16,538**	**26**	**220**	**834**	**5**
PITTSBURGH NATIONAL BANK						
1987	211	2,260	26	8	177	0
1986	164	1,315	0	5	159	0
1985	113	654	0	1	112	0
1984	80	634	0	1	79	0
Total	**568**	**4,863**	**26**	**15**	**527**	**0**
EQUIBANK						
1987	6	150	0	6	0	0
1986	18	639	3	12	3	0
1985	7	282	0	5	2	0
1984	31	802	2	20	9	0
Total	**62**	**1,873**	**5**	**43**	**14**	**0**
UNION NATIONAL BANK						
1987	7	80	0	2	5	0
1986	17	353	0	7	10	0
1985	17	319	0	8	9	0
1984	15	303	0	9	5	1
Total	**56**	**1,055**	**0**	**26**	**29**	**1**

Source: Home Mortgage Disclosure Act; definition of low- and moderate-income census tracts are based on data from *1980 U.S. Census*.

Note: Low- and moderate-income census tracts are census tracts with a 1980 median household income at 80 percent or less of the 1980 median household income for the Pittsburgh Standard Metropolitan Statistical Area, not including census tracts located in the central business district.

mortgage banking subsidiary unregulated then by either the Home Mortgage Disclosure Act (HMDA) or the Community Reinvestment Act (Pittsburgh Community Reinvestment Group 1990). Mellon Bank laid off thousands of employees and tightened its credit policies in 1987 due to heavy losses on loans made to underdeveloped Third World countries. The Mellon Bank CDC continued to operate with a small capital base and under additional pressure to finance inner city projects in Philadelphia, where the bank faced CRA protests during the 1980s, most recently from six community groups that challenged its acquisition of Philadelphia Savings Fund Society (Swaney 1990).

Pittsburgh's largest thrift institutions, historically the region's leading providers of mortgage credit, also followed this pattern. The *Atlanta Journal Constitution*'s Pulitzer Prize–winning analysis of mortgage lending by savings and loan associations in the nation's largest metropolitan areas between 1983 and mid-1988 found that Pittsburgh's savings and loans had the second worst disparity in rejection rates between white and black loan applicants. Blacks were rejected for loans by Pittsburgh savings and loans at a rate 3.8 times higher than that for whites, second only to Milwaukee's racial disparity rate of 3.9 (Dedman 1989; Barcousky 1989). The Federal Home Loan Bank (FHLB) of Pittsburgh created the Community Investment Fund in 1988 to provide cash advances to member thrifts for financing low- and moderate-income housing and community development. The advances, made at cost of funds, yielded a discount of forty basis points for the lender to be passed on to the borrower. The FHLB Pittsburgh district, which includes all of Pennsylvania, West Virginia, and Delaware, allocated $50 million annually to the program, but by the end of 1989 no thrifts had used any of the money for projects in the city of Pittsburgh.[3]

THE PITTSBURGH COMMUNITY REINVESTMENT GROUP

In late 1987, Union National Corporation, the holding company for Union National Bank of Pittsburgh, announced its intention to merge with Pennbancorp, another Pennsylvania banking company, and create a new holding company, Integra Financial Corporation. At the time, Union National Bank (UNB) was the fourth largest commercial bank based in Pittsburgh, with over $2 billion in assets and fifty-four branch offices in Western Pennsylvania. It was not a member of the Pittsburgh

John T. Metzger

Partnership for Neighborhood Development, and it was not making loans in low- and moderate-income or minority areas. The UNB made no home purchase loans in African-American census tracts in Pittsburgh during 1986–87, and in 1987 it made only two purchase mortgages in low- and moderate-income census tracts. In 1980, Pittsburgh's thirty-six African-American census tracts (those with a black population of over 50 percent) contained 11,354 owner-occupied housing units, or 11 percent of the city's total. The 102 low- and moderate-income neighborhood census tracts (those with a median household income no more than 80 percent of the median for the Pittsburgh area) contained 34,361 owner-occupied housing units, or 40 percent of the city's total (Pittsburgh Community Reinvestment Group 1990).

Based upon its analysis of Union National Bank's historical lending record through HMDA, and the experiences of neighborhood residents, the MCC concluded that UNB was redlining Manchester and other lower income and minority communities. In particular, the UNB had not made a mortgage loan in Manchester since 1981. The MCC contacted the National Training and Information Center (NTIC) in Chicago for assistance in using the Community Reinvestment Act with UNB. Shel Trapp of NTIC recommended that MCC follow a strategy and process used successfully to create neighborhood lending programs in other cities. First, MCC formed a citywide coalition. It approached the members of the Northside Leadership Conference (NLC), an umbrella organization of community groups on the North Side to which it belonged. Twelve of the fourteen NLC organizations agreed to participate in the CRA negotiations. By April 1988, seven community development corporations from other areas of Pittsburgh had joined MCC and the NLC groups to form a new citywide entity, the Pittsburgh Community Reinvestment Group, to represent low- and moderate-income neighborhoods with Union National Bank. Each organization contributed nominal dues for overhead costs, and MCC donated staff and meeting space. Table 3.2 lists the member organizations of PCRG.

The key figure in the formation of PCRG was Stanley Lowe, the chief executive officer of the Manchester Citizens Corporation and the individual who convened the coalition. Lowe had helped to found MCC in the 1970s and was an important leader within the Northside Leadership Conference. Lowe was a board member of community development corporations in the Oakland, Hill District, and South Side neighborhoods, all of which joined PCRG, and also was the director of the Preser-

80

TABLE 3.2
THE PITTSBURGH COMMUNITY REINVESTMENT GROUP, 1988–1991

CONVENER:	Manchester Citizens Corporation
MEMBERS:	Northside Leadership Conference
	Allegheny West Civic Council
	Calbride Place Citizens Council
	Central Northside Neighborhood Council
	Charles Street Area Council
	East Allegheny Community Council
	Fineview Citizens Council
	Manchester Citizens Corporation
	Northside Tenants Reorganization
	Observatory Hill
	Perry Hilltop Citizens Council[b]
	Spring Garden Neighborhood Council
	Troy Hill Citizens
	Northside Civic Development Council
	Bloomfield-Garfield Corporation
	Garfield Jubilee Association
	Hill Community Development Corporation
	Homewood-Brushton Revitalization and Development Corporation
	Oakland Planning and Development Corporation
	South Side Local Development Company
	East Liberty Development, Inc.[a]
	Eastside Alliance[a]
	Breachmenders, Inc.[a]
	Lawrenceville Citizens Council[a]
	Hill District Ministries[a]
	Lincoln-Lemington-Larimer-Belmar Citizens Revitalization and Development Corporation[a]
	Friendship Development Associates[a]

[a]Joined PCRG after negotiation of Union National Bank lending agreement.
[b]Left PCRG in 1991.

vation Fund of the Pittsburgh History and Landmarks Foundation. The Preservation Fund is a revolving loan fund for inner city historic preservation (S. Lowe 1990). As the Fund's director, Lowe had assisted many of the PCRG groups in developing and financing housing and commercial revitalization projects. The historical relationships and stature he possessed attracted many neighborhood groups to join the CRA coalition (Perlmutter 1988).

Lowe had several goals. First, MCC was in need of project and operating resources and community legitimacy. The MCC was formed

John T. Metzger

from negotiations with the Urban Redevelopment Authority during the late 1970s to establish neighborhood control over URA projects in the Manchester urban renewal area. A successful track record enabled MCC to join the Pittsburgh Partnership for Neighborhood Development as one of the founding CDCs, but URA funding cutbacks and the group's past financial management problems weakened its ability to implement community development projects. Initiating a CRA strategy with Union National Bank, while posing risks, could strengthen MCC and supply much-needed mortgage financing for Manchester.

Lowe's second goal emanated from his position as director of the PHLF Preservation Fund. The investment incentives in the Historic Rehabilitation Tax Credit were reduced by the Tax Reform Act of 1986 (National Trust for Historic Preservation 1986). The MCC and the Central Northside Neighborhood Council represent areas that include historic preservation districts, while other PCRG organizations represent neighborhoods that contain existing or eligible historic structures. Lowe and these groups believed that Pittsburgh banks could fill a gap in financing historic renovation projects in low- and moderate-income and minority preservation districts like Manchester. Finally, Lowe and other activists in the Northside Leadership Conference saw the CRA as an opportunity to leverage loans for increasingly complex and ambitious commercial real estate and economic development projects initiated by the Northside Civic Development Council, a local development corporation that worked closely with NLC (Osborne 1988: 66–67; Peirce and Steinbach 1987: 52–54).

For CDCs in other parts of the city, PCRG was an opportunity to leverage direct bank financing for projects, homebuyers, and business owners, as opposed to just CDC operating support allocated through the Pittsburgh Partnership for Neighborhood Development (Working Group on Community Development 1989). Also, in the case of Union National Bank, local financial institutions that were not members of PPND could be added to the consortium to increase the total pool of money available for CDCs. Budget reductions in the federal Community Development Block Grant and other Department of Housing and Urban Development (HUD) programs during the 1980s constrained the ability of Pittsburgh CDCs to expand their housing and economic development activities. Unable to prevent these funding cutbacks, the community groups increasingly targeted private financial institutions and state and local government as alternatives to the shrinking federal government role.

82

Stanley Lowe, as the lead spokesperson and negotiator for PCRG, served as a bridge and focal point for the broad and diverse constituencies of the coalition, which ranged from development-oriented CDCs to advocacy-oriented neighborhood groups. All of these organizations represented distinct places and boundaries that vary and differ by population characteristics such as the race, ethnicity, and income of the residents, as well as by area size and physical and economic characteristics. All of the PCRG groups shared the economic goals of increasing homeownership, adding to the supply and improving the physical condition of low- and moderate-income housing, and retaining and creating jobs. In addition, they shared the political goals of enhancing the visibility, legitimacy, and power of their organizations.

These goals were important during 1988–89, when Pittsburgh experienced several political changes. Mayor Richard Caligiuri, who had formed strong linkages with community groups, died in office in 1988 and was succeeded by City Council President Sophie Masloff. After eleven years in office and two easy reelection victories, Caligiuri had become the dominant local political figure (Sbragia 1989; Jezierski 1990). Masloff was an older machine-style politician who was less known and was aloof from neighborhood-based organizations. State Representative Thomas Murphy, one of four challengers to the incumbent Masloff in the 1989 Democratic mayoral primary, won the support of many community activists, particularly from the North Side area of the city that he represented. During the 1970s, Murphy was the director of the Perry Hilltop Citizens Council and later the North Side Civic Development Council, both of which were members of PCRG. Murphy's campaign gained strength at the end and he finished a surprisingly close second to Masloff in the hard-fought election.

Another key political change was the election of City Council members by district, instead of at-large. Pittsburgh's at-large council system had been successfully challenged and overturned by civil rights advocates who claimed that it diluted the voting strength of the African-American population, which is at least one-quarter of the city's total (Watkins 1986; Sbragia 1989). The new district system changed the politics of the Council by placing new emphasis on specific neighborhood concerns and interests, while deemphasizing the citywide outlook promoted by the old, at-large system.

The organizations in PCRG also saw the CRA negotiations as an opportunity to exert more direct control over program design and policy-making. Instead of relying on the local public sector, whose support was sometimes uncertain—particularly in the new political environment—and whose goals occasionally conflicted with those of the cDcs, the community groups themselves could be the source of new affordable housing and real estate lending initiatives targeted to low- and moderate-income areas. The leverage provided by the CRA enabled PCRG to secure greater influence in the formulation and outcomes of the public-private programs. Many believed that PCRG could become a new, strong political advocate for inner-city real estate development. This would compliment the growing role of both the URA and the PPND, and also control the power of both entities. The PCRG could negotiate with URA to reorient and target its programs to support private sector neighborhood lending initiatives, and could pressure the financial institutions in PPND to go beyond their annual cDc operating budget contributions and become more aggressive direct lenders for inner city projects. As a power base of cDcs and neighborhood groups, PCRG could be an effective counterpart to both the URA, which possessed the local government's traditional responsibilities for urban renewal and redevelopment, and PPND, which brought together the city's banks, foundations, and other funders.

The Union National Bank Lending Agreement

Upon forming the coalition, PCRG began to develop a neighborhood reinvestment program. Each organization prepared an assessment of projected credit needs in their community over the next five years. These estimates were aggregated into a citywide lending program that PCRG presented to UNB when the bank sought regulatory approval for the merger. Union National Bank initially balked at the program. Four actions by the community groups and the bank led the way to the agreement. First, PCRG kept the Federal Reserve Bank of Cleveland, which regulates Pittsburgh area banks, and the Comptroller of the Currency, which regulates national banks such as UNB, informed during the negotiations. Second, PCRG threatened to file a public protest against the merger and release information on the bank's lending record and the status of the negotiations to the media. Third, UNB hired a new president and chief executive officer, Gayland Cook, who had not been involved in formulating the bank's earlier credit policies. Fourth, UNB hired a new CRA officer, Donald Reed, and appointed him vice president for community development. Reed was from Cleveland, where he had been the key community banker in the "Bank on Buckeye" CDC/CRA program in the Buckeye-Woodland neighborhood during the early 1980s (Fulton 1987).

In June 1988, Union National Bank agreed to fund PCRG's entire program, committing $109 million over five years for home mortgages, real estate loans, and small business loans in Pittsburgh's low- and moderate-income and minority neighborhoods (Barcousky 1988). It is one of the largest neighborhood lending agreements in the country, particularly in proportion to the financial institution's asset size. By comparison, First National Bank of Chicago, which was ten times larger than UNB in asset size at the time and served a much bigger market, committed to a $120 million CRA lending program in 1984 (Swift and Pogge 1984; Weiss and Metzger 1988). Until Chase Manhattan Bank launched a five-year $200 million CRA initiative in New York in 1989 through the Chase CDC, First National's program was the nation's largest at a single bank (Willis 1990).

The Union National Bank lending agreement included $55 million in home mortgages, $6 million in home improvement loans, and $8 million in small business loans, all spread over five years, and $40 million in real estate loans for for-profit and nonprofit developers in low- and moderate-income areas, with no timing specified. These figures are outlined in Table 3.3. The UNB also agreed to join the other banks in the PPND and set aside $250,000 in a bank-affiliated foundation to write-down financing costs for real estate loans to CDCs during the first year of the program.

Conventional loans that are not insured by either the FHA or guaranteed by the Veterans Administration (VA) are an important part of the new $55 million home mortgage program. The conventional mortgages contain several built-in subsidies to promote homeownership in the targeted neighborhoods: no origination points, an interest-rate discount of fifty basis points, or 0.5 percent below the bank's prevailing rate, a 95 percent loan-to-value ratio, which necessitates only a 5 percent down payment, no private mortgage insurance requirement, a liberalized payment- and debt-to-income qualifying ratio (33 to 38 percent), and no limit on income eligibility or mortgage amount. In many sections of Pittsburgh, UNB's conventional Community Mortgage Resource Program quickly became competitive with the URA's single-family mortgage reve-

TABLE 3.3

Pittsburgh Community Reinvestment Group and Union National Bank Lending Agreement

LOAN TYPE	AGREEMENT AMOUNTS IN $ THOUSAND								
	1989	1990	1991	1992	1993	1994	1995	1996	Total
HOME MORTGAGES	10,000	15,000	10,000	10,000	10,000	7,950	8,500	9,500	55,000
Revised Dec. 1990			6,000	7,500	7,500				46,950
HOME IMPROVEMENT LOANS AND HOME EQUITY LOANS									6,000[a]
Revised Dec. 1990			3,755	4,131	4,462	4,775	5,107		22,230
SMALL BUSINESS LOANS									8,000[a]
Revised Dec. 1990			14,850	14,850	15,593	16,372	17,191		78,855
REAL ESTATE LOANS TO FOR-PROFIT AND NON PROFIT DEVELOPERS									40,000[b]
TOTAL									109,000
Revised Dec. 1990									188,035

[a]Spread over five years, 1991–1995.
[b]No timing specified.

nue bond program, the Pittsburgh Home Ownership Program (PHOP), which is available citywide and insured by FHA. Under the terms of the PCRG lending agreement, UNB also originates and services home loans through the PHOP. The URA enters into contracts with local lenders to do this. The bank's conventional underwriting ratios exceed the FHA standards used in the URA's PHOP, closing costs are less due to the absence of mortgage insurance and origination points, and the URA sets limits on mortgage amounts and requires a 10 percent down payment for sales in new construction projects. In nontargeted areas, the URA program is restricted to use by "first-time" homebuyers who have not owned a house for at least three years. The URA must also conform to federal government rules that limit the annual volume of tax-exempt revenue bond issues. The lower interest rate on URA bond-funded mortgages, ranging from 8⅛ to 8⅞ percent during 1988–90, became less of a factor when conventional interest rates dropped under 10 percent and the UNB basis point discount was then applied.

Most important, the bank's conventional mortgage program, unlike URA, does not impose income limits on prospective borrowers. This provides those CDCs which have the goal of creating mixed-income neighborhoods with a valuable financing tool to promote middle-income homeownership. In cities such as New York, Boston, and San Francisco, this reinvestment strategy, if unmanaged, might lead to wholesale gentrification of lower-income neighborhoods (Smith and Williams 1986). The demand for housing in inner city Pittsburgh is weak, however, and many CDCs are attempting to attract new residents into their depressed areas and improve the city's competitive position with the booming residential suburbs of the North Hills. The population of Pittsburgh has fallen by 32 percent since 1970, and 55,000 residents left the city during the 1980s. The community groups believe that their participation in PCRG enables them to control reinvestment in their areas and prevent any negative effects, such as displacement, from occurring. Additional protection is provided by a state antigentrification law, passed in 1989 largely in response to conditions in Philadelphia, that allows local governments to grant property tax abatements to older homeowners in neighborhoods where property values are rising (Fuoco 1989).

Some community groups have tailored UNB's Community Mortgage Resource Program to support specific neighborhood objectives. The Northside Leadership Conference and the Northside Civic Development

Council have created a special program to encourage employees of Allegheny General Hospital to purchase and occupy homes in low- and moderate-income North Side neighborhoods. Under the program, UNB provides the purchase mortgage, the hospital's foundation makes a grant to reduce the down payment to 2.5 percent, and the employee credit union services the loan. The hospital, which is located on the North Side, is the largest health care employer and the fifteenth largest employer in the Pittsburgh metropolitan area (Pollock 1990).

Representatives of PCRG and UNB meet monthly to review and monitor the implementation of the program, and this committee—the Community Development Advisory Group—meets quarterly with the newly formed Community Development Committee of the bank's board of directors to deliver a progress report. An important topic in these meetings is the marketing of the programs in the lending agreement. Both the UNB and the PCRG have taken several steps to generate demand for the loans. The bank has hired additional loan officers and mortgage originators, sponsored training sessions for CDCs and local realtors on the home mortgage programs, offered training and education seminars for minority and women business owners seeking loans, developed and distributed special brochures, and purchased advertising in neighborhood newspapers published by CDCs. To educate its employees on community economic development and prepare them to work with CDCs, UNB has sent over one hundred branch managers, commercial, real estate, and consumer lenders, and management trainees through a program operated by the Development Training Institute (DTI) in Baltimore, Maryland. The DTI is headed by Joseph McNeely, who helped found the South East Community Organization in Baltimore and worked with Monsignor Geno Baroni in HUD's Office of Neighborhoods, Voluntary Associations, and Consumer Protection during the Carter administration. Many CDC staff professionals in Pittsburgh have been trained by DTI (Peirce and Steinbach 1987: 81–82).

To increase demand for UNB's loans, PCRG has expanded eligibility for the program to include Homestead, McKeesport, and other economically depressed towns in the Monongahela River valley near Pittsburgh. Also, sections of Pittsburgh that were not classified as "low- and moderate-income" in the 1980 census but are within the service area boundaries of the CDCs in PCRG have been added to the program. To increase the bank's real estate lending in the targeted neighborhoods,

UNB invested $680,000 in loans and grants into the Preservation Fund of the Pittsburgh History and Landmarks Foundation. The Preservation Fund, headed by PCRG founder Stanley Lowe, provides short-term, low-interest "bridge" financing to CDCs to acquire inner city buildings and sites for redevelopment. The Fund is utilizing UNB's money to expand the use of its revolving loan fund to include nonhistoric housing and commercial real estate projects (Perlmutter 1990d).

Through December 31, 1990, Union National Bank made 272 home mortgage loans totaling $12.6 million to targeted areas and home-buyers in the city of Pittsburgh. Through March 1990, 57 percent of the bank's mortgages were conventional loans under the Community Mortgage Resource Program. Conventional mortgage lending was strongest in neighborhoods represented by PCRG organizations, particularly on the North Side. Ten percent of the mortgages through December 1990 were made in African-American census tracts, but three-fourths of these were concentrated in two North Side neighborhoods, Manchester and the Central North Side. The North Side of Pittsburgh, where PCRG was launched, benefited more than any other area during the first two and one-half years of the lending agreement. One hundred and forty home loans totaling $6.8 million were made in the neighborhoods of the North Side by the end of 1990. This includes ten loans made by UNB to Allegheny General Hospital employees through April 1990, one year after the special mortgage program with the hospital started. As of December 31, 1990, no residential mortgage loans made by UNB in the city of Pittsburgh under the lending agreement had defaulted. Six loans, representing only 2 percent of the total, were delinquent. Lending data on all components of the UNB reinvestment program is summarized in Table 3.4.

UNB made 111 small business loans totaling $10.7 million in the targeted communities through December 31, 1990. Forty-six percent of these loans were made in African-American census tracts, and through March 1990 48 percent were made to either minority- or women-owned businesses. Nine of these loans were delinquent, and four—amounting to $112,000 and 1 percent of the total small business loan portfolio—were in default by the end of December 1990. The bank made twenty-three direct loans and issued two letters of credit for a total of $10.4 million for commercial real estate projects. Eight of the loans and both letters of credit helped to finance projects in minority neighborhoods. The UNB made 179 home improvement loans for $2.4 million in the city of

TABLE 3.4

Loans Made by Union National Bank under the Lending Agreement with the Pittsburgh Community Reinvestment Group, as of December 31, 1990

LOAN TYPE	CITY OF PITTSBURGH		PITTSBURGH REGION		TOTAL		FIVE-YEAR LENDING	
	Number	Amount	Number	Amount	Number	Amount	Original Goal	% Reached
HOME MORTGAGES	272	$12,601,631	77	$2,845,137	349	$15,446,768	$55,000,000	28.1%
% of total	77.9%	81.6%	22.1%	18.4%	100.0%	100.0%		
% delinquent	2.2%	1.7%	0.0%	0.0%	1.7%	1.4%		
% in default	0.0%	0.0%	0.0%	0.0%	0.0%	0.0%		
HOME IMPROVEMENT LOANS AND HOME EQUITY LOANS	179	$2,425,810	452	$5,245,258	631	$7,671,068	$6,000,000	127.9%
% of total	28.4%	31.6%	71.6%	68.4%	100.0%	100.0%		
% delinquent	6.7%	6.7%	7.5%	8.3%	7.3%	7.8%		
% in default	0.0%	0.0%	0.0%	0.0%	0.0%	0.0%		
SMALL BUSINESS LOANS	111	$10,687,031	195	$26,315,731	306	$37,002,762	$8,000,000	462.5%
% of total	36.3%	28.9%	63.7%	71.1%	100.0%	100.0%		
% delinquent	8.1%	1.5%	8.7%	8.5%	8.5%	6.5%		
% default	3.6%	1.0%	0.0%	0.0%	1.3%	0.3%		

REAL ESTATE LOANS TO FOR-PROFIT AND NONPROFIT DEVELOPERS	25	$10,419,115	4	$691,000	29	$11,110,115	$40,000,000	27.8%
% of total	86.2%	93.8%	13.8%	6.2	100.0%	100.0%		
% delinquent	0.0%	0.0%	0.0%	0.0%	0.0%	0.0%		
% in default	0.0%	0.0%	0.0%	0.0%	0.0%	0.0%		
TOTAL	587	$36,133,587	728	$35,097,126	1,315	$71,230,713	$109,000,000	65.3%
% of total	44.6%	50.7%	55.4%	49.3%	100.0%	100.0%		
% delinquent	4.6%	1.5%	7.0%	7.6%	5.9%	4.5%		
% in default	0.7%	0.3%	0.0%	0.0%	0.3%	0.2%		

Pittsburgh under the lending agreement through December 31, 1990. Through March 1990, 71 percent of these loans were funded by the URA's home improvement bond issue. Twenty percent of the loans made by the end of 1990 were to African-American census tracts, and twelve loans were delinquent.

The inclusion of the bank's lending in the Monongahela River valley and other low- and moderate-income areas in the region provides a complete picture of the reinvestment program. Through the first two and one-half years of the agreement, UNB made over $15 million in residential mortgages, nearly $8 million in home improvement loans, $11 million in commercial real estate loans, and $37 million in small business loans, totaling $71 million, or nearly two-thirds of the aggregate lending target. Over one-fourth of the home mortgage and real estate lending goals had been reached, the home improvement goal was already attained, and the small business lending goal was surpassed more than fourfold. Home mortgage and real estate lending by UNB under the agreement with PCRG has been concentrated in low- and moderate-income areas within the city of Pittsburgh. The majority of the bank's home improvement and small business CRA lending, however, has been outside of the city. The inclusion of the outlying low- and moderate-income areas into the UNB program has pushed the total of loans in these two categories beyond the original five-year goals established in the lending agreement.

A key aspect of UNB's real estate lending program for CDCs has been the availability of grants from a bank-affiliated foundation to write-down project costs. During 1988–89, $250,000 of the foundation grants leveraged over $1 million of financing from the bank and $2.6 million of project funding from government and foundation sources. These grants helped to finance the construction or rehabilitation of fifty-two housing units and new retail and office space in projects sponsored by PCRG organizations. The annual $250,000 grant allocation has been renewed for two more years. Union National Bank has also deposited $100,000 into the Hill District Federal Credit Union and Dwelling House Savings and Loan, two minority-owned financial institutions located in the Hill District. The bank has installed an automated teller machine on Homewood Avenue, a low-income African-American commercial strip, and hired local residents referred by CDC-operated job training and education programs.

In December 1990, UNB and PCRG extended the agreement through 1996 and changed the aggregate mortgage lending goals. Table 3.3 shows these changes. The revised lending goals, which lower the residential mortgage targets and increase the home improvement and small business loan targets substantially, are considered by both PCRG and UNB as a more accurate reflection of the market for CRA lending in Pittsburgh after two and one-half years of experience with the lending agreement. In the future, the bank may desire more liquidity for its conventional home mortgage lending. Most of these loans are insured by neither the government nor private mortgage insurers but are "self-insured" by the bank, which keeps them in portfolio because they cannot be sold to the secondary market. The UNB has relied on the PCRG organizations to screen, counsel, and prepare borrowers for homeownership, in order to reduce the likelihood of delinquencies or defaults. So far, this approach has worked, and the conventional home mortgage lending volume is projected to grow. The "credit crunch" and stronger regulatory oversight of bank real estate lending has also not yet affected the lending agreement. The UNB has been hurt by bad real estate loans in West Virginia and Ohio, and at the end of 1990 it stopped making new real estate loans. The bank has preserved its CRA real estate lending commitment, however, and will consider financing any project sponsored or endorsed by a CDC. For example, at the request of PCRG, the Northside Leadership Conference, and the Northside Civic Development Council, the bank agreed to extend the term of a construction loan for the Rubinoff Company. The loan was for the redevelopment of Washington's Landing, a large mixed-use retail-office-residential project on Herr's Island, an abandoned site along the Allegheny River adjacent to the North Side. During 1991, Union National Bank assumed the name of its new holding company, Integra Financial Corporation.

NEGOTIATIONS WITH OTHER FINANCIAL INSTITUTIONS

The PCRG has used the Union National Bank lending agreement to establish legitimacy for CRA negotiations with other banks and thrifts in Pittsburgh. Instead of pursuing similar agreements with other financial institutions, PCRG has attempted to initiate and control a process by which specific community credit needs and concerns can be communicated and resolved, or translated into new programs and initiatives by lenders. By early 1991, PCRG institutionalized the process by creating ongoing review and oversight committees with senior bank executives and community lending officers at Pittsburgh National Bank, Mellon Bank, Equibank, and North Side Deposit Bank, in addition to Union National Bank. In doing so, PCRG was proactive and did not wait for bank mergers to occur to begin discussions. In this way, it was influenced by the new CRA policy statement released by the federal regulatory agencies in March 1989, shortly after the Federal Reserve Board denied an acquisition application by Continental Bank of Illinois on the basis of a CRA challenge. The decision, which startled the banking industry, was the first CRA protest ever upheld by the Federal Reserve. The new policy statement encourages community groups to begin CRA negotiations in advance of the regulatory applications process (Federal Reserve Board et al. 1989; Groskind and Weiss 1990).

Sandra Phillips was the link between PCRG and the policy statement promoted by the Federal Reserve Board and the other regulatory agencies. Phillips was a key figure during the 1970s and 1980s in People's Oakland, Oakland Directions Inc., the Oakland Plan, and Oakland Planning and Development Corporation, and she was an early participant in PCRG as the director of OPDC (Peirce and Steinbach 1987: 48). She was appointed to a three-year term on the Federal Reserve's national Consumer Advisory Council in 1988 and chaired its CRA committee. In January 1989, Phillips was named the first executive director of the Pittsburgh Partnership for Neighborhood Development, which until then had been informally staffed by local foundation program officers. In 1991 she was appointed to the board of directors of the Pittsburgh branch of the Federal Reserve Bank of Cleveland. In these roles, Phillips has served as an important advocate for PCRG with both bankers and regulators.

Another key factor in PCRG's post—Union National negotiating posture was the belief that additional multimillion dollar lending agreements would place pressure on CDCs to do projects that they did not have the capacity to initiate and complete. The UNB had agreed to commit all of the money for PCRG's entire reinvestment program as it was defined in early 1988, instead of funding a piece of it with the rest to be shared among the other banks. While this represented a breakthrough in CRA lending for one bank in proportion to its asset size, it placed expectations on both UNB and the PCRG organizations to achieve the aggregate five-year investment goals. Reaching the goals would demonstrate the demand for the loans and ensure that the program would be judged a success.

By 1989, PCRG identified conventional, combined home purchase-rehabilitation mortgages, minority business development financing, and real estate project loans as community credit needs not adequately addressed by the Union National Bank lending agreement. Early that year, PCRG added two new organizations—including East Liberty Development Inc., which was the only PPND-funded core CDC not involved in the UNB negotiations—and secured funding from Union National Bank and the City of Pittsburgh Community Development Block Grant to hire a staff person and operate an office. The PCRG began negotiating with Pittsburgh National Bank (PNB) and the Urban Redevelopment Authority to create a purchase-rehabilitation mortgage program targeted to selected low- and moderate-income neighborhoods (Perlmutter 1989a). In April 1989, PNB announced the Housing Recovery Program (HRP), a $1.2 million pilot program with the URA in fifteen targeted neighborhoods (Mannella 1989). Under HRP, moderate-income borrowers can secure purchase-rehabilitation mortgages with 97 percent loan-to-value ratios. The PNB finances two-thirds of the mortgage for thirty years at 8½ percent interest, and the URA supplies a deferred zero interest loan to cover the balance. The URA loans, which are repayable upon sale of the property, are funded by a $600,000 grant from the Pennsylvania Department of Community Affairs. The bank also agreed to fund PCRG and meet regularly to review and monitor HRP and the bank's existing Neighborhood Mortgage Program (NMP). The NMP is a $5 million conventional home mortgage loan program that began in 1988 simultaneously with the Union National Bank lending agreement but that PCRG did not help to create (Barcousky 1988). By November 1990, PNB and URA had committed nearly all of the HRP funds for thirty-one purchase-rehabilitation projects either closed or in process. The PNB's conventional mortgage lending in low- and moderate-income areas of Pittsburgh increased from eight loans totaling $495,000 in 1987 to twenty-eight loans for over $1 million in 1989. Pittsburgh National Bank has also taken on a leadership role among the banks in the PPND, and helped to organize a $1.9 million participation loan at cost of funds with UNB, Mellon Bank, and Equibank for the Penn-Highland retail-office renovation project in East Liberty.

Some Pittsburgh banks took proactive steps to comply with CRA before being approached by PCRG. Mellon Bank initiated a $4 million conventional home mortgage loan program for low- and moderate-income borrowers, as part of the national Community Home Buyers' Program sponsored by General Electric Mortgage Insurance Company (GEMICO) and the Federal National Mortgage Association (Fannie Mae). Under this program, lenders work with community groups to offer home-ownership counseling; GEMIC provides mortgage insurance for thirty year, 5 percent down payment loans; and Fannie Mae creates a secondary market (Federal National Mortgage Association 1990: 51–55). Mellon's program sets a maximum mortgage amount of $40,000 and includes a discount of two-hundred basis points on the bank's prevailing rate. At the urging of PCRG, Mellon is expanding the use of the Mellon CDC for debt and equity financing of minority-owned businesses. With PNB, UNB, and Equibank, Mellon used its influence to help add three PCRG representatives to the board of directors of the Minority Enterprise Partnership (MEP). The MEP is a minority business development organization affiliated with the Enterprise Corporation of Pittsburgh. The Enterprise Corporation promotes venture capital and technical assistance for local high-tech businesses, particularly start-up firms (Ahlbrandt and Weaver 1987).

In 1990, during CRA negotiations with PCRG, Equibank announced a five-year $50 million home mortgage program for low- and moderate-income neighborhoods in Pittsburgh (Perlmutter 1990e). This program was started after several months of stormy negotiations with PCRG during which the bank's president and vice chairman resigned and its stock price plunged due to a failed acquisition and bad loans (Perlmutter 1990b; Gaynor 1990a). Equibank had decided to abandon the home mortgage business in 1988 and made only three home purchase loans that year in low- and moderate-income census tracts in Pittsburgh (Pittsburgh Community Reinvestment Group 1990).

The PCRG has used the CRA protest mechanism when it is available and necessary to increase leverage and control in the negotiating process. For instance, PCRG successfully blocked the Federal Reserve application of North Side Deposit Bank to form a new bank holding company. North Side Deposit is a small bank with $186 million in assets that is headquartered on the North Side. During the 1980s, the bank expanded its presence in the booming suburbs of the North Hills. Total deposits grew by 87 percent between 1983 and 1989. Using the Home Mortgage Disclosure Act, PCRG discovered that North Side Deposit had not made a loan in an African-American census tract on the North Side since 1984 and made only two mortgage loans—both to non-owner-occupants—on the entire North Side during 1989, when it achieved record-setting profits.

The PCRG also began to approach local savings and loans during 1989. In 1984, the four largest savings and loan associations combined to make 274 conventional home purchase loans totaling nearly $9 million in low- and moderate-income census tracts in Pittsburgh. In 1988, these four thrifts made only fifty conventional loans for $1.9 million in these areas.[4] The national financial collapse of the thrift industry during the late 1980s ultimately limited the possibilities of this CRA strategy. Discussions with Atlantic Financial, Pennsylvania's largest savings and loan headquartered in suburban Philadelphia, ended when it was taken over by the Resolution Trust Corporation (McKay 1990). The contact with Atlantic Financial proved beneficial to PCRG later when Calvin Baker, the chairman of the board of Atlantic Financial, was named vice president of the Federal Home Loan Bank of Pittsburgh. Baker was in charge of the new Affordable Housing Program (AHP) created by the Financial Institutions Reform Recovery and Enforcement Act of 1989, the federal savings and loan bailout bill. The AHP provides subsidized cash advances to thrift institutions that are members of Federal Home Loan Banks to finance low- and moderate-income housing (Oravecz and Spatter 1990). During the first round of funding in 1990, two PCRG organizations, Garfield Jubilee and Perry Hilltop Citizens Council, received AHP financing through Landmark Savings Association and Parkvale Savings Bank to develop thirty-one new housing units (Gaynor 1990b).

The CRA negotiations with First Federal Savings and Loan Association, the largest Pittsburgh-based savings and loan, reached a stalemate when Pittsburgh National Bank announced its intention to acquire the institution (Perlmutter 1990a). During 1990, PCRG also publicly challenged the CRA performance of Dollar Bank, the largest mutual savings bank in Pittsburgh, and Parkvale Savings Bank (Perlmutter 1990f; 1990g). Parkvale agreed to work with PCRG to improve its CRA performance after a proposed sale of a branch was threatened. As of February 1991, PCRG's negotiations with Dollar Bank had not produced a successful outcome, despite Dollar Bank's participation in a new low-income homeownership program sponsored by Neighborhood Housing Services of Pittsburgh. The negotiations with Parkvale and Dollar created tension within PCRG, and one organization, Perry Hilltop Citizens Council, dropped out of the coalition. Perry Hilltop works closely with NHS and received financing for a housing rehabilitation project from Parkvale Savings through the Federal Home Loan Bank of Pittsburgh's Affordable Housing Program. A key problem for PCRG with the savings institutions has been that regulators from the federal Office of Thrift Supervision (OTS) have not enforced CRA when arranging mergers or branch sales. The overriding goal of the OTS in these situations has been to assist the thrifts in meeting new capital requirements.

THE ROLE OF LOCAL GOVERNMENT

The City of Pittsburgh expressed its support of PCRG in 1989 when it approved a small grant from the federal Community Development Block Grant program to the Manchester Citizens Corporation to cover some of MCC's costs related to PCRG. Later in that year, PCRG worked with the Masloff administration to create an additional pressure point for CRA enforcement. The PCRG advised the Department of Finance in the design of a new program to link the deposit of city funds with the CRA performance of the bank depositories. This process was already underway in Boston and other cities. The program rewards banks with strong community lending records through the allocation of government accounts (Perlmutter 1989b; Zehner and Valais 1990: 42–44). The point system that the Department of Finance uses in rating the banks and recommending which ones should receive deposits is shown in Table 3.5. For Mayor Masloff, this program enables her to encourage reinvestment and resettlement into the city's neighborhoods and expresses an innovative public policy thrust. It also gives her an opportunity to influence urban renewal and neighborhood development in Pittsburgh apart from the programs of the Urban Redevelopment Authority, which operates somewhat autonomously from the control of the Mayor.

The new rating system generated controversy during the CRA negotiations between PCRG and Equibank. PCRG approached Pittsburgh School Board President Barbara Burns and School Board members Ronald Suber and Richard Flanagan to use the leverage of the school system's deposits in Equibank to improve the level of lending by the bank in low- and moderate-income and African-American communities (Perlmutter 1990b). Burns and Suber had participated in PCRG as the president of East Allegheny Community Council and the director of housing for the Northside Civic Development Council, respectively, while Flanagan was the youth director for another PCRG organization, Bloomfield-Garfield

Table 3.5
City of Pittsburgh Bank Evaluation Point System

POINTS	CRITERIA
30	Cost of service
20	Quality of service
5	Awarded if the bank has special programs for servicing the credit needs of low- and moderate-income homebuyers
5	Based on the dollar volume of commercial loans made in low- and moderate-income neighborhoods
5	Based on the number and dollar volume of loans to women- and minority-owned businesses
5	Based on the number and dollar volume of loans made to nonprofit community development corporations
5	For contributions to nonprofit community development corporations
5	For involvement in support of public housing development
5	Based on the number and dollar volume of mortgage and home repair loans made to residents of low- and moderate-income neighborhoods during the previous five years
5	For contributions to municipal activities and community events
4	Based on the dollar volume of Pittsburgh municipal bonds purchased by the bank
4	For participating in high-risk development projects
3	For providing pro bono technical assistance to nonprofit community development corporations
3	For demonstrating a willingness to meet with community groups or touring neighborhoods in order to better assess community banking and lending needs

Source: City of Pittsburgh Department of Finance.

Corporation. In response, Equibank used its allies in municipal government who controlled the implementation of the program, Finance Director Ben Hayllar—who worked for Equibank prior to joining City Hall—and City Council Finance Committee Chairman Jake Milliones, to buttress its claims that PCRG's challenge to its CRA record was unfair (Perlmutter 1990c). Although PCRG and Equibank later reached an agreement on a mortgage lending initiative, PCRG declined an offer to participate in the city rating program and has instead continued to rely on bank lending information available through the federal Home Mortgage Disclosure Act. The Masloff administration has not yet released any of the data it has collected or the scores and rankings it has assigned to the banks in the quarterly reviews (Schmitz 1990). It has used the program to openly support PCRG during CRA negotiations with the two largest savings banks in Pittsburgh, Dollar Bank and Parkvale Savings Bank.

John T. Metzger

TABLE 3.6
SUMMARY OF CRA NEGOTIATIONS IN PITTSBURGH, 1988–1991

FINANCIAL INSTITUTION	OUTCOME
Union National Bank	June 1988. 5-year $109 million lending agreement December 1990. Renewal and expansion of agreement through 1996
Pittsburgh National Bank	April 1989. $1.8 million pilot housing recovery program
Mellon Bank	September 1989. $4 million community mortgage loan program
Atlantic Financial	January 1990. Thrift taken over by Resolution Trust
First Federal	January 1990. Thrift announces proposed merger with Pittsburgh National Bank
Equibank	July 1990. 5-year $50 million home mortgage program
Parkvale Savings	September 1990. City withdraws funds from thrift
North Side Deposit Bank	November 1990. Bank withdraws application to Federal Reserve to form a holding company
Dollar Bank	December 1990. City withdraws funds from thrift

The Finance Department withdrew municipal funds from both institutions after PCRG publicized the negotiations to the media (Barnes 1990; Perlmutter and Smith 1990).[5]

Finally, PCRG is working with the Urban Redevelopment Authority to develop new programs and redesign existing ones to support and leverage private sector CRA lending initiatives. An important outcome of PCRG's efforts has been the development of coalitions between banks and CDCs to lobby for increased local, state, and federal government support for community economic development. Pittsburgh banks that have invested in CDC projects are beginning to use their political power to help reformulate and expand URA and state-level housing and economic development programs to better serve CDC objectives.

CONCLUSION

Over a three-year span, the Pittsburgh Community Reinvestment Group has used the Community Reinvestment Act to negotiate for new programs and initiatives with all of the large financial institutions in Pittsburgh. The results of these negotiations through early 1991 are summarized in Table 3.6 and include one of the nation's largest lending agree-

100

TABLE 3.7
CONVENTIONAL HOME PURCHASE MORTGAGE PROGRAMS OF FOUR LARGE COMMERCIAL BANKS IN PITTSBURGH

PROGRAM ELEMENTS	UNB COMMUNITY MORTGAGE RESOURCE PROGRAM	PNB NEIGHBORHOOD MORTGAGE PROGRAM	MELLON COMMUNITY MORTGAGE LOAN PROGRAM	EQUIBANK AFFORDABLE MORTGAGE PROGRAM	EQUIBANK DOWNPAYMENT ASSISTANCE PROGRAM
AREA ELIGIBILITY	pcrg neighborhood or low/mod. tract	entire city	low/mod. tract	low/mod. tract	low/mod. tract
INCOME ELIGIBILITY	no limit	$38,700 limit in phop program area; no limit in PHOP target area	no limit	no limit	$45,000 limit
PROPERTY ELIGIBILITY	1–6 units	1–4 units	1–4 units	1–4 units	1–4 units
INTEREST RATE	fixed at .5% below UNB prevailing rate	fixed at 1% below PNB prevailing rate	fixed at 2% below Mellon prevailing rate	fixed at 1% below Equibank prevailing rate	Equibank prevailing rate
ORIGINATION POINTS	none	1 point; 2 points in PHOP target area where income exceeds $56,000	1 point	1 point	none

(continued)

TABLE 3.7 (*continued*)

PROGRAM ELEMENTS	UNB COMMUNITY MORTGAGE RESOURCE PROGRAM	PNB NEIGHBORHOOD MORTGAGE PROGRAM	MELLON COMMUNITY MORTGAGE LOAN PROGRAM	EQUIBANK AFFORDABLE MORTGAGE PROGRAM	EQUIBANK DOWNPAYMENT ASSISTANCE PROGRAM
TERM	10–30 years	up to 30 years	up to 30 years	15–30 years	15–30 years
AMOUNT	no minimum or maximum	no minimum or maximum	no minimum; $40,000 maximum with case-by-case exception	no minimum or maximum	no minimum or maximum
MAXIMUM LOAN-TO-VALUE RATIO	95%	95%	95%	95%	95%
MINIMUM DOWN PAYMENT	5% of lesser of purchase price or appraised value	5% of lesser of purchase price or appraised value	5% of lesser of purchase price or appraised value	5% of lesser of purchase price or appraised value	5% of lesser of purchase price or appraised value, with consumer loan for 50% of cash necessary to close
PRIVATE MORTGAGE INSURANCE	not required	required in PHOP target area where income exceeds $47,100	required	not required	not required

102

PAYMENT/DEBT-TO-INCOME RATIOS	33%/38%	33%/38%; 28%/36% in PHOP target area where income exceeds $47,100	28%/33%; 33%/38% in GE Capital Mortgage Insurance Program	33%/38%	33%/38%
OWNER OCCUPANCY	required	required	required	required	required
CLOSING COSTS AND PREPAIDS	paid by borrower, cannot be financed	no attorney or settlement fees and 12% discount on title insurance (not available in PHOP target area where income exceeds $47,100)	paid by borrower, cannot be financed	paid by borrower, cannot be financed	50% of cash necessary to close can be financed with consumer loan

ments and several targeted neighborhood reinvestment programs. By the end of 1990, each of the four largest commercial banks in Pittsburgh was offering below-market-rate, low down payment conventional home mortgage loans. The elements of these programs are outlined in Table 3.7. The PCRG is now funded by five different banks, with a budget exceeding $100,000. The sources of funding for PCRG's budget during 1989–91 are shown in Table 3.8.

The PCRG has become an advocacy organization for CDC real estate project financing and helps to train bank personnel on CRA responsibilities through neighborhood tours and technical assistance. It also works with the banks to develop joint strategies for marketing financial products and services and/or improving relationships and services between neighborhood branches and CDCs. Finally, PCRG plays an important role as a CRA educational organization for community economic development practitioners in Pittsburgh. Staff and board members of individual CDCs, equipped with knowledge of each bank's CRA responsibilities, obligations, and performance, have improved their ability to negotiate for private financing of projects, better branch services for residents, and stronger organizational relationships with local bankers. This role will grow in the future with the release of CRA ratings issued to banks by federal regulatory agencies and with the expansion of HMDA reporting requirements.

The Community Reinvestment Act has proven to be a powerful

TABLE 3.8
PITTSBURGH COMMUNITY REINVESTMENT GROUP BUDGET, 1989–1991

SOURCES	FUNDS ($)		
	1989–90	*1990–91*	*Total*
UNION NATIONAL BANK	33,320	35,000	68,320
PITTSBURGH NATIONAL BANK	16,000	25,000	41,000
CITY OF PITTSBURGH COMMUNITY DEVELOPMENT BLOCK GRANT	4,850	0	4,850
EQUIBANK	0	35,000	35,000
MELLON BANK	0	19,000	19,000
NORTH SIDE DEPOSIT BANK	0	2,500	2,500
MEMBERSHIP DUES	1,250	1,400	2,650
TOTAL	**55,420**	**117,900**	**173,320**

Source: Pittsburgh Community Reinvestment Group.

tool in Pittsburgh for stimulating mortgage lending to older, urban areas and for building the strength and legitimacy of community development corporations. The Pittsburgh Community Reinvestment Group is both a continuation and a new variation in the history of public-private neighborhood reinvestment in Pittsburgh. The organizations of PCRG have been able to strike new partnerships with local banks to rebuild and control the future of their communities in a way that transcends the past record of urban renewal and points to a new process for ensuring neighborhood-based growth.

NOTES

1. I thank Marc Weiss, Peter Marcuse, and Sigurd Grava for comments on earlier versions of this chapter. I benefited from the support of the Graduate School of Architecture, Planning, and Preservation at Columbia University, and the National Congress for Community Economic Development. Countless interactions with community development practitioners, lenders, and public sector officials in Pittsburgh helped me to frame the analysis in this chapter. Some of the research presented here was done while I was the coordinator of the Pittsburgh Community Reinvestment Group during 1989–90, with funding from the Manchester Citizens Corporation, the Pittsburgh Department of City Planning, Union National Bank, Pittsburgh National Bank, and with the research assistance of David Black and Danny Holmes.
2. Interview with Sandra Phillips, Executive Director, Pittsburgh Partnership for Neighborhood Development, December 5, 1989.
3. Interview with Thomas Jones, Vice President, Federal Home Loan Bank of Pittsburgh, December 7, 1989.
4. The four savings and loans are First Federal Savings and Loan Association, Atlantic Financial, Landmark Savings Association, and Parkvale Savings Association.
5. Interview with Ben Hayllar, Director, City of Pittsburgh Department of Finance, December 21, 1990

REFERENCES

ACTION-Housing, Inc. 1975. *The Neighborhood Housing Services Model: A Progress Assessment of the Related Activities of the Urban Reinvestment Task Force.* Washington, D.C.: U.S. Department of Housing and Urban Development.

Ahlbrandt, Roger S., Jr. 1986. "Public–Private Partnerships for Neighborhood Renewal." *Annals of the American Academy of Political and Social Science* 488: 120–33.

Ahlbrandt, Roger S., Jr., and Paul C. Brophy. 1975a. *An Evaluation of Pittsburgh's Neighborhood Housing Services Program.* Washington, D.C.: U.S. Department of Housing and Urban Development.

———. 1975b. *Neighborhood Revitalization.* Lexington, Mass.: D. C. Heath.

Ahlbrandt, Roger S., Jr., and Clyde Weaver. 1987. "Public–Private Institutions and Advanced Technology Development in Southwestern Pennsylvania." *Journal of the American Planning Association* 53 (4):449–58.

Barcousky, Len. 1988. "Banks to Lend More in Low-Income Areas." *Pittsburgh Post-Gazette,* June 18.

———. 1989 "Loan Exec Pledges Scrutiny of Rejections." *Pittsburgh Post-Gazette,* Jan. 24.

Barnes, Tom. 1990. "City Issues Threat Over Bank's Loan Practices." *Pittsburgh Post-Gazette,* Sept. 18.

Clark, Gordon L. 1989. "Pittsburgh in Transition: Consolidation of Prosperity in an Era of Economic Restructuring." In *Economic Restructuring and Political Response.* ed. Robert A. Beauregard. Newbury Park, Calif.: Sage Publications.

Cunningham, James V. 1965. *The Resurgent Neighborhood.* Notre Dame, Ind.: Fides Publishers.

Darden, Joe T. 1973. *Afro-Americans in Pittsburgh.* Lexington, Mass.: D. C. Heath.

Dedman, Bill. 1989. "Blacks Turned Down for Home Loans from S & Ls Twice as Often as Whites." *Atlanta Journal/Constitution,* Jan. 22.

Federal National Mortgage Association. 1990. *Fannie Mae's Low- and Moderate-Income Housing Initiatives.* Washington, D.C.

Federal Reserve Board, Comptroller of the Currency, Federal Home Loan Bank Board, Federal Deposit Insurance Corporation. 1989. *Statement of the Federal Financial Supervisory Agencies Regarding the Community Reinvestment Act.* Washington, D.C.: Federal Reserve Board.

Frieden, Bernard J., and Lynne B. Sagalyn. 1989. *Downtown, Inc.: How America Rebuilds Cities.* Cambridge, Mass.: MIT Press.

Fulton, William. 1987. "Off the Barricades into the Boardrooms." *Planning* 53 (8): 11–15.

Fuoco, Linda Wilson. 1989. "Tax Relief Supported in Gentrified Districts." *Pittsburgh Post-Gazette,* Nov. 18.

Gaynor, Pamela. 1990a. "Third Top Officer Resigns at Equibank." *Pittsburgh Post-Gazette,* June 6.

———. 1990b. "Thrifts to Subsidize Low-Income Housing." *Pittsburgh Post-Gazette,* July 17.

Groskind, Jerome D., and Marcus S. Weiss. 1990. "Regulators Turn up the Heat on CRA Compliance." *The Bankers Magazine* (May/June).

Hays, Samuel P., ed. 1989. *City at the Point: Essays on the Social History of Pittsburgh.* Pittsburgh, Pa.: University of Pittsburgh Press.

Jezierski, Louise. 1990. "Neighborhoods and Public–Private Partnerships in Pittsburgh." *Urban Affairs Quarterly* 26 (2): 217–49.

Levitt, Rachelle L., ed. 1987. *Cities Reborn.* Washington, D.C.: Urban Land Institute.

Lowe, Jeanne R. 1967. *Cities in a Race with Time.* New York: Random House.

Lowe, Stanley A. 1990. "The Pittsburgh Experience; Preservation and Displacement: Is It Inevitable?" Paper presented at Preservation and Affordable Housing Conference, Center for Urban Policy Research, Rutgers University and Preservation New Jersey. Newark, New Jersey.

Lubove, Roy. 1969. *Twentieth-Century Pittsburgh: Government, Business, and Environmental Change.* New York: Alfred A. Knopf.

Lurcott, Robert H., and Jane A. Downing. 1987. "A Public–Private Support System for Community-Based Organizations in Pittsburgh." *Journal of the American Planning Association* 53 (4): 459–68.

Mannella, Susan. 1989. "URA to Help Residents Buy, Fix Up Vacant Homes." *Pittsburgh Post-Gazette,* April 24.

McKay, Jim. 1990. "U.S. Regulators Seize Control of Atlantic Thrift." *Pittsburgh Post-Gazette,* Jan. 12.

Metzger, John T., and Marc A. Weiss. 1988. *The Role of Private Lending in Neighborhood Development: The Chicago Experience.* Evanston, Ill.: Center for Urban Affairs and Policy Research, Northwestern University.

Naparstek, Arthur, and Gale Cincotta. 1976. *Urban Disinvestment: New Implications for Community Organization, Research, and Public Policy.* Washington, D.C. and Chicago: National Center for Urban Ethnic Affairs/National Training and Information Center.

National Trust for Historic Preservation. 1986. *A Guide to Tax-Advantaged Rehabilitation.* Washington, D.C.

Nenno, Mary K., and Paul C. Brophy. 1982. *Housing and Local Government.* Washington, D.C.: International City Management Association.

Oakland Directions Inc. 1980. *The Oakland Plan: A Citizen's Planning Process, 1977–1979*. Pittsburgh, Pa.: Urban Design Associates.
Oravecz, John D., and Sam Spatter. 1990. "$3.4 Million Earmarked for Low Income Home Buyers." *Pittsburgh Press*, Feb. 7.
Osborne, David. 1988. *Laboratories of Democracy*. Boston: Harvard Business School Press.
Peirce, Neal R., and Carol F. Steinbach. 1987. *Corrective Capitalism: The Rise of America's Community Development Corporations*. New York: Ford Foundation.
Perlmutter, Ellen M. 1988. "From Agitator to Low-Keyed Mover, Stanley Lowe Convinces with Words." *Pittsburgh Press*, June 26.
———. 1989a. "Neighborhood Panel Looks at PNB Policies." *Pittsburgh Press*, Feb. 26.
———. 1989b. "3 Banks Lead Pack in Race for City Funds." *Pittsburgh Press*, Nov. 20.
———. 1990a. "Loan Fears Spur Challenge of Thrift-Bank Merger." *Pittsburgh Press*, Jan. 5.
———. 1990b. "Equibank President Calls Rap on Investments Unfair." *Pittsburgh Press*, Jan. 14.
———. 1990c. "Milliones Criticizes Attack on Equibank's Lending Record." *Pittsburgh Press*, Feb. 13.
———. 1990d. "Foundation Doubles Housing Loan Program." *Pittsburgh Press*, March 31.
———. 1990e. "Equibank to Lend $50 Million in Poor Areas to Answer Critics." *Pittsburgh Press*, July 17.
———. 1990f. "Parkvale Told to Answer Charges of Loan Discrimination." *Pittsburgh Press*, Sept. 19.
———. 1990g. "Dollar Bank Hit by Group for Few Low-Income Loans." *Pittsburgh Press*, Dec. 18.
Perlmutter, Ellen M., and Matthew P. Smith. 1990. "Dollar Bank Snubs City Business after Order for Loans in Poor Areas." *Pittsburgh Press*, Dec. 21.
Pittsburgh Community Reinvestment Group. 1990. *A Comparative Analysis of Neighborhood Lending by Pittsburgh's Four Major Commercial Banks 1984–1988*. Pittsburgh, Pa.
Pollock, Beth. 1990. "AGH Helps Employees Buy North Side Homes." *Pittsburgh Business-Times*, July 23.
Sbragia, Alberta. 1989. "The Pittsburgh Model of Economic Development: Partnership, Responsiveness, and Indifference." In *Unequal Partnerships: The Political Economy of Urban Redevelopment in Postwar America*, ed. Gregory D. Squires. New Brunswick, N.J.: Rutgers University Press.
Schmitz, Jon. 1990. "All 5 Banks Aiding City on Housing, Official Says." *Pittsburgh Press*, May 18.
Smith, Neil, and Peter Williams, eds. 1986. *Gentrification of the City*. Boston: Allen and Unwin.
Stewman, Shelby, and Joel A. Tarr. 1982. "Four Decades of Public and Private Partnerships in Pittsburgh." In *Public–Private Partnership in American Cities*, ed. R. Scott Fosler and Renee A. Berger. Lexington, Mass.: D. C. Heath.
Swaney, Chris. 1990. "Six Philadelphia Groups Assail Mellon Purchase." *Pittsburgh Business-Times*, Feb. 5.
Swift, Larry D., and Jean Pogge. 1984. *Neighborhood Reinvestment Partnership: Neighborhood Groups Lead the Way for First Chicago Corporation*. Chicago: Woodstock Institute.
Teaford, Jon C. 1990. *The Rough Road to Renaissance: Urban Revitalization in America, 1940–1985*. Baltimore: Johns Hopkins University Press.
Urban Redevelopment Authority of Pittsburgh, Department of Housing. 1990. *An Overview 1989*. Pittsburgh, Pa.
Watkins, Linda M. 1986. "Pittsburgh Blacks' Paucity of Political Clout Stirs Struggle over the City's At-Large Election System." *Wall Street Journal*, April 1.
Weber, Michael P. 1988. *Don't Call Me Boss: David L. Lawrence, Pittsburgh's Renaissance Mayor*. Pittsburgh, Pa.: University of Pittsburgh Press.
Weiss, Marc A. 1985. "The Origins and Legacy of Urban Renewal." In *Federal Housing*

Policy and Programs: Past and Present, ed. J. Paul Mitchell. New Brunswick, N.J.: Center for Urban Policy Research, Rutgers University.

Weiss, Marc A., and John T. Metzger. 1987. "Technology Development, Neighborhood Planning, and Negotiated Partnerships: The Case of Pittsburgh's Oakland Neighborhood." Journal of the American Planning Association 53 (4): 469–77.

————. 1988. Neighborhood Lending Agreements: Negotiating and Financing Community Development. Cambridge, Mass.: Lincoln Institute of Land Policy.

Willis, Mark A. 1990. "Chase CDC Launches $200-Million Program." Directions in Affordable Housing Finance 1 (2): 3.

Working Group on Community Development. 1989. Pittsburgh Renewed: Community-Based Economic Development, 1983–1989. Pittsburgh, Pa.: Working Group on Community Development.

Zehner, Andrew L., and George A. Valais. 1990. Linked Deposits: Leveraging for Economic Development. Washington, D.C.: Government Finance Officers Association.

Ziegler, Arthur P., Jr. 1974. Historic Preservation in Inner-city Areas. Pittsburgh, Pa.: Ober Park Associates.

Ziegler, Arthur P., Jr., Leopold Adler II, and Walter C. Kidney. 1975. Revolving Loan Funds for Historic Preservation. Pittsburgh, Pa.: Ober Park Associates.

David Everett   Chapter 4

CONFRONTATION, NEGOTIATION, AND COLLABORATION: DETROIT'S MULTIBILLION- DOLLAR DEAL

ON APRIL 3, 1987, after an awards ceremony in Detroit, reporters gathered in their traditional pack to buttonhole Coleman Young, the city's outspoken mayor. Their topic was one recently discussed in a Detroit City Council session: Why was so much taxpayer money needed to develop downtown hotel space in the nation's sixth largest city? Wasn't private investment possible? Young angrily called the questions "asinine." Yet, as *Detroit Free Press* reporter Patricia Edmonds wrote, the mayor proceeded to answer them: "Why? Because people have been leaving Detroit by the droves. There's been a white exodus out of this city . . . that included businesses leaving, too. The same businesses who leave this city are willing to invest money outside the city, but they're not willing to invest in the city."

Then Young leveled his combative rhetoric at a familiar target: "Our own banks have been notorious for their refusal to invest in the city, to extend loans to people who would invest in the city, or even to give mortgages to people who want to buy homes in the city. That's no secret. . . . These banks got fat and got rich off the City of Detroit, but you know, this is not a sentimental game. Ain't no such thing as gratitude in finance. It's profit" (Edmonds 1987).

Young's comments were quickly rejected by Detroit-area lenders, who argued that they had supported the city for years and would continue to do so. Still, the tirade revived a dormant belief that Young and others in the city had held for years: Detroit's financial institutions did not support their hometown. That belief reflected the same deterioration and dissent that had simmered for decades in most older industrial cities in the United States. Yet an understanding of the bank lending controversy that eventually followed Young's words begins with understanding Detroit itself.

The site of one of the nation's worst race riots in 1967, Detroit's traditional urban problems have multiplied to become some of the most severe and complex anywhere. By the 1980s, the city regularly competed for the country's highest murder rate, and it ranked among the worst in terms of infant mortality, drug use, and unemployment. Furthermore, metropolitan Detroit, with its legacy of racial conflict, evolved into one of the nation's most racially segregated areas (Gillmor 1991). To Young and some black residents of the city, therefore, it was not just that banks were ignoring their hometown; they also believed white-run banks were ignoring blacks.

Detroit's lenders, because of the city's cyclical economy, were (and still are) devoutly conservative—perhaps even more so than those in a traditionally conservative field. If they were to weather the hard times certain to come because of the city's reliance on the recession-sensitive automotive industry, then they believed in prudence even in good economic times.

With this civic legacy and in this financial environment, about a year after Young's angry comments to reporters, Detroit was to experience a controversy that, at the time, resulted in the largest single series of local lending agreements in the history of the Community Reinvestment Act (CRA). Although some institutions still resent some of the event's causes, other lenders and many community activists say the result has been both more loans for the city and better attitudes on both sides.

As in Atlanta, a major catalyst for the CRA controversy in Detroit was a series of newspaper articles. But the objective of the Free Press, which reported Young's words in 1987 and which published the later series, was broader than the traditional stickpin mortgage studies of Chicago or the computer analysis of Atlanta based on data provided by the Home Mortgage Disclosure Act (HMDA). From the beginning, the goal of the Free Press was to examine the truth or falsity of the controversial, heart-felt belief by Young and other Detroit residents that "local banks don't support Detroit."

Newspaper articles were not the only cause of the 1988 controversy. Other contributing factors were a key regulatory decision from the
State of Michigan—spawned in part by the pioneering activism of two
Detroit lawyers—and the work of a coalition of community, labor,
church, and civil rights groups that formed to negotiate increased support
from the banks.

PATH TO CONFRONTATION

Bernard Parker, Jr., a Detroit community group leader who was elected a
Wayne County commissioner in 1990, remembers that much of Detroit's
attitude about lending before 1988 was based on perception—from both
citizens and lenders.

> I don't think the community really felt that the banks
> were there to assist them. The banks were just there for
> people to deposit money or to withdraw money, but they
> were not a place to get loans—or at least that's what
> people in Detroit thought.
>   The banks had their own image of Detroit, where
> they were still trying to use the same banking procedures
> that they used twenty or thirty years ago, when people
> were working and had stable jobs. Well, the city had
> changed. It just wasn't as stable, and it wasn't much the
> same as it had been.
>
> (Parker 1990)

Amid these perceptions, the *Free Press* developed an interest in
community reinvestment issues. After Coleman Young revived the long-
standing accusations against local lending institutions in April 1987, the
paper's editors authorized preliminary interviews. Reporter David Everett
and Patricia Edmonds, the city hall bureau chief who had covered
Young's comments, began the interviews in May.

Later that year, Everett was assigned to develop an investigative
reporting project even as more public attention was directed toward local
lenders. Detroit Renaissance, a nonprofit group of business and community leaders from Detroit, had led a one-year, $750,000 study of the city's
future. Its long-awaited results, the work of more than two hundred civic
and business leaders, were released in late November as what eventually

became known as the "Detroit Strategic Plan." Like other civic improvement strategies, the plan had far-reaching recommendations. New investment pools should be created to promote development. A specific area near downtown was targeted for an innovative "town within a city" program. New education initiatives and anticrime measures were proposed (Detroit Renaissance 1987).

In addition, twenty-six members of a race relations task force had spent ten months in their work, and one key recommendation was a study of alleged housing discrimination in Detroit—including the role of financial institutions. After the report was released, Mayor Young and some of the study's authors reignited the debate about Detroit's banks by using an emotionally charged word to describe what they envisioned as the focus of the recommended study: redlining.

Less than a month later, on December 1, 1987, Detroit Renaissance selected as its new chairman Charles Fisher III, chairman and president of National Bank of Detroit and its holding company, NBD Bancorp. Known as NBD, the super-regional bank is Michigan's largest and usually ranks among the twenty-five largest in the nation. Fisher, as its key executive, was considered the city's top banker, and his institution has long been considered one of the soundest in the nation. With long ties to the General Motors Corporation, NBD also was considered one of the most powerful links in the Detroit area's industrial-financial establishment.

Discussing the Strategic Plan, Fisher and Young quickly disagreed over what the proposed housing discrimination study would find—if it ever was conducted. Fisher denied that redlining existed in Detroit. While he did not specifically oppose the study, Fisher said it "will only prove I'm right." Young, in customary bluntness, responded that he believed redlining existed in Detroit. "As far as I'm concerned, ain't no study necessary, but if there is any doubt, that study should be done" (Heron 1987).

By January, reporter Everett outlined a broad project for the *Free Press*. The goal was to document whether or not local financial institutions properly supported Detroit, and more than a study of home loans was necessary. In February, Everett was joined by city government writer Teresa Blossom, and the newspaper team later expanded again to include economic development reporter John Gallagher. Their final plan included extensive studies of three types of loans: development projects, government programs, and home mortgages. Extensive data, both statistical and anecdotal, were available for each, and it was envisioned from the early stages that computer analyses would be done in conjunction with traditional interviews and reporting.

For the mortgage part of the study, Charles Finn and Calvin Bradford of the Hubert Humphrey Institute in Minnesota were hired, in part because they were working on a similar story with an Atlanta newspaper. In Detroit, Finn would do the lion's share of the technical work, with Bradford serving as a reviewer. Basically, home mortgage and home improvement loan rates would be compared between predominantly white and predominantly black census tracts of comparable income levels. The study also would attempt to control for other factors; the goal was to make race the primary difference in the study groups. In addition to Finn's work, the *Free Press* team would compare city and suburban loan rates, and examine loan demand, branch locations, steering by real estate agents, the impact of mortgage insurance and secondary markets, and the personal attitudes of both loan applicants and lenders.

Finn had refined his HMDA computer programs since the Atlanta project to provide more information about lending rates. The Detroit study also would have the benefit of additional lending information required by Michigan law but unavailable in Georgia. Moreover, the Detroit study was to expand beyond personal computers. The *Free Press* eventually would use two mainframe computers to merge federal and Michigan state databases and to study lending rates in more detail than in Atlanta.

While the newspaper work was under way in Detroit, the sometimes timid, sometimes feisty CRA activism of the city continued. A heritage of local CRA challenges came from Erma Henderson, a long-time Detroit city council member. Henderson and her supporters used CRA challenges to promote their view that lending policies resulted in disinvestment and unwise growth patterns in the Detroit metropolitan area, but the challenges brought little publicity or change.

Another, more focused CRA effort came from James Edwards and Patrick Murray, two Detroit lawyers who, in effect, were the brains and staff of a group they called the Detroit Committee for Responsible Banking. Edwards and Murray decided to use the CRA process to present genuine legal challenges to local banks, and they seized on Comerica, the city's second largest institution, and what they believed was its complete lack of support for local development projects. They also noted a decrease in home mortgages in the city from Comerica.

In 1987, the Federal Reserve rejected an Edwards/Murray challenge to a Comerica plan to expand a Toledo, Ohio subsidiary; but by April 1988 the two lawyers had filed another federal CRA challenge. This one was against Comerica's plan to buy a Dallas, Texas bank. The two Detroit residents also filed a CRA challenge against Comerica with the State of Michigan.

State CRA challenges are unusual, but Michigan has developed some of the nation's broadest laws in the area of lending discrimination and citizen participation. The first step in this leadership had come in 1977, when the state adopted its landmark Mortgage Anti-Redlining Act—one of the nation's most elaborate state mortgage disclosure laws. Not only did this law require that banks and thrifts disclose the locations of their loans (as does HMDA), but the rule also applied to private and bank mortgage companies—information not disclosed under HMDA at the time. The state law also went beyond HMDA by requiring data on loan foreclosures and loan denials, including their location and the reasons for the denial.

In its first decade, however, the 1977 law seemed to provide the Michigan public little more than information. Activists and state officials believed federal regulators did not pay much attention to the state data. The annual reports resulting from the act appeared to be too complicated or detailed for Michigan community groups. The raw data disclosed under the law also had limitations, according to Eugene Kuthy, who was commissioner of the Michigan Financial Institutions Bureau from 1983–90. "You clearly couldn't get into the minds of the individuals doing the lending, so you couldn't prove redlining with the use of this disclosure data. You could, however, obtain strong inferences of, if not redlining, then disinvestment patterns, and that would be helpful in a challenge process" (Kuthy 1990–91). Yet if federal regulators ignored the state data, then it could not help any challenge process. What was needed was a state process in which the anti-redlining data would not be ignored.

That process was adopted in 1986, when Michigan passed an interstate banking law. In effect, a state CRA challenge process was inserted into the new law. The theory was that if deposits from Michigan were to be used to acquire non-Michigan institutions, then state regulators and the public should be able to determine whether the Michigan lender was continuing to measure and meet local credit needs. If the state or the public thought that was not being done, then the new law allowed a challenge against an institution.

According to Kuthy, the state had three grounds to act against a lender who was challenged under the state CRA: if its federal CRA rating was unfavorable; if independent information, such as the state's disclosure data, showed an institution was not providing lending support to its home area; or if an institution did not sufficiently rebut a challenger's assertions. Yet by early 1988, Kuthy had had no challenge to an interstate acquisition that afforded him the right combination of facts and allegations to use his authority. Despite all the data from the Anti-Redlining Act and despite the new state challenge capability in the interstate banking law, few state CRA protests were filed. The disclosure data still was complicated and, according to community groups, still ignored by federal regulators who were not properly enforcing their own CRA.

By March 1988, however, an opportunity for the right CRA challenge occurred when Comerica announced it wanted to buy the Texas bank. For the announcement, a top Comerica executive said, in effect, that the bank wanted to use Michigan deposits to expand in Texas. Kuthy immediately took notice. "That statement was the most classic basis for a CRA challenge that you could want," he remembers (Kuthy 1990–91).

In Detroit, Edwards and Murray filed their challenge under the state law, and Kuthy and his bureau began their review. Pursuant to long-standing information-sharing agreements, the state exchanged confidential data with federal regulators and obtained Comerica's most recent federal CRA rating. The state also began its own investigation, analyzing Comerica's CRA plan and its performance as shown in the state's loan disclosure reports. Without the public or the news media knowing it, Kuthy was beginning to gather information that eventually would lead him to make a historic regulatory decision—a decision that would become critical to Detroit's upcoming CRA controversy.

While the Financial Institutions Bureau was investigating the Comerica application and the Edwards/Murray challenge, the *Free Press* was continuing its research. The reporting trio increased its journalistic legwork, visiting more than one hundred neighborhoods in Detroit and the surrounding area. The team interviewed loan applicants and recipients, real estate agents, developers, businesspeople, bankers, banking experts, demographers, regulators, elected officials, community group leaders, economists, and just plain people. Using local, state, and federal freedom of information laws, the reporters filed and were granted formal requests for data from governments in twelve cities, eight states, and the nation as a whole. By April, as various results began to come in, the *Free Press* team grew at times to a dozen people, including editors, researchers, and computer consultants.

By May 1, the newspaper's project was at a key phase. After five months of work by the newspaper team, the *Free Press* decided to present its preliminary findings to lenders, activists, and Kuthy. Letters were sent; officials were briefed. Formal, group interviews were held in separate, hours-long sessions with Kuthy and with top executives from all of the region's top financial institutions. The process took weeks.

As the interviews continued, the Michigan public's appetite for CRA issues was whetted in early June with extensive media reports of an incident that, years later, still generates embarrassment among State of Michigan financial regulators and suspicion among Michigan lenders. What happened was that Comerica's federal CRA rating—then a secret— was disclosed to the public.

The leak came through Edwards and Murray, the two activists who had challenged Comerica's support of Detroit development projects. In a package of documents sent from Lansing, the two lawyers came upon an unexpected reference that they were not supposed to receive. Federal regulators had given Comerica a "less than satisfactory" CRA rating, putting the institution among only 2 percent of the nation's larger banks with unfavorable CRA grades.

The regulators apparently had made their move in December 1987, less than three weeks after they formally rejected the previous Edwards/Murray challenge to Comerica's Toledo expansion plans. In what then was an unknown victory for the two Detroit lawyers, the Federal Reserve (which regulated Comerica) had downgraded the bank from satisfactory to less than satisfactory (Everett and Blossom 1988).

"All we knew was that they had rejected our challenge," Edwards said. "But there really was some behind-the-scenes success that we were completely unaware of." (Edwards 1990–91).

Edwards and Murray quickly jumped on the damaging news, citing it publicly and in documents to support their current CRA challenge against Comerica's Texas acquisition. The disclosure led to threats from the Federal Reserve to end its information-sharing agreement with the State of Michigan, which said the leak was inadvertent. (After an investigation, the information-sharing agreement remained in effect.) Michigan lending institutions also privately expressed concern that the leak may have been purposeful to pressure Comerica—a charge Kuthy denied. Perhaps most importantly, the rating showed that federal regulators were among those focusing on the situation in Detroit. For Comerica, the entire episode was a sign of controversy to come.

Meanwhile, the *Free Press*'s preliminary findings began to prompt reaction even before they were published. For example, the decision to brief the institutions allowed the *Free Press*'s primary competition, the *Detroit News*, to obtain a copy of one of the paper's briefing letters and publish its own hastily written articles on lending in Detroit. In Detroit's arch-competitive newspaper war, such maneuvering was common.

Another reaction came from the institutions themselves. Unlike the quick, controversy-killing response of Atlanta's lenders to the publication of the *Journal/Constitution* series, Detroit's bankers would fight back. Among several early efforts was one from Comerica, which hired a university professor to critique the newspaper's home mortgage study. David Goldberg, a sociology professor and research scientist at the University of Michigan, conducted his initial analysis without discussing the study or its methodology in detail with Finn or with the *Free Press*. His initial report criticized the Finn/Bradford model used in Atlanta and Detroit. Specifically, Goldberg said the census data was outdated and that some neighborhoods studied by the *Free Press* had changed in racial makeup since the 1980 census. Goldberg also criticized the newspaper for excluding some tracts from some analyses, and he said mortgage lending rates could be better analyzed by regression analysis (Goldberg 1988a). Unbeknownst to Goldberg, the *Free Press* had spent weeks updating 1980 census data and visiting neighborhoods to gauge their current racial makeup. He also was unaware that some tracts had been excluded because they were no longer residential areas or for other reasons.

Though neither Goldberg nor lenders questioned the non-mortgage parts of the newspaper's project, they raised questions about the mortgage study that had not been answered by the previous work in Atlanta or by the *Free Press*'s initial research. The newspaper decided to delay publication of any articles to answer the questions and to ensure that its data was as strong as possible. Both Finn and Bradford were asked to respond to the lenders' analyses and to Goldberg's report, which also was reviewed by an outside expert familiar with both Goldberg's work and Detroit's demography. The reporting team decided to revisit some of the neighborhoods that Goldberg asserted may have changed in racial makeup. The paper also re-reviewed its mortgage demand data and census data updates and decided to conduct additional computer analyses.

One of those computer reviews was designed to address concerns that certain black census tracts in which Detroit lenders made loans were excluded from the middle-income target tracts used by the *Free Press*. In the new study, the paper analyzed the racial lending patterns of lenders in various new groupings, including one for all black tracts in Detroit. The resulting data, both before and after adjustments for income characteristics and other factors, not only supported the original Finn/Bradford methodology but provided further information on lending patterns for institutions that had made only a few loans in middle-income tracts.

The additional work improved the newspaper's study. First, the *Free Press* satisfied itself that its methodology and results were accurate and fair. Second, the resulting new analyses actually made the mortgage study stronger. While the newspaper was conducting the additional research, it also received a limited technical endorsement from Kuthy, whose staff analyzed the mortgage study in detail.

By late July, after a laborious rewriting and editing process, the *Free Press* was ready to go public. After more than a year of planning and research, Detroit's morning newspaper had found hard evidence supporting the assumptions that Coleman Young had voiced about the city's financial institutions. The project was published over four days under the title "The Race for Money."

First, the *Free Press* found racial patterns in mortgage lending. Loans were being granted about three times more often in white census tracts as in comparable black tracts, and like Atlanta, the disparity had been increasing.

Second, the paper found that local lenders had not been doing their share in the financing of major development projects in Detroit. The *Free Press* showed that Detroit's lenders lagged behind their Midwestern competitors in major development loans. For nineteen major Detroit projects since 1980, Detroit banks put up only 10.7 percent of the more than $560 million that was needed. That rate did not match other midwestern cities. Banks in Cleveland, for instance, had funded more than 40 percent of their city's recent major development projects.

Third, the newspaper reported that many of Detroit's lenders had low participation in government loan programs designed to help individuals or businesses that have trouble getting traditional loans. In that category, the *Free Press* used statistical and investigative reporting to examine six different loan programs. Local, state, and federal programs were examined, including loans from the U.S. Small Business Administration (SBA), the Federal Housing Administration, the U.S. Department of Housing and Urban Development (HUD), the Michigan State Housing Development Authority, and the Detroit Economic Growth Corp.

Local bank participation in several of those programs was then compared to that of banks in cities of similar size and of similar economic conditions. For some programs, the participation by Detroit's institutions came in dead last when compared to other cities. One SBA program, for instance, had greater local bank participation in St. Louis, Milwaukee, Pittsburgh, Baltimore, Boston, Cleveland, Chicago, and Philadelphia. For a HUD loan program, the Free Press found that the City of Detroit, with all of its housing problems, actually had returned more than $2.7 million in unspent funds to the federal government. It was unclear whether lenders or the city—or both—were to blame.

Finally, the last installment of the four-part series of articles reported on the racial makeup and home addresses of top executives and directors of each of the major financial institutions in southeastern Michigan. The paper found that most of the directors and nearly all of the executives of local lending institutions were suburban white men.

Yet "The Race for Money" never asserted overt racism on the part of lenders. In fact, the opening article about racial patterns in mortgage lending suggested just the opposite when it mentioned a range of possible causes for the phenomenon:

> Some banks have more branches near white areas. Application rates are higher in white areas. And memories of redlining—a practice critics say was common in Detroit until the 1970s—lead some blacks to seek loans from private mortgage companies because they assume banks will

reject them. The result of those and other factors appears to be that, in the 1980s, the historical but illegal practice of banks and savings and loans denying loans to blacks has been replaced by a more subtle process of discrimination that banks don't entirely control.

(Everett, Gallagher, and Blossom 1988).

The newspaper's indictment of Detroit's lenders was so broad that it called into question much more than bank support for home mortgages, which, because of HMDA, is the traditional area of study by community groups. By examining such a wide range of lending activities, the Free Press actually was able to raise questions about the compliance of the entire Detroit financial establishment with the spirit of the Community Reinvestment Act. The extent of the findings also raised questions about the performance of federal banking regulators. Despite their downgrading of Comerica's CRA rating the previous year, they were supposed to be enforcing the CRA for all lenders in the Detroit area.

ANGER, CONFRONTATION, AND NEGOTIATION

Reaction to "The Race for Money" was immediate, widespread, and strong. Some bankers expressed outrage at what it called the *Free Press*'s inaccurate, unfair, and racially charged findings. A few lenders were more measured, saying that while they disagreed with the paper's findings, they would examine their institution's practices for any possible opportunity for increasing Detroit loans.

The official reaction came in part from Congress, where members ordered investigations, and from the Michigan legislature, which formed a special investigative committee to meet in Detroit and cities around the state.

More important for the future of the CRA controversy in Detroit was the formation of an unprecedented coalition that pledged to negotiate more support from Detroit-area lenders—or force it. The breadth of the coalition made it a formidable group. Represented were the United Auto Workers (UAW), the Detroit National Association for the Advancement of Colored People (NAACP), the prestigious New Detroit civic organization, and most of the largest, most powerful local groups representing churches, community organizations, and civil rights efforts.

It was called the Ad Hoc Coalition for Fair Banking Practices in Detroit, and its threatened weapons were CRA challenges, public demonstrations, boycotts, and mass withdrawals of deposits. It was cochaired by Arthur Johnson, then president of the local NAACP, and Bernard Parker, the community leader and eventual Wayne County commissioner.

Marc Stepp, then a UAW vice-president and coalition member, issued a tough description of the group's strategy. "Pick one, maybe the worst one or two banks, and level correction action demands. And if that doesn't work, level punitive demands. That will work. Take the money out. Shut them down. That will work" (Everett and Blossom 1988). The coalition's formation was announced on July 29, 1988, two days after the *Free Press* series ended and literally as another crucial event was being announced in Lansing by Eugene Kuthy, who finally was ready with his decision about the Comerica application. That decision, in the environment created by the *Free Press*, was both momentous and unprecedented: He told the second largest banking company in Michigan that it could not expand in Texas until it submits a wide-ranging, three-year plan to increase lending in Detroit. Moreover, Kuthy said, he had to approve the plan before the Texas acquisition could take place (Kuthy 1988).

It was the first time since Michigan's interstate banking law took effect in 1986 that such severe conditions had been placed on an acquisition. Kuthy said Comerica's current CRA plan, developed after the Federal Reserve's unfavorable rating, was not enough. In his order, Kuthy criticized Comerica for planning to use Michigan deposits to buy a Texas bank: "Before a bank embarks upon a program of out-of-area lending, it should ensure that the credit needs of its local community are met." Kuthy also said Comerica had been "less than aggressive" in supporting major development projects in Detroit (agreeing in part with the Edwards/Murray challenge). He added that Comerica's advertising in Detroit "appears to be directed at middle- to upper-income suburban residents" and may be irrelevant to urban, minority customers (Kuthy 1988). The decision, Kuthy believed, established the important precedent of requiring a lender to properly determine local credit needs before it devised a CRA plan. "You simply cannot render a CRA evaluation of the performance of a bank until you have come up with the bedrock conclusion of what the local credit needs are" (Kuthy 1990–91).

The order also provided the tough regulatory ammunition that was needed to buttress the emotional reaction to the newspaper series.

For outraged community leaders, Kuthy's move represented official endorsement of their response to the newspaper's revelations. For bankers, some of whom thought the newspaper articles and CRA controversy in Detroit were only temporary public relations headaches, the order meant major changes. Not only would they have to endure headlines and legislative investigations, but they faced a state regulator who was prepared to stymie their business plans if they did not address CRA concerns.

"The importance of it was incalculable," James Edwards said of Kuthy's order. "Nothing would have happened without it. I don't even think there would have been the series of meetings which took place that resulted in these agreements with the institutions. He really stopped them dead in their tracks, and they're not used to something like that from a state regulator" (Edwards 1990–91).

Kuthy noted that the Comerica case satisfied all three grounds under the CRA provisions of Michigan's interstate banking law: Comerica had an unfavorable federal CRA rating; the state disclosure data showed the institution was not meeting local credit needs because it was not a major home mortgage lender; and the institution largely failed to rebut the Edwards-Murray allegation that it ignored Detroit development projects.

Kuthy's order completed the foundation of Detroit's CRA controversy. In six days in July, the three elements were put in place: the catalyst of a sensational, controversial newspaper series; the resulting formation of a determined, powerful community coalition; and an accompanying regulatory lightning bolt from the state.

The negotiations began with an unprecedented meeting between the community coalition and top executives of southeastern Michigan's largest banking companies. The coalition then formed teams to talk with each institution in separate sessions. The aim was to sign a CRA agreement with each lender, and the initial bargaining tool was the promise of a CRA challenge to each lender unless it had reached an agreement. By August, the coalition formally notified the lenders that it expected agreements that would total $1.15 billion in loans for the city.

Parker and Edwards, whose group became part of the Detroit coalition, remember that the group did not have the technical help that it now realizes it needed. If such assistance had been available, they said, the coalition could have suggested specific loan products or policy changes to the institutions. Without that knowledge, however, the coalition soon decided that it would negotiate lending goals, in dollar amounts, with each institution and generally allow them to devise the methods for reaching those goals.

The two major S & Ls in the Detroit area, First Federal and Standard Federal, were perhaps the most difficult negotiating targets, Parker said. As the top home mortgage lenders in the city, they did not believe they should have been included in a newspaper series that, in effect, accused the local financial establishment of not properly supporting Detroit. The talks became contentious at times, and an angry Standard Federal decided to pull its advertising from the *Free Press*. The move cost the newspaper an estimated $750,000 at a time when it was losing millions of dollars in a costly war with the *Detroit News*.

As the talks continued, CRA challenges were filed against bank expansion plans, although lending agreements eventually ended the challenges. Stepp, the UAW leader seasoned by the union's often incendiary talks with the Big Three automakers, blasted National Bank of Detroit (NBD) when it announced a new loan marketing program before it had finished its talks with the coalition. "It appears they are trying to get out in front in some public relations posture," Stepp said, adding that NBD was engaging in "dirty pool" (Everett 1988).

Beth Konrad, a first vice president for NBD, acknowledged that in 1988 lenders were defensive in their first negotiations with the Ad Hoc Coalition. "I think there was a sense that NBD, as an institution, was doing what it could be doing in Detroit" (Konrad 1990–91). As the talks continued, however, the information began to flow in both directions, she said. The defensiveness slackened, and NBD, like some of the other lenders, began to realize that at least some of what the coalition was saying was correct. "What we recognized is that there is a marketplace here that we didn't recognize or realize before. We got a real sensitivity and a new pulse for the Detroit urban market that, if it were not for the coalition, we didn't know existed." Over time, negotiations that had begun with distrust, defensiveness, and, for some institutions, bitterness, evolved into a new attitude for several lenders. It was the same progress that had come in Boston from improved personal relations. "It turned from being an adversarial relationship into joint advocacy" (Konrad 1990–91).

The talks did not stop the lenders' disagreement with the *Free Press*, however. In documents filed with the U.S. Senate Banking Committee, Detroit's biggest lending institutions criticized the newspaper's study. Comerica, especially, repeated Professor Goldberg's assertions. Yet, in one document the much-maligned bank made some startling admissions:

> It is clear to us now that we have not been nearly as effective as we would like in our marketing in the City of Detroit and this has reduced the number of loans we have made there.
>
> There are many possible reasons for this. We believe it has arisen because, in a sense, those of us who manage this bank have been overexposed to the problems the City of Detroit has experienced. . . . Those of us who live and work here do not have to look far to verify that serious problems exist. All of this has created the perception that sound market opportunities are quite limited in the City. And to an extent, they are. However, the perception is exaggerated and as our recently filed Community Reinvestment Plan makes clear, Comerica is now marketing aggressively and expects to generate larger numbers of loans in the City in coming months and years.
>
> (Comerica 1988)

Goldberg, the Comerica consultant, continued to attack the *Free Press* articles. First came an angry report shortly after the newspaper series was published. Goldberg wrote that the newspaper must have considered him a "hired shill" and ignored the information he presented to it. He also charged that the *Free Press* "became boxed in by its own efforts. Seven months is a massive investment. It is difficult to dump a study done by 'experts'" (Goldberg 1988a).

Then in September, Goldberg released his own study of Comerica's lending patterns (Goldberg 1988b). That study, using regression analysis, concluded that "Comerica does not practice discrimination in mortgage lending"—a charge the newspaper never made. The study also said that any differences in lending rates between black and white census tracts in Detroit are caused by legitimate and nondiscriminatory factors such as loan demand or income differences. Goldberg concluded his study with an assertion that "no honest person could conclude that there was discrimination in mortgage lending." The only reasons for such a belief, he said, included "mindless, knee-jerk reaction to endless media bombardment," a desire for journalistic or ballot booth rewards, or a "Big Lie" (Goldberg 1988b).

Yet Detroit's financial institutions, including Comerica, would soon pledge tens of millions of dollars because of this so-called lie. The lenders continued to complain about the *Free Press* articles, but many took action to address the problems the newspaper documented. The first to act was Comerica, which had to move quickly because of Kuthy's order. Forced into negotiations on Detroit's credit needs, the bank agreed to lend a projected $280 million in Detroit over three years. That amount would double its 1987 lending. Comerica's pact with the coalition also committed the bank to special advertising and community outreach programs, in addition to broader underwriting policies. In an agreement that proved to be a model for future agreements in Detroit, the Comerica plan contained dollar goals for different areas of lending, including mortgages, consumer loans, small business, and development.

The second agreement with the coalition came in October from First of America Bank of Southeast Michigan, a smaller bank owned by a Kalamazoo holding company. The plan was for $69 million over three years, at an estimated increase of 25 percent over the previous year. Novel to First of America's plan was the bank's "adoption" of two Detroit neighborhoods, for which it would provide special attention and lending.

As talks continued, other banks fell in line: Manufacturers National Bank committed to $270 million over three years. Michigan National Bank signed for $275.5 million. Standard Federal Bank, one of the two thrifts in the negotiations, pledged $48 million—mostly for home loans.

Finally, on April 6, 1989, after months of talks, the coalition disclosed tentative deals with the final two institutions. First Federal of Michigan, Michigan's largest thrift, pledged $61 million. Then came National Bank of Detroit, the granddaddy of them all. NBD had been tough in the negotiations. As the leading bank in Detroit and as a "superregional" bank highly respected by its peers for fiscal conservatism, the stubborn institution had resisted the coalition's pressure to sign an agreement. In the end, both sides claimed success, and joint statements were issued. Yet NBD can say to this day that it never signed a formal agreement with the coalition. It simply issued its own Detroit lending plan. The key difference between NBD's plan and the signed agreements from other institutions was that no specific dollar goals were listed. Yet in a roundabout way the dollars for Detroit could be tallied: NBD estimated its current lending rates in Detroit, and it pledged to try to beat that figure over the next three years.

The bank first disclosed that its 1988 Detroit lending totaled more than $600 million, giving NBD a "pledge" of more than $1.9 billion over three years. The institution later quietly revised the 1988 figure, cutting it almost in half to an estimated $310 million. Even at that level, NBD remained the top potential contributor to the Detroit CRA pacts.

The other institutions would grumble about the NBD exception, which was made in part because the bank and the coalition wanted to end the negotiations without a nasty confrontation. Perhaps more important, the coalition also became convinced that NBD was genuinely committed to improving its lending. Despite the stubbornness regarding a signed, number-filled agreement, a new level of trust was being developed between NBD and the coalition.

Other institutions revised their pledges after examining their Detroit performance in more detail. First of America greatly increased its commitment for 1989–91, from $69 million to more than $189 million. Comerica's projections increased to about $297 million (Financial Institutions Bureau 1990).

With NBD's plan and signed agreements from the six other big lenders in the Detroit area, nine months of often contentious talks could finally be declared complete. As with lending agreements in other cities, the Detroit community reinvestment pacts included current lending amounts plus increases. The revised total became the national record at the time for a single series of CRA agreement—nearly $2.1 billion over three years. It was a half-billion dollars more than the coalition's original goal.

OPTIMISM FOR THE FUTURE

The loans promised for Detroit were indeed astounding. Of the $2.1 billion in pledges for 1989–91, the increase over previous amounts was an estimated $300 million. Of that, about $50 million targeted new home mortgage loans. If the pledges are fulfilled, Detroit-area lenders will lend anywhere from 30 percent to 50 percent more for home buildings than they did in the previous three years—an increase that could have far-reaching impact on the city's deteriorating housing situation.

Since the 1988 controversy, the coalition has met regularly with each lender, all of which file regular reports of their progress toward the goals outlined in their agreements. Those reports show that many institutions are meeting their goals, although the home mortgage targets seem to be the most difficult to achieve in Detroit's tough economy. Small business, consumer, and development lending is above projections for some institutions.

Comerica, the bank under the most scrutiny, reported that it reached $270 million of its three-year, $280 million goal after only the second year. In its year-end report for 1989, the bank reported that it met or surpassed twelve of fifteen community reinvestment goals, including those for loans. The bank also reported that by the third quarter of 1990 it had made 128 home mortgage loans for $4.5 million, compared to 109 loans for $3.8 million for all of 1989 (Comerica 1990a–b).

Other institutions reported similar success and similar struggles with the Detroit home mortgage market, especially as a national economic recession took hold in late 1990. First of America, for instance, pledged $3 million for mortgages for 1989, but made only $2.5 million. Big increases in consumer lending, however, boosted the bank's Detroit lending for 1989 from its pledge to $32.7 million to $71.1 million. In all, the seven lenders reported more than a billion dollars in loans for 1989, compared to pledges of only $649 million for that year (Financial Institutions Bureau 1990).

Change came in ways other than dollars. Banks began to hold seminars with churches, civic groups, and even schoolchildren to promote their practices and products and to attract customers. One institution, Michigan National, appointed a woman and a black man to its board of directors to diversify its previously all-male board. Officials for government loan programs, including the Small Business Administration and the Michigan State Housing Development Authority, reported increased interest and participation from Detroit lenders. Banks began to offer help to developers, in contrast to previous years when developers had to persuade banks to help.

To fill its technical information gap, the Detroit Ad Hoc Coalition won a city grant to fund the Detroit Alliance for Fair Banking. The

David Everett

alliance is a nonprofit office that analyzes loan disclosure data and helps the coalition monitor lender performance. The alliance, which opened with two full-time staff members in 1990, offers credit counseling and help for applicants trying to qualify for loans. The coalition also helped revive the largely dormant Detroit Mortgage Review Committee, a group of lenders and community residents who review denied loans for possible reapplication. By 1990, the committee was reviewing denied loans every few weeks, and Parker said many were being granted (Parker 1990).

Despite improving relations between the community and its banks, Parker said many lenders still resent the *Free Press* series, which they believe unfairly linked lending problems to race. He credits the articles as the catalyst for genuine change in the relationship between Detroit's citizens and their financial institutions. "If it had not been for the newspaper, we would have never gotten this far" (Parker 1990). Several Ad Hoc Coalition members believe that some lenders signed the CRA agreements only under the duress of media coverage and Detroit's racially charged civic climate. They warn that any institution that fails to live up to an agreement or that refuses to negotiate new pacts will face repeated CRA challenges or other tactics.

For many institutions, however, the changes appear genuine. Parker and other coalition leaders say that not only is Detroit beginning to get more money in loans but also attitudes are changing. "In the black community in particular, there still is concern that not enough loans are coming in, but they do see that there is a different perspective from the banks. They do see that most of them are trying" (Parker 1990).

The new relationship between Detroit's banks and its residents works both ways. Comerica, still sometimes caught in controversy, proposed in 1990 that it build a new, downtown high-rise headquarters on the Detroit River. The bank suggested the city prepare a site by tearing down an auditorium built by the Ford automotive family. At a contentious public hearing in 1990 on the proposal, one of those testifying in Comerica's behalf was Parker, cochair of the coalition that so strenuously opposed the bank in 1988. "As long as they're supporting our efforts and the city of Detroit, we will support them," Parker said (Parker 1990).

Kuthy and Edwards believe the coalition's support of Comerica's building plan in downtown Detroit is the best evidence of a new relationship between lenders and the community. That Comerica would propose to stay in the city at all is an indication of a changed attitude, said Edwards, who like many local residents believed the bank wanted to leave Detroit in the late 1980s (Kuthy 1990–91; Edwards 1990–91). (While Comerica later dropped plans for its own high-rise, it pledged in 1990 to become a major tenant of a new downtown skyscraper being built near its targeted site.)

More evidence of Comerica's new attitude came in 1991, when the Federal Reserve gave the bank's Detroit operations an "outstanding" rating—the highest possible—in a new CRA evaluation program (Bowens 1991). It was a remarkable transformation for an institution that three years earlier had been rated as "less than satisfactory" by the same regulator.

The changes that began in Detroit have spread throughout Michigan. Even in cities where CRA challenges or regulatory pressures are absent, local coalitions are forming and lending agreements are being negotiated. Part of the reason, Kuthy said, is that Detroit banks operate elsewhere in the state, and they want to avoid a controversy like the one they endured in 1988.

One benefit of the new lender attitude is increased support for government-assisted loan programs in Detroit. One recent such program is "The Michigan Initiative," in which an estimated $500 million will be made available for home mortgages for low- or middle-income buyers. The program allows loans with 5 percent down and includes counseling for first-time buyers.

Bernard Parker believes that NBD, as the city's largest bank, is perhaps the most genuinely committed to the new attitudes. Not only is the bank pledging to beat all others in terms of lending performance, but the institution, by 1990, also devised some of the most creative loan products to fit Detroit's difficult conditions (Parker 1990). Chris Snow, vice president and CRA manager for NBD, points to NBD's for-profit community development corporation as one of many tangible changes in the bank's programs and policies since 1988. By 1990, the corporation had focused most of its efforts on affordable housing, with about $1.2 million in investments and construction financing. The bank also is helping develop more sophisticated community groups, so they can take advantage of the bank's new loan programs (Snow 1990–91).

Snow said the amount of NBD's average mortgage loan in Detroit is dropping, indicating that the bank is not just lending in the city's exclusive areas but reaching more modest neighborhoods. Snow is proud of the bank's use of videotapes to educate loan applicants. One series of videotapes is used in local high schools to teach future loan applicants about credit, down payments, and the dangers of bankruptcy (Snow 1990–91).

A key part of NBD's new attitude is communication. Before the 1988 controversy, the bank believed it could offer loans and wait for applicants. Today, the bank realizes it must reach out to real estate agents who never believed the institution would serve their clients. The National Bank of Detroit now buys more advertising designed to reach minority customers, and the bank has its loan officers attend local church services and meet with contractors and realtors. The institution also changed policies so that loan officers in branch offices can approve small business transactions on the spot; and branch managers can make exceptions to conventional loan policies when local situations call for them (Snow 1990–91).

The two-way attitude changes continue to develop, according to NBD's Konrad. For instance, one 1990 NBD seminar in Detroit attracted 380 persons. "This was on a Saturday—for a bank! It's an incredible change of attitude in the bank, and it's an incredible change of attitude about the bank, too" (Konrad 1990–91).

Snow said the 1988 CRA controversy allowed NBD management to shift its community involvement activities away from traditional but nonbanking activities such as donations to the symphony or charities. The bank still supports those activities, but its managers now realize they can use their professional expertise—their very reason for being—as a form of community involvement. In the process, they can do something else that banks are supposed to do: make money. "I think that was an important factor for senior management to realize, that the community groups want profitable deals," Snow said. "They know as the economy worsens, the charity goes away but the profitable deals will always be there" (Snow 1990–91).

James Edwards' reflections on the 1988 controversy are filled with tempered optimism. While the number of new loans in Detroit still is small, he believes the agreements between the lenders and the coalition reversed the downward trend. Edwards also believes that lenders who so bitterly resented the newspaper articles have since institutionalized their new commitment to Detroit. An example, he said, is Standard Federal, a suburban-based institution whose leaders were incensed at the _Free Press_ findings in 1988. "I can't think of another institution that was so offended by the idea . . . of anyone suggesting that it wasn't doing everything right," Edwards said. Now, Edwards compliments Standard Federal for hiring a new CRA official and being one of the few local lenders to participate in an affordable housing program offered by the Federal Home Loan Bank of Indianapolis. In general, Edwards said, "If I have one regret, it is that we really have only just begun to do anything about monitoring" the lenders' adherence to their CRA agreements. He suggested that other communities should be prompt to form technical organizations such as the Detroit Alliance for Fair Banking (Edwards 1990–91).

Bernard Parker suggests that community groups involved in CRA controversies in other cities extend their negotiations to include minority staffing levels at lending institutions. Parker also cautions that progress should never stop. In Detroit, for instance, some real estate agents, including those in the black community, believe that while they notice new attitudes among the city's lenders, they have yet to see any large increase in the numbers of loans being granted. Yet Parker commends others to the Detroit experience, which has led, he believes, to a new era of cooperation among most lenders and city residents.

> One thing I have found by talking to other communities is that they have a more adversarial process. They challenge the banks and sign agreements, then the community groups move on and forget how to work with the banks until the next big controversy in the next few years. They never establish a working relationship. . . . It seems like, in these other cities, they attack, negotiate, then attack again. I hope we never have to do that in Detroit.

References

Bowens, Greg. 1991. "Comerica Is Rated at Top on City Loans." _Detroit Free Press_, June 4.
Comerica. 1988. _Response to U.S. Senate Banking Committee_ (Sept.). Washington, D.C.
———. 1990a. _Community Reinvestment Plan Status Report, Fourth Quarter 1990_, 1989 Summary (Feb. 6). Detroit, Mich.
———. 1990b. _Community Reinvestment Plan Status Report, Third Quarter 1990_ (Nov. 14). Detroit, Mich.

David Everett

Detroit Renaissance. 1987. *Detroit Strategic Plan.* Detroit: Detroit Renaissance (November).
Edmonds, Patricia. 1987. "Mayor: Banks 'Got Fat,' Now Won't Back City." *Detroit Free Press,* April 4.
Edwards, James. 1990–91. Interviews with author, December 1990, February-March 1991.
Everett, David, 1988. "Coalition Leaders Say Bank Plan Is Anemic: NBD's New Marketing Proposal Called Ploy." *Detroit Free Press,* Nov. 7.
Everett, David, and Teresa Blossom. 1988. "U.S. Report Criticizes Comerica's Loan Policies." *Detroit Free Press,* June 5.
Everett, David, John Gallagher, and Teresa Blossom. 1988. "The Race for Money." *Detroit Free Press,* July 24–27.
Financial Institutions Bureau. 1990. "Summary of the Seven Largest Banks and Thrifts, City of Detroit Lending Activity." Internal Report (April). Lansing, Mich.
Gillmor, Dan. 1991. "Detroit Segregation Grows: Metropolitan Area's Black Residents become More Isolated While Other Cities Integrate." *Detroit Free Press,* April 9.
Goldberg, David. 1988. "Observations on the Scheduled Free Press Study of Home Mortgage Loans." Report for Comerica Bank (undated). Addendum report for Comerica Bank (July 29). Ann Arbor, Mich.
———. 1988b. "Discrimination in Mortgage Lending: An Examination of Several Data Sets Pertaining to Comerica, 1986." Report for Comerica Bank (Sept. 6). Ann Arbor, Mich.
Heron, W. Kim. 1987. "Fisher Gets Renaissance Post: Mayor Lauds Study." *Detroit Free Press,* Dec. 2.
Konrad, Beth. 1990–91. Interviews and correspondence with author, December 1990, February 1991.
Kuthy, Eugene. 1988. Order on Comerica Acquisition, Michigan Financial Institutions Bureau (July 29). Lansing, Mich.
———. 1990–91. Interviews and correspondence with author, December 1990, February 1991. Troy, Mich.
Parker, Bernard. 1990. Interviews with author, December. Detroit, Mich.
Snow, Chris. 1990–91. Interviews and correspondence with author, December 1990, February 1991. Detroit, Mich.

REINVESTMENT IN CHICAGO NEIGHBORHOODS: A TWENTY-YEAR STRUGGLE

THE FIRST WRITTEN REINVESTMENT AGREEMENT in the country was negotiated in Chicago between a community-based organization and a community bank. It is not surprising that the first written agreement was developed in Chicago or that this agreement was finalized in 1974, three years before the passage of the Community Reinvestment Act (CRA).

Chicago is a neighborhood town with a long-standing history of community organizing. Chicago neighborhoods have been the battleground for organizing campaigns since Jane Addams first worked to better the lives of immigrants in the neighborhood just west of the Loop. Saul Alinsky cut his teeth in the neighborhoods of Chicago and used his Chicago experiences to articulate his classic exposition of the methodology of neighborhood organizing, *Reveille for Radicals* (Alinsky 1969), a methodology that has shaped organizing efforts in Chicago and subsequently many other cities.

Chicago is also one of the most segregated cities in America. One of the nation's most severe race riots occurred in Chicago in 1919. In the years that followed, ethnic white communities, affluent WASP communities, and black ghettos evolved in different locations with little interaction. During the 1950s and 1960s, public policy institutionalized this separation when expressways were built to serve as permanent barriers between racially different neighborhoods and when public housing construction was concentrated in minority neighborhoods. The concentration of public housing in minority neighborhoods in Chicago was so blatant that in 1976, in the case of *Hills v. Gautreaux*, the U.S. Supreme Court ruled that there was sufficient basis for public housing tenants to file a lawsuit and remanded the case to a lower court for further consideration. This ultimately resulted in a consent degree that required the Chicago Housing Authority to meet established goals for placing public housing residents and developing scattered site public housing units throughout the Chicago area.

The practice of redlining was first identified and named in the Chicago neighborhood of Austin in the late 1960s. Savings and loan associations, at the time the primary source of residential mortgages, drew red lines around neighborhoods they thought were susceptible to racial change and refused to make mortgages in those neighborhoods. Using the U.S. Department of Housing and Urban Development (HUD) appraisal methodology developed by Homer Hoyt from the University of Chicago (Hoyt 1933), these lending institutions considered racially changing neighborhoods a bad credit risk because they assumed property values would decline. By extension, neighborhoods that were not racially changing but in close proximity to racially changing neighborhoods were labeled unstable and redlined. The resulting limitations on the availability of residential credit became a self-fulfilling prophecy as residents found it difficult to get a fair market price for their homes.

Because neighborhood is so central to Chicago residents' sense of home, Austin residents responded by organizing to save their neighborhood and their property values. In 1969, the Organization for a Better Austin, led by Gale Cincotta, joined with other organizations to form the West Side Coalition to fight redlining (Naparstek and Cincotta 1976). With the formation of this coalition, Chicago neighborhoods began their twenty-year struggle to overcome lenders' negative perceptions of their credit worthiness.

Reinvestment Agreements Prior to the Community Reinvestment Act

In the early days, Alinsky-style organizing tactics were used to pressure lenders into agreeing to stop redlining. Picket lines were organized. Actions were mounted that involved disruption of normal business, such as dropping hundreds of pennies on the floor of a lender's lobby at the busiest time of day and having teams of people walk in on Saturday morning to open or close an account with $1. Petition drives were mounted to secure commitments from depositors to close their accounts unless the lending institution met with the community-organization and agreed to their demands.

Many lenders met with community groups as a result of this type of organizing activity. These meetings allowed community groups to state publicly their objections to redlining and often led to the lender's agreement to stop redlining.

The first written CRA agreement was a direct result of community organizing activity that used organizing tactics and the threat of a bad public image to create a favorable negotiating opportunity. Termed an "Understanding," this document, signed in Chicago on September 19, 1974, formalized an agreement between the Bank of Chicago, a community bank that served the north lakeshore neighborhoods of Chicago, and the Organization of the NorthEast (ONE), an advocacy organization made up of residents from the Edgewater and Uptown neighborhoods along the lake. The stated purpose of the Understanding was for "implementing policies of reciprocal positive support between the bank and the surrounding community residents, businesses and institutions" (Organization of the NorthEast 1974).

In retrospect, although the Bank of Chicago/ONE agreement was negotiated without benefit of the rights given to community-based organizations under the Community Reinvestment Act, it contained many of the key elements still considered essential to a good CRA agreement. The Understanding focused on residential lending and had a term of one year with an automatic renewal provision. The bank did not commit to a dollar amount of loans in targeted areas but did agree to prioritize loans to depositors and residents within the targeted neighborhoods and to strive to establish and meet lending goals based on deposit levels. The bank agreed to use government guaranteed loan programs and to furnish ONE with a report on the geographic distribution of its deposits and loans every six months. Because this agreement was negotiated a full year before Congress passed the Home Mortgage Disclosure Act, the reporting agreement was a pioneering achievement.

The sense of partnership that later became key to formulating the neighborhood lending programs in Chicago was incorporated directly into the agreement with Bank of Chicago. In the agreement, ONE agreed to designate the bank a "Community-Responsive Financial Institution";

to seek public deposits for the bank; and to promote the bank among community residents, businesses, block clubs, and other neighborhood institutions. Quarterly meetings between the bank and the community organization were established to review progress toward the targeted goals and to modify the agreement to meet changing neighborhood needs.

Following the announcement of the Understanding with Bank of Chicago, ONE signed a similar Understanding with Uptown Federal Savings and Loan Association in October, 1974, with the Bank of Ravenswood in November, 1974, and with the Community Bank and Trust of Edgewater in December of 1974. All three agreements were modeled on the Bank of Chicago agreement. The Bank of Ravenswood's agreement was virtually identical. The Uptown Federal Savings agreement substituted a commitment to make $5 million in new single-family mortgages in the defined "restricted lending area" within the twelve-month period of the agreement for lending goals tied to deposits gathered from the community. Because the Community Bank and Trust of Edgewater had just opened in September 1974, the understanding between this bank and ONE was less specific and did not contain a stated goal in terms of either loan dollars or loan-to-deposit ratios.

After the Community Reinvestment Act was passed in 1977, there were few community challenges in Chicago prior to 1984. One reason for this was the lack of bank applications subject to the CRA. Illinois is a unit banking state that prohibited branch banks entirely during the 1970s and gave only limited branching powers to commercial banks in the 1980s. The limits on branch banking caused Illinois to have a very large number of individual banks, no applications to open bank branches, and few applications to acquire or merge with other banks. These state restrictions on banking activity limited the number of opportunities for community-based organizations to exercise their rights under the CRA.

THE FIRST NATIONAL BANK OF CHICAGO

In August of 1983, a unique opportunity to use CRA to benefit disinvested neighborhoods in Chicago arose when First Chicago Corporation, the parent of the First National Bank of Chicago, announced its intention to acquire American National Bank of Chicago. Both banks were ranked among the top ten largest banks in Chicago and First National

Bank, with assets of $36 billion, was the tenth largest bank in the country.

Woodstock Institute, a nonprofit organization created in 1973 to promote reinvestment, had been closely monitoring the potential impact of banking deregulation on reinvestment in low- and moderate-income neighborhoods and had been looking for CRA enforcement opportunities in Chicago. The Woodstock Institute realized the significance of this acquisition both in terms of the reduction of the number of large banks in Chicago and in the opportunity it presented to reopen public discussion regarding reinvestment in Chicago neighborhoods.

The Woodstock Institute researched the lending records of First National Bank and American National Bank, prepared a fact sheet with highlights of those records, and invited neighborhood-based and citywide organizations to join together to discuss the use of the CRA to open a dialogue with First Chicago Corporation about neighborhood credit needs in Chicago.

The fact that several key leaders attended that first meeting and committed to working collaboratively was critical to the ultimate success of the CRA challenge. In particular, three individuals, representing very different perspectives, attended the first meeting, made a commitment to work together and helped shape the direction and focus of the process, and the agreement. Gale Cincotta was a leader of the original redlining fights in Austin who had become the single most prominent national leader on reinvestment issues. Mary Nelson was executive director of Bethel New Life, one of the most productive community development corporations in Chicago struggling to develop low-income housing in West Garfield Park, one of Chicago's poorest communities. Jim Capraro, executive director of Greater Southwest Development Corporation, was a national pioneer in commercial and industrial revitalization. The combination of perspectives that included community organizing, low-income housing development, and commercial and industrial revitalization was key to shaping an agreement that not only created a partnership between the First National Bank and Chicago's community-based organizations but also included a sizable commitment to make both residential and commercial loans.

At the first meeting, it became clear that a citywide organizing effort would be necessary to ensure that any future actions would have the kind of grassroots support necessary to be successful. Gale Cincotta and the National Training and Information Center assumed responsibility for organizing community groups across the city. Subsequently, thirty-five neighborhood and citywide organizations, calling themselves the Chicago Reinvestment Alliance, met and formulated a draft reinvestment program request.

Eight organizations were elected by the Alliance to represent the neighborhoods in discussions with First Chicago Corporation. The negotiating team included members from four neighborhoods-based organizations that represented different sections of the city: Bethel New Life, Greater Roseland Organization, Kenwood-Oakland Community Organization, and Northwest Community Organization. It also included representatives from the two citywide membership organizations for nonprofit developers: Chicago Association of Neighborhood Development Organizations (CANDO), a membership organization that represented neighborhood commercial and industrial revitalization organizations, and the Chicago Rehab Network, a membership organization of neighborhood-based nonprofit housing developers. The negotiating team also included members from the National Training and Information Center, which provided the staff and research support for the Chicago Reinvestment Alliance, and staff from Woodstock Institute, which provided program design technical assistance and research support.

In December, the Alliance negotiating team met with Barry Sullivan, chairman and CEO of First Chicago Corporation, and five other senior officers of the First Chicago Corporation and First National Bank. The Alliance outlined the unmet credit needs in Chicago's neighborhoods and presented a comprehensive set of community reinvestment proposals. As part of the rationale for a new reinvestment program, the Alliance presented First Chicago with a five-year credit needs analysis that projected neighborhood credit needs based on estimates of the current use of residential and small-business credit. This analysis supported a request for a $500 million targeted loan program.

The result of the initial meeting was a decision to work together to develop a mutually acceptable community reinvestment program before the deadline for submitting comments on First National Bank's CRA record to the bank holding company's regulator, the Federal Reserve.

During the first two months of 1984, representatives from the Chicago Reinvestment Alliance met nine times with First Chicago's negotiating team. At the first meeting, an important agreement was reached. Both the bank and the Alliance agreed not to talk with the press. This allowed the negotiations to be conducted face to face and not through the newspapers. The fact that both sides honored this agreement created an atmosphere of trust between the two parties that was a key factor in keeping both sides committed to the process of negotiation.

Each negotiating session was organized around a specific type of community request. By agreeing to one topic per meeting, the group was able to focus on specific issues and work toward consensus on the action needed. The topics included multifamily housing loans; single-family housing loans; small-business loans; loans for mixed-use buildings; the effectiveness of the bank's existing community development corporation; and the need for grants to support community development organizations. As each type of credit or community development need was discussed, the organizations that had the most familiarity with the issue prepared and made a presentation. This format was very successful because the presentations were specific and actionable.

For example, long-term mortgages were generally not available for older apartment buildings in the city. When this credit need was discussed, the Chicago Rehab Network and several individual nonprofit housing developers described their success in rehabilitating older buildings for low-income residents. They then described the problems presented by the lack of long-term mortgages, and outlined the specific underwriting barriers that made it difficult for nonprofit developers to qualify for the few sources of mortgages that were available. The bank took each of the presentations very seriously. Between meetings they researched the nature of specific problems and returned to the next meeting with an assessment of the ways the bank could respond to the problem. This dialogue progressed into a framework for the agreement.

Although the negotiating sessions were well organized and effective, early in the process it was not clear that the Alliance was convincing the bank management of the need for credit and the potential for good loans in low-income neighborhoods. Once again, the bankers' lack of experience with Chicago neighborhoods was a barrier to coming to an agreement about reinvestment. To give the bank a more accurate view of Chicago neighborhoods, the Alliance took First Chicago's chief negotiator on two neighborhood tours—one focused on successful nonprofit multifamily housing rehab projects and the other focused on successful neighborhood commercial/industrial redevelopment projects. The neighborhood tours showcased the high level of professional development skills of nonprofit developers, the quality of their workmanship and management, and their integral role in weaving together the ancillary support systems needed to maintain a stable community. The positive impressions created by the two tours were pivotal in the discussions.

Throughout the negotiating process, the Alliance team met at least weekly to assess the progress of the discussions and to review and develop negotiating positions and strategies. In addition, the Alliance hosted periodic meetings to which a broad range of neighborhood-based and citywide organizations were invited to provide input.

Toward the end of the negotiations, the negotiating team met with the mayor and the commissioners of the Department of Housing and the Department of Economic Development to inform them of the progress in the negotiations, to seek support, and to lay the groundwork for involving the city in the emerging community/bank partnership. Harold Washington, Chicago's first black mayor, had been elected in 1983 by a coalition of black, Hispanic, and liberal voters. The new mayor had made it clear to bankers that doing business with the city would require ensuring that black and Hispanic neighborhoods would benefit. Therefore, securing the city administration's support for the agreement was not difficult. Because First National Bank was one of the City of Chicago's two main banks, the city administration's support for the Chicago Reinvestment Alliance proposal was very significant.

Throughout the negotiations, the Alliance continued to protect its right to protest the bank's application under the Community Reinvestment Act. Early in the process, the bank and the Alliance agreed to ask the Federal Reserve Board for an extension of the period for comments on the reinvestment performance of the bank. A request for denial of the bank's application must be filed during the comment period and the Alliance wanted to preserve its right to file such a request. Despite the continuing progress of the negotiations, the Alliance contracted for representation with lawyers from a public interest law firm, Business and Professionals in the Public Interest (BPI)—the same firm that successfully represented Chicago Housing Authority residents in the Gautreaux lawsuit against HUD. The fact that the Alliance was represented by professional legal counsel seemed to further impress the bank with the seriousness of the effort.

Along with Woodstock Institute and other Alliance members, BPI worked to prepare a CRA challenge and to review the various drafts of the agreement with the bank. However, BPI lawyers did not attend the negotiating sessions. The decision by the Alliance not to invite BPI to the meetings was made for two reasons. The first was that the Alliance was concerned that bringing their lawyer to the negotiations would change the positive atmosphere of trust that had been established between the parties. The second reason was that BPI advised the Alliance that the bank would want its lawyers involved if the Alliance brought BPI lawyers to the table and that the involvement of lawyers could change the nature of the discussion and possibly the outcome. Since the Alliance was continuing to make progress with the bank, they decided not to risk having the BPI lawyers attend the meetings.

THE NEIGHBORHOOD LENDING PROGRAM

In February, 1984, First Chicago Corporation and the Chicago Reinvestment Alliance jointly announced a five year, $120 million agreement that initiated a unique partnership between First National Bank and community-based organizations in Chicago. The focus of the agreement was a commitment by the bank to make the types of loans most needed and to target low- and moderate-income neighborhoods as the market for those loans. The new initiative was called the "Neighborhood Lending Program."

Sixty million dollars of the commitment was for permanent mortgages for older apartment buildings—mortgages which at that time were not generally available from any bank or thrift in Chicago for older inner city apartment buildings. An allocation of $5 million was made to permanent financing for mixed commercial/residential properties. Mixed-use properties with retail stores or offices occupying the first floor and apartments on the second and third floors are one of the most common building types in Chicago neighborhoods. Yet in 1984 it was virtually impossible to secure long-term financing for these buildings. An allocation of $15 million was made to create special acquisition/rehab mortgages for single-family (from one to four units) buildings. These mortgages allowed new owners to buy and fix an older building and pay for the cost over the life of a long-term mortgage. Finally, there was an allocation of $20 million for commercial loans to businesses with sales less than $5 million and an allocation of $20 million to buy Small Business Administration loans made by other banks.

Perhaps the most unique feature of the neighborhood lending program was the formal partnership established between the bank and two citywide community organizations; CANDO and the Chicago Rehab Network were given responsibility for loan packaging. It was their job to ensure that less sophisticated borrowers had assistance in preparing the documentation and information required by the bank's application and loan evaluation process.

This arrangement did three things. First, it ensured that low-income borrowers would not be denied a loan because the quality of their application compared unfavorably with other applications. Second, it created a business relationship between the bank and the two organizations that represented neighborhood nonprofit developers. Third, it provided a collaborative effort to ensure that local marketing efforts were effective and appropriate.

To monitor the agreement, a review board composed of six community representatives and six bank representatives was established. The review board was given the charge of monitoring the lending and philanthropic activity of the bank under the terms of the agreement, reviewing modifications in the program, and making recommendations to solve disputes involving neighborhood issues.

Within the four-month period following the announcement of the First Chicago CRA agreement, the Chicago Reinvestment Alliance was able to negotiate a similar five-year CRA commitment with Harris Bank and the Northern Trust. Harris Bank agreed to initiate a Neighborhood Lending Program with a commitment of $35 million. The Northern Trust, the smallest of the three banks, agreed to implement an $18 million Neighborhood Lending Program. Within the space of six months, a total of $173 million was committed to loans in Chicago neighborhoods. In 1989, each of the three banks renewed and increased its commitment to the Neighborhood Lending Program, bringing the total commitment for the second five years to $200 million (Bradford 1990).

SIGNIFICANCE OF THE NEIGHBORHOOD LENDING PROGRAMS

The announcement of the three neighborhood lending programs generated a great deal of publicity both in Chicago and nationally. Because of their size and comprehensiveness, these programs represented a significant step forward in the struggle to fight redlining. As a result, the three agreements and the process that was used to develop them became a model for the wave of agreements that swept the country during the last half of the 1980s, as bank acquisition and merger activity generated numerous opportunities for CRA challenges and the banking landscape was redrawn in communities across the country. Several factors contributed to the significance of these agreements and made them a good model that other cities have effectively utilized, as demonstrated by subsequent agreements reported in this volume and in other cities around the nation. Perhaps the most important feature of the Chicago agreements was their comprehensiveness in terms of the types of loans and the geographical area that the program covers. Because redlining was first defined as a problem with residential single-family mortgages, the main emphasis in CRA agreements prior to 1984 had been on residential single-family home loans. The Neighborhood Lending Programs included both commercial and residential loan products, and the majority of the residential loan commitment in the agreement was for multifamily mortgages.

The inclusion of both commercial and multifamily loans in the agreements was an acknowledgment of the range of loan products offered by large commercial banks and their inclusion resulted directly from the expertise gained from the participation of Chicago community-based developers. During the late 1970s and early 1980s a number of local nonprofit community development corporations were formed in Chicago. These organizations bought and rehabilitated buildings for low-income housing, worked to retain and attract businesses in their neighborhoods, and in some cases, entered into joint ventures with for-profit developers to get new development in their neighborhood. Many of these organizations had become very sophisticated developers and were frustrated by the lack of loan products to meet their needs as developers or the needs of other developers and businesses in their neighborhood. Without the participation of sophisticated and mature community development corporations in the Alliance, it is unlikely that agreement would have been reached on the variety of commercial and multifamily residential loan products or on the underwriting guidelines necessary for nonprofit developers to use those products.

The fact that commercial and multifamily loan products were a central part of the request to the bank made it much easier for First National Bank to come to agreement with the Alliance. Because First National Bank of Chicago was a retail-oriented bank, it did make a significant number of single-family mortgages every year. However, in 1983 residential mortgages were not a major product line for any commercial bank, including First National, and a request from the Chicago Reinvestment Alliance for an agreement that focused primarily on single-family residential loans would have made it difficult for the bank to respond with a large commitment.

Another advantage of the mix of commercial and residential loans in the agreement that the Alliance did not anticipate was the opportunity to negotiate a lower interest rate for multifamily mortgages to nonprofit developers. The community-based developers were very concerned about the fact that subsidies for low-income housing were disappearing. These developers were clear that although lower interest rates could not substitute for housing subsidies, a one- or two-point difference in the interest rate on a long-term mortgage for an apartment building could significantly lower the cost of housing. The Alliance felt strongly that below-market-rate loans for nonprofit developers had to be included in the agreement. At the same time, the bank was clear that it did not want to make loans that were priced below its cost of funds or that would undercut the loan market in Chicago.

The impasse was resolved by negotiating with the bank to consider the overall interest rate on the entire commitment as the rate that would be required to meet the bank's conditions. Because commercial loans are generally priced higher than residential loans, a selected portion of the multifamily mortgages could be priced at a lower rate of interest without forcing the bank to commit the entire package at below market rates or at a price below its cost of funds. In addition, because nonprofit borrowers were a unique and limited group, it was possible for them to be offered below-market-rate mortgages without affecting the overall Chicago loan market.

The Neighborhood Lending Programs were designed to apply not just to the city but to the entire metropolitan area. This was another ground-breaking feature of the programs that was copied in several cities, with Pittsburgh's program incorporating even broader regional components. Defining each program as a metropolitan area program acknowledged that a large commercial bank serves more than just the city. The broader geographical definition also addressed the fact that it is difficult, if not impossible, for individual neighborhood-based organizations to have enough clout to negotiate with a large bank. However, both the Alliance and the bank were concerned that Chicago's Neighborhood Lending Programs specifically benefit neighborhoods that had been disinvested. In order to ensure that the agreements achieved that objective, residential loan products were targeted to low-income areas as defined by an income formula—census tracts with median income levels at or below 80 percent of the metropolitan area median income level. Commercial loans were not similarly targeted because there was not a geographical connection between commercial loans and low-income residential areas.

At the time the Chicago Reinvestment Alliance agreement with First Chicago was announced, it was the largest agreement of its kind and contained the most detailed description of the terms of loan products, underwriting guidelines, and interest rates. This agreement was not a handshake and it was not just a statement of good intentions. In fact, the agreement itself was so detailed in terms of underwriting criteria and interest rate commitments that the bank requested that it not be publicly released. A summary of the key provisions was prepared and released with the announcement. The level of detail in the agreement was a direct result of the serious intent of the Alliance and the bank to develop a business partnership that could last over the five-year period of the agreement and accomplish the goals that had been mutually defined.

THE RESULTS

The commitment to reinvest in Chicago neighborhoods that was negotiated with the Neighborhood Lending Programs of First National Bank of Chicago, Harris Bank, and the Northern Trust has had a significant impact on the availability of credit for neighborhood development in Chicago, in the relationship between the banking industry and Chicago neighborhoods, and in the use of the Community Reinvestment Act throughout the country.

The announcement of the three Neighborhood Lending Programs generated renewed lender interest in the market for loans in neighborhoods across the city. The fact that three of the largest banks in Chicago announced their intention to make small-business loans made smaller community banks more aggressive in lending to their small-business customers so that they would not lose the business. The availability of long-term mortgages for multifamily buildings helped push the corporate community into investing in the Chicago Equity Fund, which packaged corporate investments into limited partnerships that gave nonprofit developers the equity they needed to acquire and rehabilitate buildings. Moreover, community-based organizations in other cities were inspired to replicate the successes in Chicago.

Enough time has elapsed since the Neighborhood Lending Programs were announced to look at how well the partnership has worked. A recent evaluation of the three programs concluded: "The Neighborhood Lending Programs have had considerable success in achieving their individual goals. They have developed new loan products and served markets not previously served by these lenders. They provided loans for a wide range of housing and commercial/industrial real estate needs. Finally, and most significantly, they have established working partnerships between the lenders and the community groups involved in the programs" (Bradford 1990).

During the initial five-year term of the agreements, 572 loans totaling $117.5 million were made. At the five-year anniversaries of the Neighborhood Lending Programs, each of the three banks willingly renewed and increased their commitment to the Neighborhood Lending Programs. In each case, the bank indicated that it had experienced no direct loan losses and that the delinquency rates were well within acceptable standards. Clearly, the success of this lending record demonstrates the accuracy of the Chicago Reinvestment Alliance premise that there are good loans in Chicago neighborhoods. The positive loan experience should also begin to reverse the negative perception of the riskiness of reinvestment in low-income communities.

While the Neighborhood Lending Programs have been successful by most measures, during the first five years there has been a variety of problems that have tested the partnership and the program design. In each case, the review board structure has proven to be a flexible and effective forum for discussion and for reaching consensus on the best solution to the issue.

The first issue that developed was the request from neighborhood-based developers to become qualified as loan packagers. Because this request had not been anticipated in the program design, the review board had to develop a process and qualifying guidelines to certify new loan packagers. This process has worked smoothly and several new organizations have become certified packagers.

Probably the most difficult issues have been the unevenness of the loan demand and the difference of opinion about how to address this problem. The demand for residential loans has been stronger than the demand for small business loans and the strongest loan demand has been for mixed-use loans. To ensure that the residential lending goal for multifamily loans was met, First National Bank decided in 1984 to start making loans directly without using the Chicago Rehab Network or CANDO as loan packagers. This decision was not wholeheartedly endorsed by the review boards and caused a program design change that provided for an endorsement of the loan and the borrower by a local community group. This change gives the review board a measure of community opinion about each project while allowing each bank the ability to move faster to meet their lending goals.

A second controversial issue centered on the degree to which some multifamily loans made through the Neighborhood Lending Programs may have contributed to gentrification and the displacement of low-income residents of the community. While there was not overall consensus about either the degree to which loans from the Neighborhood Lending Programs contributed to this problem or the definition of this issue, it continued to be a serious concern among many nonprofit housing developers, and particularly among those in two specific neighborhoods. Again, the review board provided a forum for the kind of in-depth discussion over time that was needed to develop a consensus about an appropriate response. A shift in the program design was made in order to allow the lender and the review board to examine rent levels in each project and ask for community endorsement for any project. While this has not totally allayed concerns about gentrification, it has given the review boards a method by which to estimate the projected cost of housing that is built using neighborhood lending loans.

Jean Pogge

The Neighborhood Lending Programs have demonstrated that re-investment is possible without significant loan losses, that bank/community partnerships do work and that the Community Reinvestment Act is a valuable tool for community groups. While much remains to be done to revitalize low- and moderate-income communities in Chicago, those communities now have access to the credit that is needed to continue the process of rebuilding.

REFERENCES

Alinsky, Saul. 1969. *Reveille for Radicals*. New York: Vintage Books.
Bradford, Calvin. 1990. *Partnerships for Reinvestment: An Evaluation of the Chicago Neighborhood Lending Programs*. Chicago: National Training and Information Center.
Hoyt, Homer. 1933. *One Hundred Years of Land Values in Chicago*. Chicago: University of Chicago Press.
Naparstek, Arthur J., and Gale Cincotta. 1976. *Urban Disinvestment: New Implications for Community Organization, Research and Public Policy*. Washington, D.C.: National Center for Urban Ethnic Affairs; Chicago: National Training and Information Center.
Organization of the NorthEast. 1974. "Understanding between Organization of the NorthEast and Bank of Chicago." Chicago: Unpublished document.

Michael L. Glabere   Chapter 6

MILWAUKEE: A TALE
OF THREE CITIES

MILWAUKEE'S RESPONSE TO REDLINING AND DISINVESTMENT reflects the
city's three distinct personalities. Milwaukee has been characterized as a
slow, conservative city; a well-run, congenial metropolis; and a seriously
segregated community notwithstanding a strong progressive tradition
(Norman 1989). As a conservative city, Milwaukee has been ten years
behind the rest of the country in recognizing and responding to disinvestment problems. As a well-run city, Milwaukee has borrowed the best
solutions from the rest of the country. A segregated yet in many respects
progressive Milwaukee has seen race as the driving force in the formation, dissolution, and, hopefully, what now appears to be a reformation
of public and private sector efforts to address redlining by financial institutions. All three characterizations accurately reflect the city's history.
These three themes interact in Milwaukee's reinvestment struggles.

    Reinvestment in Milwaukee, like in many other cities, has in-
volved several diverse actors and a range of activities. While the reinvestment movement grew out of Milwaukee's redlined inner city neighborhoods, once established that movement quickly aligned itself with its
counterparts in other cities, local public officials, local lenders, and interested citizen groups. Relationships over time have been both collegial
and adversarial. Reinvestment efforts have met with both success and
failure. While productive partnerships have evolved, it is clear that law
enforcement has been a critical stimulant to the emergence of voluntary
collaborative relationships. If reinvestment in Milwaukee has developed
a little later than elsewhere, it appears to be solidifying as part of the
city's institutional fabric. Though racial tensions persist, the many social

costs of racial divisiveness are increasingly recognized by all sectors of the community. Nowhere are these perceptions more evident than among those directly involved in Milwaukee's reinvestment debate.

THE EARLY YEARS: 1964–1984

To understand the dynamics of the most recent surge of reinvestment activity in Milwaukee, it is necessary to review the history of the city from two perspectives. One is the demographic changes and their impact on neighborhoods. The other is the experience of the community in responding to disinvestment, in terms of both success and failure. The institutional memory of community organizations plays a critical role in the strategies that have been adopted in recent history.

Milwaukee, like the rest of the country, experienced a resurgence of social protest in the 1960s, over civil rights, housing, and education issues in particular, and a blossoming of community organizing in general. This was a time that saw dramatic changes in the racial and economic character of the city. Between 1960 and 1970 the white population in Milwaukee declined by 11.8 percent. In 1960 the city was 8.4 percent black; by 1970 the percentage had increased to 14.7 percent. High-wage factory jobs were moving to the South, and their disappearance had the greatest impact on the central city. During the 1960s the median family income in the city fell from 96 percent of the suburban level to 91 percent (Lankevich 1977). As the black population increased, particularly in north- and west-side neighborhoods (now predominantly black), and as urban development displaced numerous poor, mostly minority, families, financial institutions began to relocate to the outlying and suburban neighborhoods. The reinvestment movement in Milwaukee has its roots in community response to the flight of these institutions from the west side of the city.

In 1964 the Park State Bank announced that it was closing its west-side office. It was not the first, nor the last financial institution, to leave the west side of the central city, but the response to this move left an impact still felt today. Over a period of four years, three community-based organizations emerged and still exist. The campaign to keep a bank in the neighborhood laid the groundwork with Senator Proxmire for the Community Reinvestment Act (CRA) legislation of the 1970s and changed Wisconsin banking laws. The end result of four years of organizing work was the establishment of the Midtown State Bank on the west side by the holding company that now controlled the Park State Bank (*Midtown Times* 1968a). Not long after, the North Milwaukee State Bank was established as the first African-American bank in the city of Milwaukee. This was a result of a separate effort by the National Association for the Advancement of Colored People (NAACP) and other African-American organizations to spur local control over investment activity in the African-American community. Both of these openings were significant victories for disinvested neighborhoods, but they did not stem the tide of institutional and capital flight. The same newspaper that touted the opening of the Midtown State Bank also denounced the closing of seven First Wisconsin branches and three savings and loans (*Midtown Times* 1968b).

During the 1970s the demographic changes which began in the 1960s accelerated, compounded by the aftereffects of riots and white flight. By 1980 nonwhites constituted over 25 percent of Milwaukee's populations. City policy emphasized downtown development, to the detriment of neighborhood stability (Norman 1989). The West Side Action Coalition (WAC) was formed in early 1973 to address issues confronting west side residents. It was an umbrella organization made up of eighty-nine member groups including churches, senior citizens, block clubs, and parent-teacher associations. Its structure and function came directly out of the Alinsky school of organizing, and it remained active for four years. It attacked redlining and discrimination in housing on two major fronts. The first was a concerted campaign focused on Federal Housing Administration (FHA) loans and their use in blockbusting neighborhoods. The second was a campaign entitled "Savings for the Westside Campaign". The focus of the campaign was to reward financial institutions that did not redline the neighborhood by funneling community deposits to them. A major objective of the WAC strategy was to persuade lenders to give preference to homeowners rather than absentee investors (Heidkamp 1974) though WAC published many studies and analyses of lending patterns, over time the strategy failed to result in greater investor commitment to the neighborhood.

The campaigns of the west side were focused on white or predominantly white neighborhoods and did not result in similar activity in minority neighborhoods. Organizing in the African-American community at this time was primarily focused on delivery of the Great Society

Michael L. Glabere

programs and education. Housing efforts focused on the need to end discrimination and segregation in housing patterns (Lankevich 1977) The antiblockbusting campaigns of the west side were of little interest to people who were working to open up segregated areas of the city to racial minorities, and the desire of white-controlled financial institutions to leave the African-American community was viewed by some segments of that community as a positive step toward community control of resources. The campaigns to promote homeownership over absentee landlords did not include an effort, or a tacit acknowledgment of the need, to make homeownership opportunities available to racial minorities. Two reports issued as part of the WAC campaign, *Redlining in Milwaukee* (Heidcamp and Sandy 1974) and *Redlining: Update* (Snyder 1977)—both sponsored by the Council on Urban and Rural Life—failed to make any reference to race in their discussions of the causes and impacts of discriminatory lending practices. Even the discussion in these reports of the devastating impact of appraisal practices made no reference to racial effects. It is not surprising that to this day west side organizations are viewed with suspicion by African-Americans in Milwaukee, long after the organizations have ceased to be white-dominated and controlled.

It was concentrated media attention, coupled with efforts at the state and local levels, that moved local elected officials to take action. In September 1974 the mayor's office, in partnership with the Savings and Loan Council of Milwaukee County, announced the formation of the Milwaukee Area Mortgage Opportunity Plan (MAMOP). The plan was formed as a direct result of the protest activity and allegations of community organizations. Its purpose was to provide an appeal panel for mortgage applicants who were denied a loan and felt that it was due to redlining or discrimination. Twenty-nine savings and loans and several banks signed up to participate. By March 1976 MAMOP had heard only one complaint and had found in favor of the applicant (*Milwaukee Journal* 1976). The loan was subsequently approved. Ted Snyder, chairman of Milwaukee Alliance of Concerned Citizens (a member organization of WAC) admitted that the idea of a grievance procedure was good, "but we were quite aware of the fact that it was used as a decoy when we were going after state regulations against redlining" (*Milwaukee Journal* 1976). The major impact of MAMOP seemed to be that lenders no longer used property location as the reason for a loan denial, substituting some other "rational economic" reason, while still denying loans in the same neigh-

152

borhoods that had long been redlined. In commenting on the attitudes of fellow lenders who admitted to redlining, Fred Banholzer, president of Republic Bank and chair of MAMOP, said, "They say, you're right, I do discriminate. How else do you think I'd keep from getting bad loans?" (*Milwaukee Journal* 1976). (MAMOP exists to this day and has continued to be as ineffective in nurturing reinvestment as it was in its formative years.)

Nothing could better demonstrate the failure of a strategy that relied exclusively on voluntary collaborative efforts and informal persuasion than the announcement by Midtown State Bank in 1979 that it wished to abandon the west-side neighborhood that had struggled to create it in the first place. Cooperation West Side Association (COWSA), an Alinsky-style neighborhood-based organization, had formed around the organizing effort to establish the bank and now was faced with the task of organizing to prevent the loss of Midtown, the one remaining bank in the neighborhood. Effective community organizing, including the use of law enforcement tools, proved to be essential complements to the more informal and voluntary tactics that had previously been utilized.

The first sign that the bank was not happy with its location came in September 1979 from Alderwoman Betty Voss, who informed COWSA that the bank was having problems getting repairs made. Voss assure COWSA that the bank was not intending to move and that the building was basically sound and in good repair. In October 1979 the bank's board of directors voted to not renew the bank's lease and to withhold rent. The bank then proceeded to file an application with State Banking Commissioner Eric Mildenburg and with the Federal Deposit Insurance Corporation (FDIC) requesting permission to relocate to the downtown area. The bank ran notices of its application in the financial pages of the *Milwaukee Journal*, and as expected they were overlooked by the neighborhood organization.

The neighborhood and COWSA became aware of the proposed closing on December 21, 1979, when the bank's owner, John Kelly, announced the move in the local media. By this time permission had been granted by the state banking commissioner and the deadline for requesting a formal FDIC hearing had expired. In spite of this, COWSA was determined to fight the move. Having already seen three banks leave its neighborhood in the last fifteen years, the organization knew that the loss of the one remaining bank could deal a fatal blow to any hopes of redevelopment.

Initial meetings with the bank and the state banking commissioner were unproductive, leaving COWSA with the realization that the only hope of preventing the move lay in forcing the FDIC to hold formal hearings. Congressman Henry Reuss persuaded the FDIC to agree to informal hearings, however these would not carry the regulatory capacity to prevent a move. Then COWSA organized a picket line at the bank and began to sign up depositors who committed themselves to withdrawing their funds if the bank left the neighborhood. The aim was to create a media atmosphere that would result in the FDIC agreeing to a formal hearing, and in this COWSA was successful. As a result of the media attention a downtown bank approached COWSA with the offer of legal help and with information that a second downtown bank had filed a formal protest with the FDIC within the legal time period. In addition, Legal Action of Wisconsin offered its assistance to COWSA. Armed with this knowledge and these resources COWSA demanded a formal hearing, and the FDIC agreed to meet the demand. After further pressure theFDIC moved the hearing from Washington, D.C. to Milwaukee and set the stage for COWSA to go to work.

By the day of the hearing COWSA had the signatures of 1,300 depositors on its petitions. It also had enlisted the help of three major downtown banks and an attorney and had prepared a forty-page brief. Excerpts were used from the bank's charter hearing in which the bank's officers stated the need for a bank in this area. Neighborhood residents pointed out that for most of the bank's history the majority stockholders of the bank had owned the building and that they were at least in part to fault for any building problems. Representatives of COWSA used Home Mortgage Disclosure Act (HMDA) data to establish lending patterns as evidence that the bank had not fulfilled its responsibilities under the Community Reinvestment Act and therefore was not entitled to move. Residents who had been discouraged or denied loans presented personal testimony. Moreover, the bank's statements at the hearing about the neighborhood were used as evidence by COWSA that the bank did not want to serve the neighborhood as the law required. The bank's main contentions at the hearing were that the building was in such poor shape that the bank could not be expected to continue there and that the neighborhood was run down and not appropriate to a good business atmosphere.

The FDIC staff was impressed by critics of the move. In early March 1980, COWSA learned that the FDIC had sent a letter to the bank giving tentative denial of permission to move. On May 20, COWSA was informed by the bank that it had withdrawn its proposal to move and looked forward to working with COWSA. According to the FDIC this was the first time that a community organization had prevented a bank from leaving its neighborhood. Paul Cochran, president of Midtown Bank stated: "You and other members of COWSA did exactly what I would have done in your place and I congratulate you in your efforts. It is now evident that it took something like this for the bank, civic groups, businesses, and the people to recognize that we really do need each other" (COWSA 1979–80).

Members of COWSA had set out to retain a bank in their neighborhood and had succeeded. During the campaign the organization emphasized that it did not view this as a struggle with the bank but as a struggle to retain the necessary capital to redevelop the neighborhood. Letters and documented phone calls show a constant effort to keep lines of communication open with the bank. This assured the bank that COWSA did not want to destroy it but in fact wanted to establish a working relationship. Bank officials understood this and personal animosity was kept at a minimum (COWSA 1979–80).

This struggle marks a turning point in Milwaukee's response to disinvestment. The transition in the method of retaining capital in the neighborhood occurred at the same time that the neighborhoods in Milwaukee, especially on the north and west sides, were changing rapidly. As the 1980s began, the same west-side neighborhoods that had spent two decades working to stabilize as working-class neighborhoods were now working poor and mostly minority neighborhoods. Blockbusting was no longer an issue. The struggle to prevent the flight of capital had been lost and so now the struggle was to force the reinvestment of capital in the neighborhood. The neighborhoods of the west side and the near south side of Milwaukee had now reached the same state of disinvestment that the African-American community had been in for at least the last twenty years.

Milwaukee had accumulated a twenty-year history of citizen activity to address discrimination in lending. The organizations that had been the most active in reinvestment struggles had a core of experienced leaders. Yet restructuring in the local economy impoverished many central city neighborhoods that had become primarily minority communities in the two previous decades. These conditions set the stage for the most recent chapter in Milwaukee's history, one which reflects successful reinvestment initiatives despite continuing economic pressures particularly in the central city.

MATURATION OF MILWAUKEE'S REINVESTMENT MOVEMENT: 1984–1990

The summer of 1985 marked the beginning of the new strategy for reinvestment in Milwaukee. Midtown Bank, now known as FirstMil Bank, notified COWSA that it wished to move its main office from Thirty-fourth and Lisbon to Thirty-ninth and Lisbon. Cooperation West Side Association was faced with the decision to fight the move or to use the opportunity to improve the neighborhood. Using HMDA and the force of the CRA, COWSA was able to make a compelling case that FirstMil had a poor record of serving the neighborhood and should be denied permission to move. This was a strategy the organization had used in the past, but now it took a different turn. Using the leverage of the ability to block the move, COWSA entered into negotiations with the intent to permit the move ultimately. At stake was the price of the move. By August 21, 1985, a $1.3 million three-year set-aside program targeted to the COWSA neighborhood was successfully negotiated with First Milwaukee Bank. The agreement established quarterly review procedures and limited use of the money to people who resided in the neighborhood (FirstMil 1985). This agreement marked the first dollar commitment for reinvestment purposes by a private institution in Milwaukee. In exchange, the bank was permitted to move its offices.

With this agreement COWSA completed the shift from a capital retention to a reinvestment strategy. However, the problem of disinvestment was not limited to the COWSA neighborhood, and the resources of COWSA would not be sufficient to succeed in campaigns against larger institutions in the city. National Peoples Action (NPA) and National Training and Information Center (NTIC) staff in Chicago had been consultants to COWSA for several years and now worked with Milwaukee organizers to formulate a strategy for developing a broad based reinvestment campaign in Milwaukee. Outreach aimed at recruiting organizations which would be geographically and racially diverse. In March 1986 fourteen community based organizations met and formed the Milwaukee Community Reinvestment Coalition. They reached a consensus on the need to secure reinvestment dollars for the central city and to increase the number of loans to racial minorities in the metropolitan area. The initial goal was to gather information and work on expanding participation in the coalition. However, fortuitous events would dictate the direction and actions taken in a short period of time.

On June 19, 1986, several coalition members were contacted by Liz Wolff from Phoenix, Arizona. Wolff worked for the Arizona Association of Community Organizations for Reform Now (ACORN), which had filed a formal protest to the proposed acquisition of Thunderbird Bank of Phoenix by Marshal and Ilsley Bank (M & I) of Milwaukee. One extension of the comment period had been granted at the request of ACORN but M & I had refused to negotiate with ACORN and seemed confident that the federal regulators would permit the acquisition. Staff from NPA had suggested that the Acorn reinvestment challenge might be assisted through local action in Milwaukee. The CRA coalition met on June 25 and decided to support the Phoenix challenge by issuing a Milwaukee protest of the lending activity of M & I. On June 26, a request for extension of the comment period was forwarded to the Federal Reserve in Washington, along with documentation of the poor lending record of M & I in the central city of Milwaukee.

While the extension of the comment period was denied, the act of challenging the acquisition led M & I to reconsider its posture of refusing to negotiate. The added clout of an interstate protest raised the possibility that public hearings would be granted and meant that the purchase would be delayed no matter what the outcome of the hearings. Over the next two months meetings were held in Milwaukee and in Phoenix between M & I and the respective community organizations. The Milwaukee coalition was operating with a distinct disadvantage in that the Federal Reserve Board was not granting them legal status as a protesting body. The negotiators for the bank were able to exploit this to their advantage. After an initial round of negotiations in Milwaukee and in Phoenix, M & I adopted a high profile media strategy. They announced their final offer to ACORN on July 25, committing to lifeline rates (e.g., low or no service charge checking accounts, cashing of government checks for bank customers), and little else (*Milwaukee Sentinel* 1986). On August 11, M & I unilaterally announced a $50 million loan program targeted at the central city of Milwaukee. The CRA coalition members were shocked and in a letter to the federal reserve stated "we do not feel that the program as currently outlined will have a significant impact on improving M & I's CRA record. It is our position that unless M & I is willing to discuss loan terms the program will not meet the credit needs of low and moderate income families" (CRA 1986). The Federal Reserve Board approved the acquisition on September 3, 1986, in spite of the continued protest of the community organizations.

To the public this challenge was portrayed as a success for the community in Milwaukee. After all, $50 million for the central city was not insignificant. In private, coalition members knew that the bank had outmaneuvered them. The major lesson learned was that the press had to be used to the coalition's advantage, or it would be used against them. One other disturbing aspect of the campaign was the hiring of Bob Nicol as the first CRA officer for the bank at the end of August, 1986. Nicol had been the executive director of a coalition organization and a central member of the negotiating team. His hiring caused many rifts within the coalition and accusations of "selling out" became points of contention between members. This dissension had a major impact on the challenges and negotiations that followed.

On August 28, the CRA coalition was informed of pending applications by Marine Bank of Milwaukee to purchase Community State Agency of Bloomington, Minnesota, and Marine Bank of Mt. Pleasant, Wisconsin. The CRA Coalition responded by filing for an extension of the comment period and requesting that Marine Bank enter into negotiations to produce a CRA agreement. At the same time, the Harambee Ombudsman Project decided to break from the coalition and file a separate challenge to Marine Bank. This decision was a direct result of the animosity caused by the hiring of Bob Nicol by M & I. It also reflected the same racial tensions that had permeated the last twenty years of group activity in reinvestment organizing.

The Harambee Ombudsman Project is an African-American block club–based community organization situated in the core of the minority community. Ed McDonald, its executive director at the time, had been one of the negotiators for the M & I challenge and was also part of the organizing core of the coalition. According to McDonald, "our leadership on the board of directors didn't trust the west-side organizations to negotiate a fair deal for our community" (McDonald 1990). The Harambee Project, Harambee Housing Project, and the Inner City Redevelopment Corporation (ICRC) filed a request for public hearings at the same time that the coalition asked for an extension of the comment period. While the loan numbers for the CRA coalition case might have been debatable, the Harambee protest showed that a community of 35,000 people had received only one mortgage for less than $50,000 in three years of lending activity (Harambee 1986). The fact that this community was also 90 percent African-American left the bank with a public relations disaster as the media began to play the race angle of the lending pattern, with the encouragement of the community organizations.

Marine Bank first attempted to play one group off of the other. This attempt failed, as the CRA coalition refused to negotiate on behalf of Harambee (unless Harambee asked it to), and Harambee refused to settle unless an agreement was reached with the coalition. The basic demands for each negotiating group were identical, with the exception that Harambee was demanding a loan program targeted at its specific community and was also demanding the establishment of a branch bank in its neighborhood. This last demand was especially significant since the neighborhood had not had an active branch bank for the last twenty years.

After three meetings with the Harambee group, each one well-covered by print, radio, and television media, the Marine Bank indicated it would enter into agreement. On October 22, 1986, the Harambee agreement was signed. One condition of the deal was that Harambee's protest would be withdrawn only after the bank signed an agreement with the CRA coalition. Marine agreed to establish a branch bank, contingent on a feasibility study, to lend $6 million over five years in the Harambee community, and to establish a monitoring committee that would review the bank's underwriting guidelines and ensure that the loans were made. On October 30, 1986, the bank signed the CRA coalition agreement. This committed the bank to make $25 million in loans in the Community Development Block Grant Area (CDBG), in addition to the $6 million for the Harambee community. The total agreement included $31 million over five years as well as a process for ongoing monitoring and modification of the bank's activity. The dollars were targeted at the low-income areas of the city. The press had played a major role in publicizing the community organizations' efforts and pushing the negotiations forward; but there was one other factor that had lent urgency to the bank's desire to settle and that became apparent only later.

In the summer of 1987 Banc One of Columbus, Ohio, announced its intention to purchase Marine Bank of Milwaukee. Initially, this sparked a bidding response from M & I bank to counter the offer to purchase. After consideration, the board of Marine Bank opted to accept the offer of Banc One. All of this was watched quite closely by community organizations in Milwaukee and in Ohio. Banc One had been the target of several reinvestment campaigns, resulting in agreements in several cities in the midwest. During that summer, the CRA coalition met to develop its strategy for responding to the acquisition. The Harambee groups had rejoined the coalition in order to provide a united front for action. The goals of the community groups were, at a minimum, to get a signed commitment to honor the CRA agreements of Marine Bank and to expand the agreements where possible. The first meeting between the coalition and Banc One officials ended in conflict. The bank stressed that it had an exemplary CRA record, claiming the acquisition would only enhance reinvestment in Milwaukee. The coalition members demanded that a meeting be held with George Slater, the CEO and chairman of Marine Bank, and with the CEO of Banc One. The bank agreed to send Slater and Roman Gerber, executive vice president of Banc One, with authorization to cut a deal. The coalition prepared to stage a high profile media event. The meeting was held at the North Division Neighborhoods office on October 2, 1987, in the core of the African-American community and surrounded by boarded-up buildings. A picket line was set up and the bank officials were forced to walk through it, with the television cameras documenting picketers chanting "Honor the Agreements" and "Reinvestment Now." The meeting was cordial and somewhat productive, however no firm commitments were made. At a press conference immediately after the meeting, the coalition unilaterally announced that the bank had agreed to honor all past commitments and was now negotiating improvements to the previous agreements. Mr. Slater, who was listening to the announcement, verified these statements in front of the cameras. From there the negotiations went fairly smoothly. On December 3, 1987, the coalition and Banc One entered into a formal agreement which strengthened and consolidated the two Marine agreements. The $31 million goals were retained. Improvements to the agreement included a firm commitment to opening the Harambee branch bank, low-cost lifeline checking and savings accounts, free cashing of government checks, and the support of several marketing and development initiatives in the central city. The CRA agreement was filed with the Federal Reserve Board as a part of the application to purchase Marine Bank, and became a part of the legal document that was approved by the regulators.

In 1988 the merger of the two banks went forward, the branch bank was opened, and progress was made toward getting the loans out to the community. The CRA coalition was occupied with serving on the advisory committee of the deal, and each individual organization could truthfully say that their human resources had been stretched to the point where new ventures were not feasible. For a brief period of time in the spring the state legislature considered instituting a state CRA. However, there was very little legislative support, in part because the CRA coalition did not have the resources to mount a campaign. Consequently, the issue was dropped. It remains unclear what costs or benefits have been incurred by the community and lenders in the failure to secure passage of a state CRA in Wisconsin.

Bill Dedman's January 1989 article in the Atlanta Journal/Constitution made redlining and reinvestment a major topic of discussion among leading politicians, lenders, the media, and community groups in Milwaukee (Dedman 1989). The report detailed the mortgage loan rejection rates for blacks and whites and reported the ratio of black to white rejection during the mid 1980s for major cities around the nation. Among the fifty cities included in this study Milwaukee had the highest disparity in the rate of rejection between the two races. While nationwide, blacks were rejected twice as often as whites for mortgage loans, the ratio in Milwaukee was almost four to one. The reaction in Milwaukee was immediate and loud. Community leaders demanded action from their elected officials, and on April 18, 1989, Milwaukee Mayor John Norquist and Wisconsin Governor Tommy Thompson announced the formation of the Fair Lending Action Committee (FLAC). The committee was comprised of community leaders (primarily members of the CRA coalition), lenders, realtors, and government representatives. Several members from the African-American community were added after the NAACP took issue with the background and racial composition of the original panel. Its stated purpose was "to identify the reasons for the disproportionate amount of mortgage loan application rejections for black residents in Milwaukee and to recommend remedies that will facilitate greater loan availability for minority and low income people, which may include commercial lending" (Fair Lending Action Committee 1989a).

Early in the meetings of the group it became apparent that redlining as a geographic phenomena was not going to be addressed directly in the recommendations. Members of the committee instead focused on race-based lending goals in order to address racial, rather than geographic discrimination. The members of the committee who were concerned with community redlining knew that their neighborhood concerns would likely be addressed by race-specific remedies because of the highly segregated housing patterns in Milwaukee, as long as the lending goals were high enough. "Since Milwaukee minority populations are concentrated in neighborhoods clearly in need of major revitalization efforts, by creating greater access to minority financing options we would be simultaneously meeting much of the needs in blighted neighborhoods" (Fair Lending Action Committee 1989b).

While FLAC was negotiating its recommendations, financial institutions were still actively looking to grow through mergers and acquisitions. In June 1989, First Financial Savings Bank, the largest savings and loan in the state, announced that it intended to acquire Illini Savings and Loan Association of Fairview Heights, Illinois. Fairview Heights is located just outside of East St. Louis. This acquisition was occurring as a part of the savings and loan bailout program, and as such had a great deal of regulatory attention paid to it. For First Financial it represented an opportunity to enter the Illinois market in a painless fashion and then use the unlimited branching laws of that state to expand. To several community organizations in Milwaukee this represented an opportunity to move the reinvestment struggle to the arena of savings and loan institutions.

Several African-American organizations worked together to protest the acquisition by First Financial. The CRA coalition was invited to participate; however, due to staff and resource limitations coalition members decided not to enter into this challenge. Milwaukee United for Better Housing (MUBH), a church-based housing developer, led the effort and called upon the member organizations of its board of directors, the NAACP and the Milwaukee Realtists, to participate. Both the NAACP and the Realtists had affiliate chapters in East St. Louis which agreed to file a separate challenge in Illinois to support the Milwaukee effort (MUBH 1989). John Seramur, president and CEO of First Financial, personally handled the negotiations and reached agreement with the organizations in two meetings. The press was present and supportive of the community organizations, and Seramur responded by negotiating in good faith and agreeing to almost all of the community organizations' demands. On August 2, 1989, a $20 million agreement was reached for reinvestment in Milwaukee's inner city. This agreement went further than the previous agreements by including a commitment to affirmative action hiring and a written plan to implement it. This marked the first time that a CRA agreement had addressed the issue of minority employment in financial institutions and its impact on lending practices.

In October 1989, FLAC issued its report on lending in Milwaukee and its recommendations (Fair Lending Action Committee 1989c). The committee concluded that mortgage lending was disproportionately low among blacks and in predominately black neighborhoods as compared to whites and predominantly white neighborhoods. There were many recommendations on marketing, outreach, and partnership formation. The most significant recommendation of FLAC was to set voluntary racial lending goals for Milwaukee lenders.

The recommended goals were directed to all Milwaukee area lenders and addressed mortgage, commercial real estate, and business loans. The specific goals called for each lender in 1990 to make 5 percent of all loans and 5 percent of the dollar volume of all loans in the metropolitan area in each of these three categories to racial minorities. The goals for 1991 and 1992 were set at 10 percent and 13 percent, the latter number being the percentage of racial minorities in the population of the four-county metropolitan area according to the 1980 census. The numerical-goals statement was the most contentious issue in FLAC's deliberations. Many lenders, both on and off the committee, claimed they were unrealistic. Yet, when the report was issued, every member of FLAC signed the document and, at least publicly, endorsed its findings and recommendations.

By design, FLAC was a voluntary, community-wide initiative. Specific, concrete activities that evolved directly from a particular FLAC recommendation are difficult to pinpoint. Still, lenders often point to areas where they exceeded FLAC goals as evidence of their successful reinvestment efforts and they see failure to meet the goals as evidence that there are areas where more can be accomplished. So, in some respects, a standard has been set. Perhaps more important, personal and professional relationships among lenders, community groups, elected officials, and the public were developed that led to a variety of reinvestment programs in Milwaukee.

163

Michael L. Glabere

WHAT HAS BEEN ACHIEVED?

Clearly there have been pronounced impacts from the reinvestment movement in Milwaukee. Lenders have made commitments to inner-city lending and have learned the value of having community-based organizations as partners in that effort. Politicians have reached some understanding of the critical role of government in promoting balanced development. Most important, the financial industry has become more accessible to low-income people. Table 6.1 summarizes the key elements of the agreements secured in Milwaukee subsequent to CRA challenges.

Between 1986 and 1989, commitments had been secured to increase lending in the central city by $102 million over a five-year period. Advisory committees to evaluate underwriting guidelines had been established as a mutually beneficial means of doing business. A branch bank opened up in the Harambee community for the first time in twenty years and has since proven to be one of the most effective branches in generating new accounts. It has even announced plans to expand to accommodate the level of demand.

The most important measure of the impact on lending institutions is the change in actual lending in redlined neighborhoods. Lending is evaluated from HMDA reports by examining the changing percentage of an institution's metropolitan-area mortgage loans to the city's target area; depressed neighborhoods identified by Milwaukee's Comptroller's Office from housing and income data. Lending is also evaluated by examining

TABLE 6.1
MILWAUKEE LENDING AGREEMENTS SIGNED BETWEEN 1985 AND 1989

LENDER	$ MILLION	YEARS	OTHER COMMITMENTS
FIRSTMIL (LIBERTY)	1.3	1985–1988	Advisory committee
M & I	50	1986–1991	Advisory committee, discounted loan terms
MARINE BANK/ BANK ONE	31	1986–1991	Advisory committee, discounted loan terms Branch bank, lifeline rates, CDC marketing
FIRST FINANCIAL	20	1989–1994	Advisory committee, discounted loan terms, lifeline rates, minority employement

164

loans to minority areas, census tracts whose populations are 50 percent or more minority. By comparing lending patterns in 1984, immediately prior to the initiation of negotiations, and with those in 1989 after the agreements were signed, it is clear that the CRA challenges and subsequent negotiations were effective.

In 1984 the industry average for total loans made in the target area was 10.1 percent. By 1989 this figure had dropped to 4.2 percent. The lending institutions that had signed agreements showed a much different pattern from the industry as a whole. Liberty Bank increased from 2.3 percent to 10.0 percent, Bank One stayed virtually the same at 5.8 percent. First Financial increased from 21.8 percent to 24.5 percent and M & I decreased from 7.9 percent to 4.7 percent. In all cases the institutions with agreements were above the industry average and either increased or else showed a much smaller decrease than the rest of the industry. The patterns for lending to minority census tracts indicates the same kind of effect. The industry average fell from 12.3 percent in 1984 to 6.0 percent in 1989. At the same time Liberty increased from 0 percent to 23.5 percent, Bank One Milwaukee increased from 7.6 percent to 8.4 percent, First Financial increased from 25.8 percent to 29.3 percent and M & I showed a decrease from 7.2 percent to 6.3 percent. Once again, all of the challenged institutions were above the industry average and, with the exception of M & I, showing increased lending activity in minority census tracts.

During the time when challenges were taking place in Milwaukee, the industry as a whole was disinvesting from the central city at an ever increasing pace. The institutions that had been challenged and have signed reinvestment agreements have all risen above the industry average for lending to low-income and minority neighborhoods. These institutions have either increased the percentage of their loans in depressed areas or experienced a slight decrease while the average for the rest of the industry declined dramatically.

The attitudes of many lenders toward the inner city were also affected by the reinvestment agreements. Neighborhood groups are frequently credited by lenders for teaching them about lending in the inner city. Several stress the importance of good communication with neighborhood organizations in order to more effectively ascertain the credit needs of the community. Joe Blonigen, CRA officer for First Financial expresses it this way: "The communication is good. What this did is it makes it more formal as far as having in writing that we will meet needs and the goals will be there" (Blonigen 1990). As Tim Elverman, vice president of government relations for Bank One, more colorfully stated: "We knew the community organizations that made up this coalition were not a bunch of wackos" (Elverman 1990). Elverman credited the importance of CRA in encouraging lenders to support community investment, which also turns out to be profitable. "You don't lose money doing CRA, it's the right thing to do. It also is good business strategy." Yet he acknowledges that "without the law, the bank would never have done these things on its own" (Elverman 1990).

Community organizers emphasize that there is greater access to loans through their organizations; but it is unclear whether there is an increase in the ability of low-income people to interact with the bank individually. "I'm not familiar with whether there has been much success in connecting individuals with lending institutions in terms of securing loans," says Chuck Mrousek, secretary for the CRA coalition. "But again, in terms of their non-profit lending they clearly have provided very attractive loans" (Mrousek 1990).

THE STILL UNCERTAIN FUTURE

Clearly there have been some immediate positive impacts resulting from the lending agreements. The long-term impact on disinvested neighborhoods will depend on the future directions of developments that emerged in the wake of these agreements.

For instance, in 1991 Milwaukee enacted a linked deposit ordinance similar to those previously implemented in Boston, Pittsburgh, and several other cities. Officially labeled a "socially responsible investment program," this legislation requires depositories of city funds to demonstrate—by their lending, employment, and related practices—a commitment to reinvestment in the city. In addition, several new public/private partnership efforts aimed at economic development and housing production have developed over the past five years. Financial institutions have made substantial contributions to the Housing Partnership, the Housing Assistance Corporation, Milwaukee Neighborhood Partnership Incorporated, and the Neighborhood Development Corporation during their formation. Many lending institutions have initiated their own community reinvestment efforts, guided not only by the requirements established in the CRA and other legal mandates but also by an emerging perception of the linkages between the needs of the city and their own self-interest. It remains to be seen if these activities will blossom into meaningful reinvestment vehicles for distressed neighborhoods. Still, the willingness of the lenders to initiate and participate in these kinds of programs has been an encouraging indication of changes in their attitude toward their business and their community.

This is not to say that advocacy efforts have ground to a halt. Indeed, FLAC has evolved into the Milwaukee Area Mortgage Opportunity Committee (MAMOC), founded by the Wisconsin Savings and Loan League and including lenders and neighborhood-based housing developers as participants. Its purpose is to build upon the FLAC recommendations and pursue collaborative means of improving lending to distressed neighborhoods and to minorities in general.

At the same time, the Fair Lending Project (FLP), a coalition of labor unions, community organizations, churches, and civil rights groups has formed to pursue both voluntary and, where appropriate, adversarial tactics (including CRA challenges) for similar objectives. Early in 1991 FLP secured a $25 million five-year reinvestment commitment from Norwest Bank, of which one key component is a commitment to increase minority employment. A few months later, Equitable Savings Bank launched a $7 million reinvestment program that incorporated several new marketing plans based on FLP initiatives. Brochures describing bank products and services are to be distributed in several languages including Spanish, Laotian, and Hmong. The bank agreed to finance direct mailings through several inner-city organizations. Bank officers will work with five central-city employers to assist their employees in purchasing homes near their places of work. Moreover, the bank will initiate affirmative action programs to increase minority employment and will contract with more minority-owned vendors. Other lenders have approached FLP to develop similar programs, and the project monitors lending throughout the community in anticipation of further challenge opportunities. The project has been funded by a local private foundation and by city with the full endorsement of the mayor. Unfortunately, the mayor's endorsement leaves some African-American organizations skeptical of the project, making their participation somewhat tenuous.

The future of reinvestment activity in Milwaukee is sure to contain the same discords as its past. The proliferation of partnerships with

Michael L. Glabere

private industry as a leading participant represents an extension of the conservative approach long-favored by city founders to resolve social problems such as discrimination. Yet, the city's willingness to look beyond its borders for solutions reflects a more progressive tradition that emphasizes efficient and equitable service. Nonetheless, the overriding issues for some time to come are likely to be racial inequalities and what to do about them.

There is reason to believe that communication channels are opening up among groups that have long been adversaries, and there is reason to hope that more equitable lending practices will result, leading to the redevelopment of long depressed communities. It is clear that the threat of CRA challenges and related law enforcement is critical for nurturing the collaborative relationships that are emerging. Many questions remain, but one matter is clear. How the city manages reinvestment will be a powerful determinant of Milwaukee's future.

REFERENCES

Blonigen, Joe. 1990. Interview with Joe Blonigen, Vice President, Mortgage Compliance and Training for First Financial Bank, Oct. 19. Milwaukee, Wis.
COWSA. 1979–80. Papers, correspondence, and notes. COWSA archives, Milwaukee, Wis.
CRA. 1986. Letter to Franklin Dryer from the CRA Coalition, Aug. 28, 1986.
Dedman, Bill. 1989. "Blacks Turned Down for Home Loans from S & Ls Twice as Often as Whites." *Atlanta Journal/Constitution*, Jan. 22.
Elverman, Tim. 1990. Interview with Tim Elverman, Vice President for Government Relations, Bank One Wisconsin, Sept. 14. Milwaukee, Wis.
Fair Lending Action Committee. 1989a. "Mission Statement." In *Equal Access to Mortgage Lending, The Milwaukee Plan*. Milwaukee, Wis.: Fair Lending Action Committee (October).
———. 1989b. "Needs Statement." In *Equal Access to Mortgage Lending. The Milwaukee Plan*. Milwaukee, Wis.: Fair Lending Action Committee (October).
———. 1989c. *Equal Access to Mortgage Lending. The Milwaukee Plan*. Milwaukee, Wis.: Fair Lending Action Committee (October).
FirstMil. 1985. *FirstMil Bank Lending Agreement*. Milwaukee, Wis. (Aug. 21).
Harambee. 1986. Collection of research papers in Harambee files, Milwaukee, Wis., relating to lending activity of Marine Bank.
Heidkamp, Ann, and Stephanie Sandy. 1974. *Redlining in Milwaukee: Who Is Destroying the Westside?* Milwaukee, Wis.: Council On Urban Life.
Lankevich, George J. 1977. *Milwaukee: A Chronological and Documentary History*. Dobbs Ferry, N.Y.: Oceana.
McDonald, Edward C. 1990. Interview with Edward C. McDonald, Nov. 23. Milwaukee, Wis.
Midtown Times. 1968a. "New Bank Rises in Midtown Area." Jan. 18.
———. 1968b. "'Bright Future for Midtown' Says Ertl." Jan. 18.
Milwaukee Journal. 1976. "Redlining Hubbub Simmers Down." March 7.
Milwaukee Sentinel. 1986. "M & I to Offer Special Services in Response to Arizona Protest." July 25.

Mrousek, Chuck. 1990. Interview with Chuck Mrousek, Secretary for the Milwaukee CRA Coalition, Oct. 11. Milwaukee, Wis.

MUBH. 1989. Letters, phone logs, and papers, First Financial Challenge, Milwaukee United for Better Housing archives. Milwaukee, Wis.

Norman, Jack. 1989. "Congenial Milwaukee: A Segregated City." in *Unequal Partnerships: The Political Economy of Urban Redevelopment in Postwar America.* ed. Gregory D. Squires. New Brunswick, N.J.: Rutgers University Press

Snyder, Theodore. 1977. *Redlining: Update.* Milwaukee, Wis.: Council on Urban and Rural Life.

Larry E. Keating   Chapter 7
Lynn M. Brazen
Stan F. Fitterman

RELUCTANT RESPONSE
TO COMMUNITY PRESSURE
IN ATLANTA

IN THE CITY THAT CRADLED the civil rights movement enough time has
passed for redlining to be replaced with reinvestment; but the record in
Atlanta is mixed. Though some lenders continue to resist significant
change in their basic business practices, important positive developments
have occurred.

Atlanta banks and financial institutions resisted pressure from the
Atlanta Community Reinvestment Alliance (ACRA) for two and one-half
years, until the publication of a four-part front-page series in the *Atlanta
Journal/Constitution* detailing the extent and persistence of racial discrimination in mortgage lending. Within two weeks, financial institutions that had
earlier proposed and then withdrawn an offer of a $10 million consortium
loan pool were at press conferences announcing a $65 million program. The
creation of the Atlanta Mortgage Consortium in May 1988, the passage
of the area's first fair housing law, and some reformation of previous
discriminatory practices in lending were all outgrowths of the effort.

Still, racial discrimination persists. Banks and financial institutions continue to close offices in African-American sections of the central city while opening new branches on the expanding white periphery
of the metropolitan area. Three years later, the struggle continues.

THE ATLANTA COMMUNITY REINVESTMENT ALLIANCE

As community organizing around the issue of redlining gained national
momentum, the Chicago-based National Training and Information Cen-

ter (NTIC) obtained a grant to assist community groups in several major cities where no such effort had begun. Atlanta was one of those cities.

At the end of 1985, following notable success by community groups in Chicago, Shel Trapp—an NTIC organizer—contacted the Georgia Housing Coalition, offering to meet with community groups in Atlanta to do a workshop on the Community Reinvestment Act (CRA).

About a dozen community activists from nearly as many organizations spent a January 1986 Saturday morning learning about CRA. At the end of the meeting they agreed individually to take responsibility for collecting CRA statements and Home Mortgage Disclosure Act (HMDA) data from Atlanta's major lending institutions and to meet again in a few weeks. That Saturday morning was the beginning of a loosely knit affiliation of community groups and nonprofit organizations that called itself ACRA.

Over the next several months ACRA members compiled information, colored in census tract maps to display lending patterns, conducted public meetings, and invited low-income neighborhood groups from Fulton and Dekalb counties to hear about the group's findings. At the community meetings, ACRA gathered information on problems community residents had encountered with area banks. Surveys were distributed to residents throughout many of Atlanta's low-income and predominately black neighborhoods.

From the beginning ACRA was an informal organization. It was not incorporated and it had no by-laws, no budget, and no staff. The Georgia Housing Coalition provided the glue and other participating organizations and individuals volunteered their time. The group's brochure listed nine organizations as founding members: Atlanta Community Housing Resource Board, Atlanta Neighborhood Housing Services, Capitol View Neighborhood Association, Capitol View Manor Community Group, Emmaus House, Georgia Housing Coalition, Interfaith, South Atlanta Land Trust, and Youth Leadership Atlanta (Atlanta Community Reinvestment Alliance n.d.). From the beginning attorneys from Atlanta Legal Aid, acting privately, also assisted the group and played leadership roles.

The ACRA coalition represented the diversity of metropolitan Atlanta's low- and moderate-income housing interests—housing development organizations, advocacy groups, social service agencies, neighborhood groups, public housing tenants, attorneys, and others. From its

Larry E. Keating, Lynn M. Brazen, and Stan F. Fitterman

inception, ACRA intentionally sought to be multiracial and involve participation from throughout metropolitan Atlanta's low-income and minority neighborhoods. When asked about his first impressions of ACRA, Bob Kennedy of the Atlanta Federal Reserve Bank responded, "I thought, finally, we have someone representing all these [low-income housing] issues" (Kennedy 1988).

The core leadership of ACRA included Craig Taylor, director of the South Atlanta Land Trust; Lynn Brazen, board member of the Georgia Housing Coalition and vice president of the Capitol View Manor Community Group; Dennis Goldstein, an attorney with Atlanta Legal Aid; Duane Stewart, chair of Neighborhood Planning Unit M; Eugene Bowens, president of Interfaith; Steve Brazen, board member of Interfaith and director of Catholic Social Services; Aaron Worthy, director of Atlanta Neighborhood Housing Services and president of Atlanta Community Housing Resource Board; and the state coordinator of the Georgia Housing Coalition—originally Joan Cates and later Ginny Montes. Each of these individuals had spent many years working in metropolitan Atlanta's low-income communities. More than a dozen other individuals played significant roles at different points in ACRA's three-year history, and several hundred individuals attended public meetings and workshops conducted by ACRA.

The alliance never developed its grass-roots participation as completely as it initially intended. It lacked the staff and resources to do the kind of organizing necessary to create and sustain participation by a large number of people. The focus of the group on CRA research and negotiations supplanted organizing and further coalition building. The leadership of ACRA also found that some other organizations, the Association of Community Organizations for Reform Now (ACORN) and African-American ecumenical and civil rights groups were reluctant to join in alliance efforts (Dedman 1987). Despite these shortcomings, ACRA's efforts did involve contact with a relatively broad cross-section of Atlanta's low-income and minority communities.

In early analyses of the major lending patterns of regulated institutions serving Fulton and Dekalb counties, ACRA showed a clear and consistent pattern of little, if any, lending in low-income and minority neighborhoods. What the group could not clearly discern, with its limited research capabilities, was whether that pattern was a function of income or race or both. All of the institutions studied made significantly fewer loans in predominately black, low-income census tracks than in predominately white, upper-income census tracks.

Armed with this information, the group requested a meeting with the Atlanta Federal Reserve Bank to discuss their findings and ask the regulators what could be done. Howard Dillon, then head of the bank's supervision and regulation functions, and two staff members met with two ACRA representatives. The meeting was a big disappointment to ACRA. Dillon blithely brushed aside ACRA's information and allegations and simply stated that he just knew that lenders would not redline. While Dillon's staff expressed some interest in ACRA's findings—and had clearly never undertaken such an analysis themselves—the message from the top was clear: ACRA could not count on any support from the Federal Reserve Bank.

Despite this response ACRA members, fortified by their own research and by conversations with CRA alliances in other cities, knew there was a problem. They began to develop an action agenda, a description of the actions they wanted local lenders to take in order to meet the credit needs of their communities. The agenda included below-market home loans with less restrictive underwriting criteria, provisions for credit counseling and referral, a commitment of funds for affordable, multifamily housing, increased marketing in minority-owned and low-income community-oriented media, a lifeline checking account, low-cost government check cashing, an expansion of the types of identification accepted to open a checking account, formation of a community development corporation, expanded minority business lending, and charitable contributions for nonprofit community development organizations. By the summer of 1986, ACRA was ready to pursue this agenda.

The First Trust Company Challenge

The group began to monitor acquisitions and mergers involving Atlanta banks, activity that would require the filing of an application with a federal regulatory agency. The alliance anticipated that the threat of a CRA protest to such an application would make the banks more responsive to its concerns. In late summer of 1986, ACRA members learned that SunTrust Bank of Florida was planning to acquire Trust Company Bank of Georgia, and ACRA requested a meeting with the president of Trust Company Bank.

173

The first meeting was held in October in a community center in south Atlanta. Members of ACRA spent a great deal of time preparing for this first meeting. Approximately a dozen representatives of various community groups attended. Trust Company was represented by Lending Officer Jim Mynatt, Public Relations Officer Willis Johnson, bank CRA Compliance Officer Jim Graham, and a senior officer from Trust Company of Georgia. Three representatives from the Federal Reserve Bank of Atlanta also attended, including William "Bill" Estes, the newly appointed head of supervision and regulation.

The meeting was conducted formally, beginning with presentations of large colored maps and detailed statistics of Trust Company's lending patterns by census tracts. Next the group presented Trust Company with a proposed community investment agreement listing actions the group wanted the bank to take to improve its lending performance in Atlanta's low-income and minority communities. The list was composed of most of the elements of the ACRA action agenda (i.e., below-market home loans with less restrictive underwriting, provisions for credit counseling and referral, etc.). Representatives of ACRA asked Trust Company to respond to the proposals at a follow-up meeting scheduled for the next week.

Trust Company's lead representative at the follow-up meeting was Wade Mitchell. He laid ACRA's proposal on the table and flatly told the ACRA representatives that Trust Company was not about to negotiate an agreement with the group. The ACRA representatives, prepared to discuss alternatives to their initial proposals, were shocked by the stonewalling response from Trust Company. In spite of the threat of a CRA challenge, Trust Company was only prepared to meet with ACRA representatives to discuss the group's concerns. They made it very clear that they would not enter into any agreement.

Over the next several weeks, ACRA representatives met with Trust Company representatives to discuss the group's concerns. Trust Company made a number of small concessions—it paid for advertisements in minority media and agreed to accept suggestions from ACRA about additional forms of identification that could be accepted to open an account. The bank participated in two or three mortgage loans made to minority families through one of the nonprofit groups involved in the leadership of ACRA. The talks seemed to be making some progress, and ACRA decided not to file a CRA complaint, based on the "good faith" negotiations that had taken place and on Trust Company's willingness to continue those discussions. The merger between Trust Company and SunTrust Bank was approved by the Federal Reserve shortly thereafter.

At this point ACRA members made a conscious decision not to involve the media. Members of the group had mixed feelings about the impact as well as the potential for media coverage. Some felt that media attention might impede the negotiation process. Others questioned whether the *Atlanta Journal/Constitution* would deal seriously with ACRA's concerns and be willing to criticize Atlanta's banking establishment. Affordable housing and community development had never received much coverage in Atlanta's news media and the coverage housing had received had led to pressure which subsequently contributed to career changes for two previous housing reporters (Celia Dugger and Susan Faludi). In the fall of 1986 there was no housing beat reporter.

The Carras Proposal

The members of ACRA knew that community development corporations (CDCs) were a relatively unfamiliar concept to the bank and that a specific CDC proposal needed to be presented. Consequently they pooled their financial resources and hired a consultant, James Carras, to help them develop a CDC proposal. Carras had worked with forming CDCs in other parts of the country and had led a workshop on CDCs in Atlanta that was attended by several ACRA members.

The Carras proposal to create the Metropolitan Atlanta Community Development Resource Center was developed out of Carras' experience and with input from ACRA on the unique needs and conditions in Atlanta. The proposal had four goals:

1. To develop affordable housing opportunities in Atlanta for low and moderate income residents in conjunction with nonprofit development organizations.
2. To provide loans, loan guarantees, grants, and technical assistance to projects that will produce stable revenues for the sponsoring community development organization and increase the value of its assets.
3. To build stronger relationships between the private sector and community development organizations and to help private lending institutions find feasible development projects of acceptable yield.

4. To encourage and support the development of "human capacity" within community development organizations in order for them to meet their development objectives through a business discipline.

(Carras 1986)

Carras formally presented his proposal to Trust Company Bank early in December 1986 at a meeting attended by representatives of Trust Company Bank, the Federal Reserve Bank of Atlanta, and ACRA.

The bank produced mixed responses to the proposal. While they acknowledged the need for such a vehicle, they were not willing to form the CDC and finance it on their own. It is unclear what was driving the bank's response at this time. Relying on its own staying power and ACRA's lack thereof is a possibility. Sufficient profitability to justify costs was a concern (Kennedy 1988). Frequent references to two failed local efforts at nonprofit development were often used to counter successful community-based development examples from Atlanta and other cities (Montes 1988). Given the politics of Georgia, it is also possible that because Carras was an "outsider" from Massachusetts his connection to the proposal put it at a disadvantage (Montes 1988). However, Trust Company did agree to present the Carras proposal to the other major Atlanta banks to see if they would consider cooperatively sponsoring the CDC. Trust Company's effort eventually proved unsuccessful.

The Federal Reserve's Bob Kennedy in retrospect believes that, because of the closed circles of Atlanta's business elite, a collaborative effort was likely to fail without the personal backing of at least some of the presidents of the largest banks (Kennedy 1988). In addition, staff of Central Atlanta Progress, a development group funded by downtown business and a leader in many of metropolitan Atlanta's business partnership efforts, expressed reservations about the concept of a community development corporation.

Trust Company Bank may have been a poor choice for the first attempt; but ACRA members had hoped that Trust Company's very profitable financial situation and its image as a community leader and good corporate citizen would make it more responsive than other institutions. They undoubtedly underestimated the extent of Trust Company's motivation to minimize their affirmative lending responsibilities. While ACRA emphasized that affirmative lending did not translate into reduced profits, Bob Kennedy of the Federal Reserve Bank of Atlanta noted,

"Trust Company is an extremely profit motivated bank. They live and die by their profit goals" (Kennedy 1988).

Although the banks refused to sponsor a CDC they did respond to one aspect of the Carras proposal and began working on the formation of a loan consortium. During the spring and summer of 1989 discussions with ACRA involved plans to form a loan consortium to provide slightly below market-rate loans with less restrictive underwriting criteria for single-family purchase, rehabilitation, or purchase/rehabilitation loans to low- and moderate-income families who could not qualify for the banks' regular lending programs. For a moment it appeared that some progress might be made.

Trust Company took the lead in developing the consortium, using its House Money program as a model. By March 1987 the bank had developed a description of the consortium that included both a single-family and a multifamily program. It envisioned a commitment of $50 million from ten financial institutions (Trust Company of Georgia 1987).

Later in the fall the institutions which Trust Company had convened to form the consortium had reduced the proposal to include only a single-family program and a commitment of $10 million. Converting the shrinking proposal to action would have to wait until the spring of 1988, when publication of Bill Dedman's articles in the "Color of Money" series generated enough publicity to prod the banks into making a commitment. The newspaper series documented discriminatory lending patterns and had a significant impact on lending in Atlanta.

Negotiations with Trust Company Continue

The alliance continued its negotiations with Trust Company. Early in 1987 Trust Company had agreed to undertake a credit needs study and had hired a private consultant to conduct the study. Members of ACRA were invited to review the study design and suggest changes. The study was completed in the spring of 1987, but ACRA and Trust Company representatives differed on their interpretation of the results, particularly as they affected the bank's decision not to offer any kind of lifeline product.

In March 1987, at the same time it was attempting to organize a lending consortium, Trust Company formally assigned a staff person to oversee and market their House Money program. House Money had been a special lending program for southside, inner-city communities with below market rates and slightly relaxed underwriting requirements. While it did not meet all of ACRA's ideals for a lending program, it was seen by ACRA as a start. House Money had been in existence since 1978 but had never made more than three to seven loans a year; ACRA pointed out that there was no point in having a program if it was not actively promoted. The bank's choice for this new responsibility was Willie Yancy, who also had responsibility for Trust Company's minority business lending. Following the "Color of Money" series, Trust Company began to promote the program, put an experienced loan officer in charge of it and made 269 loans from June 1988 through August 1991 (Trust Company Bank n.d.).

Negotiations with Georgia Federal Savings and Loan

Frustrated by slow progress with Trust Company and suspecting that other lenders had similarly poor lending records, ACRA members began in early 1987 to consider approaching another institution. Their choice was Georgia Federal.

Georgia Federal was chosen for several reasons: initial studies had shown a discriminatory lending pattern; it was a savings and loan and therefore required to place with more emphasis on home mortgages than a commercial bank; and it was regulated by the Federal Home Loan Bank Board rather than the Federal Reserve. At the community meetings held by ACRA, many individuals and organizations indicated that they held accounts at Georgia Federal or had lending experience with Georgia Federal, giving that savings and loan some standing in low-income communities. In addition, Georgia Federal had just undergone significant changes in upper management as a result of new ownership. Because of these features, ACRA members decided that they would try initiating discussions with Georgia Federal without the threat of a CRA challenge.

The first meeting with Georgia Federal took place in August 1987. From the beginning negotiations with Georgia Federal contrasted favorably with ACRA's experience with Trust Company. Instead of the stonewall that ACRA encountered with Trust Company, the Georgia Federal representatives, headed by Ed Asbury, listened and looked for ways to respond to ACRA's requests—requests similar to those presented to Trust Company. Within a couple of months Georgia Federal had offered an adjustable-rate mortgage with low closing costs and no points in certain lower-income neighborhoods, developed a low-cost checking account, cut the price of money orders at some of its inner city branches, and offered loan counseling at its central city branches.

The Second Trust Company Challenge

Although Trust Company and ACRA continued to meet, by fall 1987 it was clear that very little progress was being made. Then SunTrust Bank applied to the Federal Reserve for permission to acquire SunTrust Bank-Card. This time ACRA decided to issue a formal challenge. The *Atlanta Journal/Constitution* carried a small one-paragraph article about the challenge in the business section of the paper (Dedman 1987). It was the first coverage of CRA issues provided by the paper and went largely unnoticed by the reading public. A few days later ACRA called a press conference in front of Trust Company's downtown headquarters. No one attended except representatives of ACRA and Trust Company. The local media had not yet recognized the significance of the redlining issue.

At ACRA's request, the Federal Reserve Bank agreed to host a meeting between Trust Company and ACRA. After ACRA members presented their concerns and Trust Company representatives stated their response, Bill Estes of the Federal Reserve expressed his pleasure that there was open dialogue between the parties. Yet there was no intervention by the Federal Reserve to encourage the bank to respond to ACRA's concerns. SunTrust's application was approved shortly afterwards and ACRA's subsequent appeals to the board of governors were to no avail. Although discussions with Trust Company continued into the early months of 1988, no significant action was taken by the institution until the publication of the "Color of Money" series in May.

The Waning of ACRA

Following the approval of the SunTrust acquisition, ACRA began to dissolve as an organization. This was partially a result of the limited progress that ACRA members experienced in their negotiations with Trust Company and the lack of progress toward forming a loan consortium. It was also a result of decisions by the Georgia Housing Coalition.

Early in 1988 the Georgia Housing Coalition decided to continue its CRA research and challenge efforts under its own name. The coalition had provided the staff for ACRA, but the board of directors of the coalition felt it had too little control over ACRA decision-making. At the time of the dissolution other coalition members who had been active in ACRA

179

decided to focus their energies on the formation of a metro-wide community development corporation.

Georgia Housing Coalition members and a few others obtained assistance from the Fulton County Department of Planning and Economic Development in forming the proposed CDC. The new CDC was patterned after the Carras proposal to provide technical assistance and lending services. The proposal eventually evolved into an organization called the Metropolitan Atlanta Community Development Corporation. Although the organization was created and it garnered a commitment for some financial support, it became trapped in the middle of mayoral politics in the summer of 1989 and never got off the ground. (Its initial funding had come from the Fulton County Commission, from whence Chairman Michael Lomax was launching a mayoral bid. City politicians, not wanting to offend the poll-leading Maynard Jackson campaign and conscious of Jackson supporter Walt Huntley's [head of the Atlanta Economic Development Corporation] opposition to the CDC proposal, decided not to fund the CDC, thus leaving the metropolitan CDC without city participation.)

THE "COLOR OF MONEY" AND A MORE CONCILIATORY APPROACH BY ATLANTA LENDERS

At the same time ACRA was dissolving into its constituent organizations and the Georgia Housing Coalition was pushing further CRA research, the Atlanta anti-redlining effort was receiving an infusion of new resources. Bill Dedman, an investigative reporter hired by then *Journal/Constitution* editor Bill Kovachs, began to research CRA activities for the newspaper. Simultaneously, Stan Fitterman, a graduate student at the Graduate Program in City Planning at the Georgia Institute of Technology and a member of ACRA, decided to research mortgage loan flows for his master's degree thesis. In addition to Dedman and Fitterman, Calvin Bradford, then a senior fellow at the Hubert Humphrey Institute of Public Affairs, and Charles Finn, a research associate at the Humphrey Institute, provided input on the development of the methodology and the technical aspects of data manipulation and then periodically reviewed the results. In effect, the Dedman-Fitterman combination provided the CRA effort with a research staff and a direct link to the media.

The research methodology compared the number of loans per census tract—directly available from HMDA statements—with socio-economic data for each census tract to determine whether something other than the creditworthiness of borrowers was driving the availability of credit.

As Dedman was putting the series together he sought to involve the two men who were the likely candidates for the 1989 mayor's race—Michael Lomax and Maynard Jackson. Lomax was chair of the Fulton County Commission and had begun making electoral moves. Jackson, who was Atlanta's first African-American mayor (1973–81) and who had served for the legal limit of two consecutive terms, had returned to Atlanta from his Chicago bond lawyer's business and was beginning to make the circuit of church and civic organization appearances.

Their responses to the pending publicity were contrasting opposites. Lomax who ultimately ran with significant white power-broker backing, agreed to participate in the human interest side of the developing story, recounting his own personal difficulties in securing a mortgage loan for his Adams Park home in southwest Atlanta. Jackson, who as Atlanta's first black mayor had earlier broken some of the cozy ties between City Hall and the white business elite and who thereby had developed a reputation for antagonism toward that elite, declined to participate in prepublication series development.

A brief interruption of the relatively quiet scene produced by the fading away of ACRA and the unpublicized research activities of Dedman and Fitterman occurred just before Christmas when ACORN staged a protest and held a red ribbon across the front doors of Georgia Federal's main office to draw attention to the group's claims that the institution was redlining Atlanta's inner-city neighborhoods. The ACORN action made the local news and was the first redlining story written by Dedman (Dedman 1987). The protest by ACORN drew the ire of the ACRA group, since ACRA invited ACORN to join in the alliance and felt that Georgia Federal had been responsive to CRA negotiations.

The "Color of Money" series was originally scheduled to run in December 1987, but completing the analysis extended into early 1988. The remnant shell of ACRA maintained negotiations regarding establishment of a loan consortium. Because ACRA and most of the housing advocacy community were aware of the results of the research, because significant public pressure was anticipated when the series was published, and also because ACRA had effectively dissolved, former coalition members were reduced to waiting until the series generated a public outcry.

As the series underwent a succession of deadline postponements tension rose. In March 1988 the financial institutions withdrew the $10 million offer for a mortgage consortium. April and spring brought increasing worries. Had the previously ubiquitous white power structure squashed the story? Dedman kept saying "no"; there was one small technical reason for the delay and then there was another technical reason for the delay, but in a town where the two previous housing reporters had been effectively pink-slipped, activists worried.

On Sunday, May Day, 1988, the series broke—filling four of the five front-page columns, announcing "Atlanta blacks losing in home loans scramble" and featuring Fulton's Michael Lomax, "If I can't get a loan, what black person can" (Dedman 1988a).

The evidence on which the series was based was incontestable—every home purchase loan and home improvement loan made by every bank and savings and loan in metropolitan Atlanta between 1981 and 1986 had been analyzed. The researchers had categorized 109,000 loans by the race and income of the area in which they were made. Comparing middle-income black neighborhoods with middle-income white neighborhoods, the ratios of mortgage loans per 100 owner-occupied structures in white and black neighborhoods varied from a low of 2.2 (i.e., there were 2.2 loans per 100 owner-occupied structures in middle-income white neighborhoods for every loan per 100 owner-occupied structures in middle-income black neighborhoods) in 1982 to a high of 6.0 in 1986 and 5.9 in 1983 (Fitterman 1988).

The research further documented that most savings and loans had no offices in black areas, that offices taking home loan applications were almost all located in white areas and that demand for mortgage loans in black areas, while less than demand in white areas, was not low enough to explain the discrepancy in loan ratios (Fitterman 1988).

Initial reaction from the banking community was defensive. "It's a myth that banks have a map with a red line on it," said Jim Graham, vice president of SunTrust, the parent of Trust Company (Dedman 1988a). "Much of the housing in predominantly black areas is substandard, requiring rehabilitation to qualify for mortgage lending," said Willis Johnson, another spokesman for Trust Company (Dedman 1988a).

By Monday, reaction in the banking community was beginning to turn from defensive denial to conciliation. "I think anytime that there's a perception of a problem, that there must be a problem. I think obviously there's a perception of a problem, and we need to address it," said Lee Sessions, executive vice president of Citizens and Southern (C & S) Bank (Dedman 1988d).

Some state and local politicians were quick to enter the fray, while others, perhaps mindful of the business/black electoral coalition's capacity for retribution, were uncharacteristically silent or conciliatory. City Council President Marvin Arrington led a drive in the city council to form an "action committee" of politicians, bankers, and citizens to investigate lending practices. "Hard recommendations" were sought by Arrington in twenty days (Dedman 1988d). The first metro Atlanta local fair housing law—which had worked its way up to the Fulton County Commission the week before—was passed by the commissioners on Thursday (Hendricks 1988).

Mayor Andrew Young oscillated between his governing coalition partners and the conclusions to the research. "I would hate to think we've slipped. It's the kind of thing you want to hope we've moved beyond. If there is serious redlining, it's not good for the city," he said. Young went on to say that he hoped that city regulation would not be necessary and that the banks had responded earlier to his personal pleas for loans to Underground Atlanta and the Democratic National Convention (both of which were business elite/city government projects) (Dedman 1988c).

Commissioner Lomax began to beat a retreat back toward his eventual mayoral campaign financial backers. On the "Today" television show he said, "I'm not very concerned about the fact that we've had the problem [in the past]. I'll really be judging our community on how we respond to it in the future." Later he said in a response to Dedman's query regarding linked deposits, "I've never encouraged that in Fulton County. My preference would be to raise the issue with the banks in a positive way" (Dedman 1988b).

Maynard Jackson, also responding to a linked deposits query by Dedman, was less conciliatory but conciliatory nonetheless:"I like to try to negotiate things first. You're talking about conservative institutions. That's not going to change. There are probably banks that are going to be more responsive than others; we have to find those institutions and work with them, organize their efforts. To whatever extent we can legally and economically leverage city money, I'm willing to consider that" (Dedman 1988c)

The response from the mayor, candidates for mayor, a city council president, and public relations departments was a prelude to the response that had been sought for two and one-half years. Now that discriminatory practices had been incontestably documented and now that the public was aware of the extent and longevity of redlining, what moves would the banks make to mollify political and public opinion?

The dissolution of ACRA, the nearly autonomous conduct of the research on lending patterns by the newspaper and academics, the lack of an organized response by civil rights groups, and Atlanta political traditions that accord the business elite most of the stage had left the financial institutions with no one to negotiate with but themselves. Thirteen days after the initial article in the "Color of Money" series, the largest banks announced a $65 million program for mortgage and home purchase loans focused on the city's black southside. In addition, the banks pledged to "keep Southside branches open on Saturdays, accept loan applications there, solicit more real estate agents in black and integrated areas, begin offering government-backed loan programs, and advertise on media outlets with large black audiences" (Dedman 1988e).

The $65 million commitment was composed of a $20 million pool generated by nine banks and three separate commitments of $25 million from C & S, $10 million from First Atlanta Bank, and $10 million from Trust Company (Dedman 1988e). Yet, bellying up to the bar was not, the banks pointedly emphasized, an admission of guilt. This convoluted logic was most clearly expressed by Bill Van Landingham, president of C & S, who said, "No, it's not an admission of any racism. I think it was a recognition of what was actually happening in the lending" (Dedman 1988e). Slightly more coherent but equally misleading was the comment by First Atlanta President Raymond Riddle, "This economic issue has been made to appear that it is a racial issue and the story has gone all over the nation with the implication that this form of discrimination is taking place in Atlanta" (Dedman 1988e).

Signaling the official end to this episode, the newspaper's lead editorial on May 16 opened with admonitions to civil rights groups and churches to chill out: "Hold the tough talk, NAACP. Cancel your boycott, Concerned Black Clergy. Atlanta banks and savings and loans know how to make friends and keep friends. With money. Lots of it." While not saying that the banks' denials were denials, the editorial went on to point out that, against the $765 million in black bank deposits, the $65 million pledge was a beginning and not a complete solution (Editors, *Atlanta Journal/Constitution* 1988).

The series had belatedly mobilized segments of Atlanta's black community. Groups like the Southern Christian Leadership Conference (SCLC) and Concerned Black Clergy, who had declined to play a significant role in ACRA's early organizing efforts, led the black community's response to the articles. Reverend Joseph Lowery, president of the SCLC, convened the major black church and community leadership to develop a "Black Empowerment Campaign." The group, calling itself the Coalition for Economic Justice, organized a citywide "bank-in" by preachers on July 5 to move deposits from Atlanta's major white-owned lending institutions and into two small, minority-owned institutions. While this effort gained some media exposure, the impact of the gesture had relatively little effect on the major lenders.

The Empire Real Estate Board and the local chapter of the professional organization of black realtists called for more loans to black families and businesses and more bank outreach to black real estate brokers. The professional organization of black real estate appraisers called for equal treatment and a larger share of the banks' appraisal business. For the most part, lenders were responsive to these demands and expanded their contacts with the black professional realtists and appraisers, but without making specific commitments to any individuals or groups.

A member of the Empire Real Estate Board was appointed to the Atlanta Mortgage Consortium advisory group, Reverend Lowery played a leadership role in later discussions with C & S Bank as it merged with Sovran, and other black leaders were consulted by local lenders as part of the lenders' community outreach efforts. Still, the black community's opportunity to capitalize on the momentum of the articles was largely lost. Because all of the organizing efforts lagged behind the "official" end of the episode and because no organization was able to commit the staff time necessary to sustain the initial community interest, within a few months the issue had moved to the back burner.

The majority of the efforts by the black community focused on the issue of racial discrimination, not affordable housing and economic development. Many of the individuals and organizations that had been active in ACRA supported the efforts of the SCLC and other black groups, but the issue of affordable housing and development of lower income neighborhoods was usually a secondary agenda for the African-American organizations whose origins had been, and remained, in civil rights. As a result, no new long-term relationship developed between the groups active in ACRA and the civil rights groups.

As with all events political, what did not happen is as important as what did happen. The committee appointed by Council President Arrington disappeared for nearly a year after holding an initial series of hearings and subdividing itself into six subcommittees. Prodding from the newspaper and threatened resignations from committee members led to the publication of a quickly assembled and unendorsed twenty-seven-page summary of the subcommittee recommendations in spring 1989. Reflecting both the more complex and extensive array of problems faced by low-income and minority communities and the attraction of other interest groups (primarily commercial and development interests) to a previously "hot" issue, the subcommittee recommendations covered a broad array of possible actions that could help minority businesses and communities.

The homeownership subcommittee gently rattled the city's sabre by suggesting shifting city deposits to financial institutions that followed the recommendations. By now the compilation of subcommittee recommendations was a dead issue as there was no subsequent political call for them to be implemented. The council president released the report and both mayoral candidates in the summer 1989 campaign sidestepped the issue.

THE ATLANTA MORTGAGE CONSORTIUM AND FURTHER NEGOTIATIONS

The enduring response has been the mortgage loan pool, the Atlanta Mortgage Consortium (AMC). The consortium established an advisory board with representation from several of Atlanta's political jurisdictions, low-income housing groups, and black community groups. Several of the individual banks established similar advisory groups.

The $20 million pool established by AMC offered fixed-rate mortgages at 9.25 percent interest, slightly below then-current rates. The single-family, owner-occupied loans were capped at $60,000, could go up to 97 percent of appraised value, did not require private mortgage insurance, had no loan origination fees, had no discount points, had lower closing costs tied to direct out-of-pocket expenses, required only a $50 nonrefundable application fee—which was subsequently applied to closing costs for a successful application—and permitted a 35 percent ratio of mortgage payment to income and a 50 percent ratio of total debt to income.

During the first fourteen months of operation, the consortium dispersed $10 million to 224 successful applicants, an average of $44,640 per loan. There were no defaults during this time period and only two loans were over thirty days in arrears. More applications were rejected (227) than were accepted (221). Other than information provided by Trust Company's House Money program, no data were available from individual banks regarding the extent and characteristics of the mortgages funded by the individual pledges (Murff 1990).

Between late July 1989, when a follow-up article appeared in the *Atlanta Journal/Constitution*, and October 1989 the consortium dispersed the remaining $10 million to 184 applicants (an average loan value of $54,350), and in November 1989 the consortium established a second pool of $24 million. During the first eight months of the Phase Two program, 71 loans totaling $3 million (an average of $42,240) were made. Phase Two terms were stiffer—the $50 nonrefundable application fee was increased to $250 and no longer was applied to closing costs, and the ratio of mortgage payments and other monthly obligations to gross income was reduced to 42 percent from an earlier 50 percent (Murff 1990).

In 1989 and 1990 the consortium made 531 loans to a population which was 63.7 percent African American, 58.2 percent female-headed households and 71.6 percent unmarried. Median incomes were approximately $22,480 and median purchase prices were $47,730. Median total housing expenses increased from prepurchase $350 per month to $486 per month. A little over $25 million in loans was disbursed.

The consortium's advisory board represented different segments of the community and put pressure on the AMC board to provide credit counseling and homebuyer education to AMC borrowers, to expand the outreach efforts for the program, and to increase the size of the mortgage pool. Homebuyer education was eventually added as part of the second phase of the AMC program and has since been credited with increasing

the number of eligible borrowers and reducing the consortium delinquency rate. To date the effectiveness of the mortgage pool has not been
increased by the establishment of a secondary market for the loans.

Advisory board members initially pressed for an elimination of
the geographic targeting of the AMC program, encouraging AMC to make
loans to eligible individuals regardless of the location of the housing. The
AMC board, however, was determined to limit the loans to low-income
census tracts. Eventually the board agreed to expand the target areas to
include low-income areas within higher income census tracts.

It is important to note that there was not unanimity among the
advisory board members on every issue. Some board members wanted to
raise the income and mortgage limits in order to address the needs of
more middle-income black homebuyers seeking to finance move-up
homes. Some board members felt the debt ratios should be lowered while
other wanted them to remain high. A few wanted the loans to remain
geographically targeted while others wanted lower-income families to
have a full range of choice of neighborhoods in which they could purchase a home and still qualify for an AMC mortgage.

The Federal Reserve has maintained some research oversight on
AMC and it has focused on the debt ratios. Ron Zimmerman, vice president of the Federal Reserve Bank of Atlanta has been highly critical of
the Atlanta Mortgage Consortium from the outset, particularly the high
total debt ratios allowed.

> The review of the AMC loans has dramatically illustrated
> the detrimental effects that high consumer debt can have
> on a loan applicant's home purchasing power regardless
> of the level of gross income and the difficulties high con-
> sumer debt can create for the lenders seeking to serve the
> applicant's credit needs. Moreover, it is apparent that,
> even if the 28 percent of gross income permitted for
> housing expense under the conventional standards is
> available, an applicant's income may be too low for this
> percentage of income to support the purchase of decent
> housing in the local market area.
>
> (Zimmerman 1990)

Zimmerman also notes that the new Home Mortgage Disclosure Act reporting requirements do not include information on the level of con-

sumer debt, making it difficult to analyze the actual effect upon loan declinations and loan defaults.

From the outset many lenders, some ACRA members, and the Federal Reserve expressed concern that AMC's less restrictive underwriting would result in a high delinquency rate. In addition, ACRA members noted that delinquencies probably would have been higher without the homebuyer education and counseling programs they had recommended. In fact, over AMC's three-year history the overall delinquency rate has been consistently higher than the industry average. The industry average was 5.28 percent in the second quarter of 1991, but AMC's overall delinquency rate was 12.34 percent at the end of October 1991.

However, two critical features of the AMC program must be considered when comparing the program's delinquency rate with the rest of the industry. First, the AMC portfolio is not directly comparable to an industry average that is composed of a broad range of loan types and borrower incomes. A more accurate comparison could be made if the delinquency rate for loans made to lower-income borrowers by all institutions were compared to AMC's delinquency rate.

Second, the delinquency rate for AMC loans made under the second phase is significantly lower than under the first phase. While AMC's overall delinquency rate was 12.34 percent at the end of October 1991, Phase One loans had a delinquency rate of 15.31 percent and the Phase Two rate was only 7.38 percent. Supporters of AMC point to the tighter underwriting requirements of the Phase Two program and more importantly to the required homebuyer education program implemented in Phase Two but not provided in Phase One.

Although the ACRA organization was no longer in existence, many of ACRA's member organizations still worked together through the Georgia Housing Coalition and through informal means. Dennis Goldstein, with Atlanta Legal Aid, continued to monitor lending by Trust company and Georgia Federal and continued to investigate the lending activity of other Atlanta institutions.

In the fall of 1989, the groups came back together around the proposed merger of C & S Bank and Sovran Bank. Representatives from the Georgia Housing Coalition, Interfaith, SCLC, and Atlanta Legal Aid met with William "Bill" Van Landingham, president of C & S, Lee Sessions, head of the Atlanta C & S, and other staff to discuss their concerns about the proposed merger and about C & S's lending policies. The discussions were cordial but generally unproductive. In January 1990 the groups contacted the Federal Reserve Bank of Atlanta and filed formal challenges to the merger. A change in leadership at the *Atlanta Journal/ Constitution* meant that the paper no longer carried the CRA banner. The only significant press coverage the challenge received was in *Georgia Trend*, a relatively small circulation business magazine (Thiel 1990). Once again, the Federal Reserve Bank approved the merger, with little comment on the concerns raised by community groups.

The *Atlanta Journal/Constitution* underwent several changes in the year following the publication of the Pulitzer Prize–winning series. Editor Bill Kovachs resigned ostensibly in a dispute regarding control of the Washington bureau, but many observers thought the issues were deeper. Bill Dedman moved on to the *Washington Post* within a few weeks of Kovachs' resignation. Dedman was replaced by Amy Wallace on the housing beat. Wallace learned her beat, published the July 1989 evaluation of the consortium's performance, and had begun to participate in a research update when she moved on to the San Diego bureau of the *Los Angeles Times* in August 1989.

By the time Wallace left the newspaper, new management had shifted the substantive content of the papers to an "infotainment," *USA Today* format. Wallace was not replaced on the housing beat—instead the function was dispersed among several younger reporters whose primary responsibilities lay in other areas.

One of the changes instituted by Kovachs which lingered beyond his, Dedman's, and Wallace's departure was the research unit. A preliminary update of the research covering calendar year 1988 was completed by Michele Murff, a graduate student in city planning at the Georgia Institute of Technology, and the newspaper's research unit in October 1989.

The newspaper, believing that the aggregate ratio of white to black loans had declined into the 4.0–4.5 range, explained that the reason they were not going to publish an update was that "the banks had not had enough time to respond" (Morris 1989). Whether the decision was based on the change in the newspaper's content and focus, or on the pressure financial institutions had put on the paper, or on the convergence of economic and political power in Atlanta, or on the stated reason, the update was not published.

ACCOMPLISHMENTS AND REMAINING CHALLENGES

Murff's research was less damaging than the newspaper had thought. The aggregate ratio for the seventeen most active institutions (not directly comparable with the previously discussed aggregate ratio for all financial institutions) for lower-, moderate-, middle- and higher-income households had declined to 2.5. Nine of the fifteen white-owned banks improved their individual performances, five institutions had higher ratios, and one was unchanged. Of the six largest mortgage originators (over 1,000 mortgages per year and over 80 percent of the mortgages financed by the seventeen institutions), four improved, one was unchanged, and one declined. The two most politically active banks, Trust Company and C & S, both improved. Nevertheless the three largest mortgage originators, in spite of their improvement, still compiled ratios of 8.1, 3.1 and 3.0 (Murff 1990)

Interpretation of the results is confounded by the lack of a complete picture of mortgage loan flows. It appears that recessionary housing markets in 1982 and in 1988 produced similar ratios (for all financial institutions the 1982 ratio was 2.2; in 1988 the ratio was 2.5 for the seventeen largest, regulated originators). An untested hypothesis is that conditions in slow markets drain proportionately more white consumers to unregulated lenders. Partial support for this line of inquiry is provided by the fact that there was a 30 percent decrease in loans to white households between 1986 and 1988. Nevertheless, the 74 percent increase in loans to black census tracts in 1988, when coupled with the apparent decline in the aggregate ratio and the improved records compiled by a majority of the institutions, imply that the regulated segment of the mortgage market has become less discriminatory.

There has been change in Atlanta's lending community since ACRA had its first meeting with Trust Company Bank in 1986. Several of ACRA's early concerns have been addressed, though some have not. More loans have been made in Atlanta's lower income neighborhoods, but a significant disparity between lending in white and black neighborhoods remains.

In the more than three years since the "Color of Money" was published, and in a manner similar to events in Detroit, relationships and dialogue between Atlanta's white bankers and the city's housing

Larry E. Keating, Lynn M. Brazen, and Stan F. Fitterman

groups and minority groups have expanded. Several nonprofit housing groups have obtained loans for their projects and charitable contributions from Atlanta lenders. The Atlanta Mortgage Consortium continues to offer below-market-rate loans with more lenient underwriting. The consortium has taken some steps to finance a limited number of multifamily deals and is cautiously developing a formal multifamily lending program. The AMC and many individual financial institutions have aggressively undertaken homebuyer education programs to prepare low-income and minority families for homeownership. The fair housing law passed by Fulton County remains on the books, but fair housing enforcement is severely underfunded.

Yet much has stayed the same. The senior management and boards of directors of the major Atlanta banks remain solidly white. Minority borrowers continue to experience declinations for loans at a rate much higher than that of white borrowers (Federal Reserve 1991). Sources of funding for rental housing—the only real option for most very-low-income families—remains nearly nonexistent. The City of Atlanta and Fulton County have put only negligible funds into affordable housing and pay lip service to the needs. The local media refuses to publish the latest research, instead offering a few sentimental human interest stories on housing matters, and rarely prints the terms "CRA" and "redlining."

Pressure from ACRA and the publicity surrounding the "Color of Money" series helped to produce two needed reforms—the mortgage consortium and the fair housing law—in an inequitable and discriminatory system. The reforms appear to have reduced the extent of discriminatory practices, but the underlying problems have not been affected substantially. Indeed, the momentum for change has been supplanted by a return to the status quo.

References

Atlanta Community Reinvestment Alliance. N.d. "Atlanta Community Reinvestment Alliance Brochure." Atlanta: ACRA.
Carras, James A. 1986."A Proposal to Create the Atlanta Community Development Resource Center." Atlanta. P. 9.
Dedman, Bill. 1987. "2 Citizen Groups Clash on Bank's Loan Policies." Atlanta Journal/ Constitution, Dec. 19.
———. 1988a. "Atlanta Blacks Losing in Home Loans Scramble" and "Fulton's Michael Lomax, 'If I Can't Get a Loan, What Black Person Can?'" Atlanta Journal/Constitution, May 1.

————. 1988b. "Banks Need 'Color-Blind' Policies to Uphold City's Image." *Atlanta Journal/Constitution*, May 3.

————. 1988c. "City Hall Clout Could Sweeten Home-Loan Pot." *Atlanta Journal/Constitution*, May 4.

————. 1988d. "Panel Appointed to Probe Banks' Lending Practices." *Atlanta Journal/Constitution*, May 5.

————. 1988e. "Banks to Lend $65 Million at Low Interest." *Atlanta Journal/Constitution*, May 13.

Editors. 1988. "Banks Act Swiftly to Close Lending Gap in Black Areas." *Atlanta Journal/Constitution*, May 16.

Federal Reserve. 1991. Bank Study (Oct. 21). Atlanta, Georgia.

Fitterman, Stan F. 1988. "Mortgage Redlining in Metropolitan Atlanta." Master's thesis, Graduate Program in City Planning, Georgia Institute of Technology, Atlanta. Pp. 23–27.

Hendricks, Gary. 1988. "Fulton Approves Fair Housing Law." *Atlanta Journal/Constitution*, May 5.

Kennedy, Robert. 1988. Interview with Robert Kennedy, Federal Reserve Bank of Atlanta, Feb. 19. Atlanta.

Montes, Virginia. 1988. Interview with Virginia Montes, Georgia Housing Coalition, Feb. 29. Atlanta.

Morris, Dwight. 1989. Interview with Dwight Morris, *Atlanta Journal/Constitution*, Oct. 3. Atlanta.

Murff, Michele. 1990. "Mortgage Redlining in Metropolitan Atlanta: An Update." Master's thesis, Graduate Program in City Planning, Georgia Institute of Technology, Atlanta. Pp. 8–10.

Thiel, Paul. 1990. "Holding up a Big Bank Deal." *Georgia Trend* (June), 12–18.

Trust Company Bank. N.d. "Specific Examples of Trust Company's Community Development Activities." Atlanta: Unpublished.

Trust Company of Georgia. 1987. "Proposal for Financial Institution Consortium for Inner City Financing." March. Atlanta: Unpublished.

Zimmerman, Ronald. 1990. "Lessons Learned from the Atlanta Mortgage Consortium." Atlanta: Federal Reserve Bank.

CALIFORNIA:
LESSONS FROM STATEWIDE
ADVOCACY, LOCAL GOVERNMENT,
AND PRIVATE INDUSTRY
INITIATIVES

THE HISTORY OF REINVESTMENT ADVOCACY and programmatic response in California derives from diverse antecedents rooted in the late 1970s.[1] These early efforts included separate but roughly parallel initiatives by public sector, advocacy, and industry groups. By the late 1980s a state-wide coalition of advocacy, consultant, and technical assistance organizations, in conjunction with representatives of California local governments, had negotiated community lending commitments from large and small lenders statewide totaling more than $350 million. By 1990, the success of these community lending commitments negotiated by a state-wide coalition, combined with a resurgent awareness among regulators, lenders and elected officials of the harmful effects of discriminatory lending practices on local and neighborhood economies, had produced an array of responses reminiscent of the early 1980s. These responses include industry initiatives, city programs, and continued monitoring of community lending agreements by an evermore sophisticated core of community development practitioners and reinvestment advocates. In 1991, three major California banks—Bank of America, Security Pacific and Wells Fargo—had made ten-year broad commitments to "community lending" exceeding $10 billion.

This chapter reviews the history and achievement of the last decade of community reinvestment activism in California. It describes early, disjointed efforts, the emergence of a statewide advocacy coalition and the resultant local and statewide lending initiatives underway in 1992. This chapter concludes with observations on the lessons of the last twelve years, a suggested statewide community reinvestment agenda, and strategies to realize that agenda.

1978–1981: A CHECKERED START

Early reinvestment efforts in California were spawned by several sectors responding to both statewide and local concerns. One initiative, the Savings Association Mortgage Company (SAMCO), was a product of collaboration between the Federal Home Loan Bank of San Francisco and a consortium of savings and loan associations statewide. The SAMCO initiative used low-cost loan advances from the Community Investment Fund (CIF) of the San Francisco Federal Home Loan Bank to provide permanent financing to affordable, multifamily housing projects. A second effort entailed a series of legal challenges by the Legal Aid Society of Alameda County alleging discriminatory mortgage lending practices in that county, centered around Oakland, California. The Legal Aid Society of Alameda County challenges resulted in several early lender agreements. A third initiative, the San Diego City/County Community Reinvestment Task Force, was an early joint public and private sector effort to monitor mortgage lending within that county.

Savings Association Mortgage Company

Eleven savings and loan associations initiated the Savings Association Mortgage Company in 1971 to assist in the creation and financing of affordable housing. SAMCO is now a statewide organization with eighty-nine members, including five banks that were admitted as members in 1990. Fifty of its members are stockholders in SAMCO.

SAMCO initially focused most of its lending activities on the single-family mortgage market for inner-city areas within the San Francisco Bay Area's nine counties. From 1971 through 1975, brokers originated mortgage loans, warehoused them into approximately $2 million pools, and then sold them to stockholders in percentage blocks. Under this program SAMCO created twenty-one mortgage pools totaling $30 million.

From 1976 through 1979, SAMCO itself originated single-family loans in five pools totaling $20 million.

Beginning in 1980, SAMCO shifted its focus away from single-family loan pools to permanent financing for government-assisted programs and other housing project financing. SAMCO offers permanent thirty-year adjustable rate loans at .75 to 1.5 percent below market rates, using Community Investment Fund advances from the Federal Home Loan Bank. The loans can adjust every ten years with a 4 percent cap over the life of the mortgage. About half of its loans go to nonprofit housing corporations. The remainder go to private developers.

Each individual loan application is reviewed by the SAMCO Board of Directors, which meets monthly. Once approved by the board, the loan is offered for participation purchase to member institutions. After the loan is purchased, a commitment letter is issued to the developer. SAMCO staff then process the loan and service it on behalf of the pool participants. SAMCO is self-supporting based on its loan activities.

SAMCO's lending has increased during recent years from $25 million in permanent financing in 1988 to $38 million in 1989 and over $45 million in 1990. SAMCO currently has $90 million in loans on the books, equivalent to over 4,500 housing units. Over its life, SAMCO has lent more than $200 million in loan funds, facilitating the production of over 7,000 units. There have been very few delinquencies: less than one-tenth of 1 percent versus an average industry standard of 2 to 5 percent.

Early Challenges and Agreements
by the Legal Aid Society of Alameda County

The Legal Aid Society of Alameda County, in coalition with a number of community organizations in the Oakland and the surrounding East Bay Area, filed several early challenges against northern California thrifts alleging discriminatory home lending practices. These early challenges resulted in mixed outcomes and are briefly reviewed below.

In 1978, American Savings and Loan Association (American) sought to open a branch office in Oakland. The Legal Aid Society of Alameda County filed four administrative complaints challenging countywide discriminatory lending practices by American on behalf of United Neighbors in Action, an Oakland-based community group, as well as neighborhood residents who had been denied loans by American. These complaints were among the first actions of this kind nationwide.

The complaints were filed before four regulatory agencies: Federal Home Loan Bank Board, U.S. Department of Housing and Urban Development, California Business and Transportation Agency, and California Fair Employment Practices Commission.

The complaints alleged that American's lending practices violated numerous state and federal laws, including the Community Reinvestment Act of 1977, by denying loans due to geographical location of the property, racial composition of the neighborhood, and race of the applicant.

The complaints detailed discriminatory experiences of six complainants who were denied loans by American and provided statistics which documented American's redlining practices. They also demonstrated American's poor performance in comparison to the five other savings and loan institutions in Alameda County. The challenges noted discriminatory lending patterns in census tracts with 45 percent or more black and Spanish-surnamed populations. American's record in these areas was noted to be declining in contrast to the other thrifts.

United Neighbors in Action, which performed the research, said, "American's lending patterns consistently are among the worst of all savings and loan associations. Community groups in Los Angeles and San Diego will tell you the same thing" (Legal Aid Society of Alameda County, 1978).

The complaints sought relief from each of the four government agencies, specifically requesting that:

1. American be ordered to cease its unlawful redlining practices;
2. American institute lending programs to rectify past and ongoing harms caused by this unlawful practice;
3. Appropriate remedies and sanctions be ordered;
4. The State not deposit Treasury funds in American and disallow any branching and mergers of American offices unless and until American fully rectifies its illegal practices.

Mark Taper, president of American, agreed to make up deficiencies in Alameda County in a settlement under the seal of the court. The suit was a private agreement, not subject to public review, and included single-family home lending mortgage purchase. Steve Ronfeldt, attorney with the Legal Aid Society, called it "a good agreement," acknowledging

David Paul Rosen

that keeping it private was undesirable, but the only way American executives would agree to the settlement.

Also in 1978, the Legal Aid Society of Alameda County, together with the ad hoc Committee for Community Reinvestment in Oakland, filed a complaint against Northern California Savings and Loan Association (Northern California). The complaint documented a consistent low-lending volume to low- and moderate-income areas and census tracks in Oakland and Alameda County. From the period 1974 to 1978, the Legal Aid Society and the committee documented that Northern California's lending rate to these neighborhoods averaged half the industry rate statewide and that the S & L consistently ranked among the worst lenders in the state. Complainants requested that the State Department of Savings and Loan undertake an immediate investigation of Northern California's lending practices and that the department suspend any decision on Northern California's branching application pending resolution of the investigation, and completion of an administrative hearing.

As a result of the complaint, Northern California agreed to finance $3.5 million in home rehabilitation loans to mortgage deficient neighborhoods within the city of Oakland at low interest rates. Eligibility for the program was limited to persons whose family income did not exceed 120 percent of the area median income, with priority given to applicants whose family income was below the median level. Additionally, Northern California agreed to offer aggregate financing of $3.5 million to qualified borrowers under the Department of Housing and Urban Development (HUD) Section 8 Moderate Rehabilitation Loan Program, in cooperation with the Oakland Housing Authority. Preference was to be given to smaller property owners and minority developers with a demonstrated expertise in the construction and rehabilitation of residential properties. Federal Housing Administration (FHA) and Veterans Administration (VA) family home loans were to be offered to Oakland residents, subject to "the availability of funds."

Additionally, Northern California agreed to a marketing program which would solicit loan applications from Oakland residents in mortgage deficient neighborhoods. Finally, subject to State approvals, Northern California was to establish a service office in West Oakland.

In 1980, the Legal Aid Society of Alameda County, representing a broad coalition of eleven community groups, filed an administrative complaint seeking enforcement of the fair lending laws and objecting to Fidelity Savings and Loan Association's applications for two branch offices and a relocation of an existing office. The complainants, including the Committee for Community Reinvestment in Oakland, National Urban Coalition, Asian Law Caucus, and Oakland Better Housing, first tried to negotiate with Fidelity to resolve its deficiencies, but these efforts proved unsuccessful.

The complainants found that while the industry rate of lending to mortgage deficient areas had increased since the enactment of the anti-redlining laws in 1976, Fidelity's rate of lending had become progressively worse. In fact, of the state's major lenders, only Fidelity showed a decreasing rate of lending to very low- and low-moderate income areas. Their analysis showed that Fidelity had the poorest fair lending record in the state. Fidelity was ultimately acquired by Citibank, and became Citicorp Savings, providing the New York banking giant's first toehold in the lucrative California market. No community lending agreement or commitment was reached upon Citibank's acquisition of Fidelity.

San Diego City/County Community Reinvestment Task Force

In the early 1980s, the two jurisdictions of the city and county of San Diego established the Community Reinvestment Task Force. This task force has received support from each jurisdiction's Community Development Block Grant (CDBG) budgets. The CDBG allocations support a staff person whose primary responsibilities are to evaluate annually lender residential loan performance in low-income and minority areas and to staff the task force. The task force is comprised of community, government and lender representatives, and meets periodically to review the annual performance reports. The task force has recommended linked deposit policies be established in local jurisdictions within San Diego County. The staff director has also provided technical assistance and support to state legislative efforts affecting reinvestment policy. He has also contributed substantial pro bono time to participation in the California Reinvestment Committee (CRC), a statewide ad hoc consortium of government, community organizations, nonprofit development organizations, consumer, and other reinvestment advocates formed in 1986 over the merger of Wells Fargo Bank and Crocker National Bank.

David Paul Rosen

THE CALIFORNIA REINVESTMENT COMMITTEE AND STATEWIDE ADVOCACY

Wells Fargo Bank

In the spring of 1986, Wells Fargo Bank announced its intention to acquire Crocker National Bank. At the time, Wells Fargo was the fourth largest bank in California (behind Bank of America, Security Pacific Bank, and First Interstate Bank) with roughly $20 billion in assets. The acquisition of Crocker Bank would double Wells Fargo's assets. More importantly, it would establish Wells Fargo, a San Francisco–headquartered bank, in southern California, with a substantial branch system and customer base in Los Angeles and San Diego. The acquisition signaled Wells Fargo's intention of remaining one of the few dominant banking institutions in California through 1990, capable of facing interstate banking challenges from the large, money-center banks of New York.

Attorneys with the Legal Aid Society of Alameda County, community development practitioners, community reinvestment advocates, and local public agency officials, largely concentrated in the San Francisco Bay Area, recognized the Wells Fargo–Crocker merger for the watershed it represented in California banking history. This recognition was sharpened by the then-ongoing debate in the state capitol about California's forthcoming terms for interstate banking. This debate was precipitated by the U.S. Supreme Court's reversal of the McFadden Act in 1985, which effectively lifted restrictions on interstate banking activity. Not coincidentally, Citibank, which had acquired Fidelity Savings and Loan Association in 1981 to establish a California retail banking toehold, was actively engaged in the interstate-banking lobbying effort in Sacramento.

More importantly, these community reinvestment advocates viewed the proposed merger as an opportunity to redefine the community reinvestment debate in California throughout the coming era of bank deregulation. Organized under the name California Reinvestment Committee (CRC), these advocates recognized the imperative need to create a statewide coalition if they were to credibly address statewide community credit needs. As a result, a small group of community development practitioners and reinvestment advocates reached out to organizations representing those interests in southern and rural California. Participants included the San Diego City/County Reinvestment Task Force, coordinated by Jim Bliesner; the deputy administrators for finance and housing of the Los Angeles Community Redevelopment Agency, the largest re-development agency in the state; representatives of rural California non-profit housing development corporations; the National Housing Law Project; the National Economic Development and Law Center; and the City of Oakland's Office of Community Development. Other partici-pants included a representative from the Center for Community Change and the Northern California Association for Non-Profit Housing. Pro bono assistance was provided by community development consultants.

The California Reinvestment Committee had the benefit of an initial, single focus on the Wells Fargo–Crocker merger. The CRC adopted a collective negotiation strategy which included direct commu-nication with the Federal Reserve Board in Washington, D.C.; preparing preliminary data on Wells Fargo's and Crocker's separate home lending records, using Home Mortgage Disclosure Act (HMDA) data (which docu-mented deficiencies in both Wells Fargo's and Crocker's performance); offering a proposed reinvestment lending agenda as a business oppor-tunity of mutual benefit to the newly merged bank and the state's low-income and minority neighborhoods; and preparations to file a legal challenge opposing the merger.

The collective negotiation strategy resulted in a series of meetings between the CRC and top executive management of Wells Fargo Bank. The CRC structured an agenda around three main goals: lending for af-fordable housing; small business and community economic development enterprise lending; and consumer banking.

These discussions resulted in a $41 million annual commitment from Wells Fargo to specific lending targets in these three areas. A press release from the CRC dated April 29, 1986, detailed provisions of the bank's Community Lending Program:

- $18 million in construction and permanent financing for multi-family and "for sale" housing affordable to families at or below 80 percent of the median income, adjusted for family size. The bank will make "best efforts" to include housing units to families below 50 percent of the median income. It will consider "price concessions, including below market rates and reduced fees" to help make units affordable, par-ticularly where subsidies are provided by other partners to a given project.

- $18 million in Small Business Administration guaranteed and California-guaranteed loans to small businesses. Of that amount, $3 million is targeted exclusively for minority-owned firms providing affordable housing or economic development activity in poor and minority neighborhoods.
- $2 million in home improvement loans on one to four unit buildings in locally designated community development programs and areas.
- An increase in bank community personnel for both low-income housing and small-business lending and marketing.
- Access to bank executives for local government, nonprofit housing developers and minority-owned firms for housing and economic development loans.
- Continued periodic meetings between bank management and the reinvestment committee to evaluate the progress of the special Community Lending Program, and to discuss changes as needed.
- An evaluation of a basic banking service account affordable to low income consumers with low minimum deposit requirements.
- Direct deposit of government checks (e.g., paychecks, unemployment and welfare checks) with the needed cooperation of the state and the counties.

One of the notable features of the Wells Fargo community lending agreement was that it counted only that portion of affordable housing lending which finances units affordable to families earning less than 80 percent (low income) and 50 percent (very low income) of the area median income. These definitions comply with most HUD programs for the targeting of housing subsidies. Thus, if Wells Fargo extended a $10 million construction loan on a project where only 10 percent of the units were affordable to low- and very low-income households, then only $1 million would count toward the bank's $18 million annual affordable housing lending goal.

The CRC felt this targeted method of accounting for affordable housing loans was among the most important features of the agreement it negotiated with Wells Fargo. Another key provision of the agreement was continued access and periodic meetings with top management of the bank to evaluate and review the progress of the Community Lending Program and to discuss changes as needed. In fact, this monitoring process has proven critical to improving Wells Fargo's program.

Over the next several years, members of the CRC met with key Wells Fargo lending executives in the fields of housing and commercial lending. Over that time, mutual respect grew among Wells Fargo's executives, CRC members, community development practitioners, nonprofit housing development corporations, and local public agencies involved in low-income housing and neighborhood revitalization efforts. At one point, Wells Fargo's Real Estate Industry Group had significant concerns about lending on single-room occupancy (SRO) hotels as a type of low-income housing. Members of the CRC were able to demonstrate how SRO hotels should be underwritten differently than commercial tourist hotels, and how SRO hotels represented a much more secure type of lending than first imagined by Wells Fargo's executives.

Significant questions were raised about the adequacies of Wells Fargo's small-business and minority-business lending programs. The bank had been largely inactive in Small Business Administration (SBA) guaranteed loan programs until 1986, and its SBA loan production remains far short of the activity of much smaller institutions in California.

Nevertheless, Wells Fargo took assertive steps to carry out its loan commitments. It hired line lending executives in northern and southern California with direct responsibility for loan production in both housing and commercial development. In 1989, it created a new Business Loan Division, with responsibility for making smaller commercial loans to small businesses, nonprofit organizations, businesses located in enterprise zones, and minority-owned businesses.

These efforts paid off with promising results. For the period January 1, 1990 to October 31, 1990, Wells Fargo exceeded in most categories of its community and economic development loan program targets. For 1990, the annual low-income housing lending goal had increased to $60 million, and by the fall of 1990 the bank had far exceeded that amount with commitments totaling more than $108 million in twenty-eight projects. That volume more than doubled the bank's total low-income housing lending in 1989, which saw commitments of nearly $50 million in nineteen projects. In 1989, a total of 236 units affordable to families with less than 50 percent of the area median income and 410 units affordable to families with less than 60 percent of the area median income, for a total of 646 low-income units, received construction financing from Wells. Table 8.1 summarizes the five-year record of Wells Fargo's low-income housing construction lending from 1986 to 1990.

David Paul Rosen

TABLE 8.1
WELLS FARGO BANK, 1986-1990

AFFORDABLE HOUSING REAL ESTATE LENDING			COMMERCIAL BANKING GROUP CRA LENDING		
	Commitment Amount ($ Mil)	Goal Credit ($ Mil)		Loan Goal ($ Mil)	YTD Commitments ($ Mil)
1990[a]	108,134	60,000	1990[a]	60,000	66,090
1989	57,347	49,993	1989	16,500	64,198
1988	28,814	20,250	1988	18,000	38,352
1987	28,874	25,643	1987	18,000	38,790
1986	26,207	21,903	1986	18,000	19,563
Total	249,376	177,789	Total	130,500	226,993

Source: Real Estate Industries Group, Wells Fargo Bank, San Francisco, Calif.
[a]For the period 1/1/90 to 10/31/90.

During this period, Wells Fargo lent a total of nearly $250 million, exceeding their goal of $178 million.

In Wells Fargo's 1990 Community Reinvestment Act statement, the bank indicates that since June of 1986, when it negotiated its initial commitment with the CRC, it had committed a total of $137 million in interim and permanent financing in 118 transactions. More than 4,000 affordable housing units have been financed through the program since its inception. Of the 4,122 units supported with Wells Fargo's financial commitments, the statement notes that more than 1,500 are affordable to residents earning 50 percent or less of the area median income, and more than 2,600 are affordable to those with 80 percent or less of area median income. In fact, a large percentage of the units contained in the 80 percent of the area median income level are affordable to families earning 60 percent or less of the area median income, based on eligibility for the low income housing tax credit.

On March 20, 1990, Wells Fargo adopted a seven-year goal of at least $1 billion in special loans through its Community and Economic Development Loan Program. The commitment was made as a result of discussions with the Greenlining Coalition, a coalition representing diverse minority interests in northern California and working under the coordination of Public Advocates, a nonprofit, public interest law firm in San Francisco. Wells Fargo summarized the program by setting lending targets in the categories indicated in Table 8.2 (Wells Fargo Bank 1990b).

TABLE 8.2
WELLS FARGO COMMUNITY LENDING: ANNUAL VOLUME TARGETS (1990)

LOAN TYPE	AMOUNT
Loan to moderate income multifamily housing activities	$60 million
Economic development • SBA 504 real loans/certified • Development company • Community business "enhanced product" • Community business "standard product" • Community development loans • Small business	$60 million
Low income 1–4 unit subsidy family	$3 million
Low income finance terms (LIFT) consumer	N/A

The lending for multifamily housing has been limited almost exclusively to construction loans. Wells Fargo shows no signs at this writing of changing that emphasis. The "economic development" loans are a
mix of SBA and bank loan products, most of which are secured by real
estate. The bank indicates it will make loans ranging from $25,000 to
$500,000 to targeted types of businesses, for example, minority- and
women-owned, nonprofit, or those located in an enterprise zone.

SUBSEQUENT AGREEMENTS, ATTEMPTED AGREEMENTS, AND AN EXPANDING COALITION

The California Reinvestment Committee has remained actively involved
in negotiating and monitoring lending agreements with numerous California lenders, large and small. While somewhat mixed, the results of
these efforts are impressive for the volume of community lending commitments made in the area of affordable housing. The results of these
efforts are summarized below.

Citicorp Savings

In 1986, Citicorp filed to acquire Great Western Bank and Trust of
Phoenix, Arizona. The California Reinvestment committee sought a series of meetings with both California and New York Citicorp executives
in an effort to secure a community lending commitment in response to

David Paul Rosen

the proposed Great Western acquisition. Associated Communities Organized for Reform Now (ACORN) was simultaneously negotiating with Great Western representatives in Phoenix for community lending commitments to that area. Once again, CRC proposed three main areas of community lending commitment:

- Basic banking services, including low-cost checking accounts, free cashing of government checks, bilingual banking services, and establishing a procedure for community consultation on branch closures.
- Low-income housing credit commitments, including a specific dollar amount or number of units constructed, periodically renewable, affordable to households at or below 50 percent of the area median income; concession in rates, fees and terms used to finance such housing; and review and revision of loan underwriting criteria as necessary to stimulate the production of creditworthy housing projects by nonprofit developers and public agencies.
- Small business and economic development credit commitments in an annually renewable dollar amount for small businesses and economic development loans in low-income and minority neighborhoods, including measures to carefully target the provision of such credit to those neighborhoods with the greatest credit needs, as well as a review and revision, as needed, of loan underwriting criteria needed to stimulate credit underwriting in this area.

No agreement could be reached between representatives of Citicorp and CRC. Subsequently, the Legal Aid Society of Alameda County, on behalf of CRC, filed a complaint with the Board of Governors of the Federal Reserve System in Washington, D.C., protesting Citicorp's acquisition of Great Western. Dated July 3, 1986, this complaint reviewed Fidelity's documented discriminatory lending practices through the time of its acquisition by Citicorp in 1982. The complaint further documented deficiencies in Citicorp/Fidelity's home lending record in the San Francisco/Oakland Standard Metropolitan Statistical Area (SMSA). The complaint noted that at the Federal Reserve Board's hearing for the Citicorp acquisition of Fidelity in 1982, then Citicorp Executive Vice President Edwin Hoffman testified that Citicorp would equal the lending records of other financial institutions within one year after acquisition: "I want to reiterate that we stand ready to have that comparison made and, in fact, welcome it and would only suggest that because we think we're going to do so well that you broaden the universe of people [to which we are compared]" (Federal Reserve Board 1982:154). In fact, by 1986, the most recently available HMDA data from 1984 showed that Citicorp had compiled at best a mixed record of home lending, with significant deficiencies in many minority and lower-income neighborhoods. The Legal Aid Society concluded that

> Citicorp Savings, according to unrevised 1984 HMDA statistics, has demonstrated a positive lending pattern in very high minority and very low income census tracts. These positive statistics, however, are not enough to offset Citicorp's poor affirmative lending records to 16 to 79 percent minority tracts and tracts with incomes of 80 to 120 percent of the SMSA median. When Citicorp's deficiency of $2.7 million in loans to higher minority areas is combined with its deficiency of $1.8 million in loans to lower and middle income areas, the result is a total deficiency of $4.5 million.
>
> Since Citicorp spent a total of $26.6 million in home loans in the Bay Area, the amount of this cumulative deficiency is significant.
>
> (Sweet et al. 1986)

In response to the Legal Aid Society and CRC complaint, Ellis Bradford, then assistant secretary to Citicorp, wrote to the Board of Governors of the Federal Reserve System defending Citicorp's record and accused the protestants of having "proposed the sort of fishing expedition" criticized by the court in *Connecticut Bankers Association v. the Board of Governors* (627F.2d 245,252, DC Cir. 1980) (Bradford 1986: 7). In fact, the Board of Governors approved Citicorp's acquisition of Great Western without requiring substantive community lending commitments.

Subsequent to the acquisition, Citicorp's community lending record in the area of low-income housing has been uneven. Some community development practitioners observe that Citicorp's affordable housing lending commitments in California have proven to be a direct function of the quality of the loan officers employed by the institution. Citicorp Savings did institute a philanthropic program of modest grants to non-profit housing development corporations in the Bay Area. During the 1986 discussions, the institution refused to consider business lending, arguing that it only had a thrift charter to operate in the state at that time. However, Citibank had conducted corporate finance operations for some businesses in California prior to the 1986 challenge. During 1985 and the first half of 1986, the period of its acquisition of Great Western, Citicorp reported its "Community Investment Program Accomplishments":

1985
- Eleven first mortgages in the Oakland flatlands; $560,000 in financing provided.
- Six multifamily project loans totaling $6.5 million and funding a total of 181 housing units (number of affordable units unspecified).
- Charitable contributions to thirteen community and housing oriented nonprofit organizations totaling $239,000.

1986
- Eight mortgages in the Oakland flatlands; $529,000 in financing provided.
- Five multifamily affordable housing projects involving 109 units at a total of $3.9 million in construction and term financing (number of affordable units unspecified).

The most notable shift in Citicorp's 1989 community investment statement is the increase in accounting for mortgages in "neighborhoods designated by the Federal Home Loan Bank as having low- or moderate-income and/or minority families, as well as areas identified by the California State Department of Savings and Loan as having a very low loan volume." Citicorp reported that in 1988 they made a total of 2,518 loans involving $350 million in mortgage financing. A total of 295 units of housing were financed with $4.2 million in construction or term financing during 1988, with, once again, the number of affordable units among that total unspecified. During 1988 Citicorp made twenty-two grants to a variety of housing and community development nonprofit organizations totaling $212,000. To this date, as a matter of policy, Citicorp has not made a published commitment to loan production in either the field of multifamily or single-family lending.

California First Bank/Union Bank

On February 17, 1988, California First Bank of San Francisco announced that it would pay approximately $750 million to acquire Union Bank of Los Angeles. This acquisition represented the record investment in a U.S. bank (Union Bank) by a Japanese-controlled bank (California First). The Bank of Tokyo Limited owned 77 percent of California First at the time, and Standard Chartered PLC of Great Britain owned Union Bank. By 1988, Japanese-owned banks had expanded their market share to about 13 percent throughout the United States. At the time, California First was primarily a retail bank with 135 branches, while Union Bank, by contrast, was a commercial bank with 32 branches serving middle-market companies with assets between $2 million and $125 million.

By 1987, California First had assets of $6.1 billion, compared to Union's assets of $9.1 billion. The new bank became the fifth-largest bank in California. The acquisition attracted the attention of the business and financial press because of the signal it sent regarding Japanese bank interests in California. The business press has observed that Bank of California (Mitsubishi Bank), Sanwa Bank, Sumitomo Bank, and California First (now renamed Union Bank) came to dominate the entire middle tier of banks in California by the late 1980s.

Once again, the acquisition attracted the interest of the CRC and that of a newly formed organization, the Greenlining Coalition. The Greenlining Coalition is a San Francisco-based, ad hoc consortium of minority group representatives, coordinated out of the offices of Public Advocates. Union Bank executives and representatives of CRC and the Greenlining Coalition negotiated and published a community lending commitment in 1988 satisfactory to all parties. At the time, the $86 million, two-year commitment was the largest negotiated in California. Among its targets, Union Bank agreed to provide:

- $20 million per year in affordable housing financing.
- $10 million per year in home loans to families at 50 percent to 80 percent of the area median income.
- $2 million per year in consumer loans.

David Paul Rosen

- $10 million per year in sba loans to minority and low-income persons.
- $6 million per year in direct business loans to minority and low-income persons.

TABLE 8.3
1990 COMMUNITY SERVICE ACTION PLAN: REAL ESTATE CONSTRUCTION
LOANS AS OF AUGUST 31, 1990

	NO.	AMOUNT ($)
MODERATE- AND LOW-INCOME HOUSING LOANS		
Fresno, moderate-income apts.	120	2,625,000
Livermore, low-income apts.[a]	34	1,760,000
Jamestown, senior citizen apts.	51	1,891,500
Cloverdale, senior citizen apts.	34	1,524,840
Bakersfield, low-income sfrs	14	1,282,000
Oceanside, moderate income apts.[a]	72	4,200,000
Pacoima, low-mod. income sfrs	60	5,040,000
Bay Area, Low Income Housing Fund	Credit Line	1,000,000
TOTAL	385	19,323,340
LOW-INCOME CONSUMER LOANS		
Northern California	84	828,000
Los Angeles–Orange	104	824,000
San Diego	321	1,501,000
TOTAL	509	3,153,000
MINORITY BUSINESS LOANS		
Northern California	100	7,154,000
Los Angeles–Orange	65	6,735,000
San Diego	32	1,316,000
TOTAL	197	15,205,000

Source: Union Bank, San Francisco, Calif., 1990.

[a]Part of a larger project.

Notes: Average loan size is $77,183. Minority business loans are not made to start up a company unless on a fully-secured basis. The typical borrower has been in business at least three years and made a profit at least two of the last three years, including the present. The number of loans may include multiple loans to the same borrower and do not include any government-guaranteed loans. Totals do include gap funding of sba 504 loans, which will be repaid from the sale of sba debentures in the future.

210

Union Bank also agreed to provide free cashing of government checks, including public assistance warrants. In addition, the agreement provided for free checking accounts for persons receiving public assistance who accepted direct deposit of their benefits. By September, 1990, Union Bank published the results of its early community lending activity. These results are summarized in Table 8.3.

Other significant features of the 1988 Union Bank agreement included commitments to expand affirmative action contracting, hiring of minority and women executives, and representation of minority constituents on the bank's board of directors. The Greenlining Coalition was particularly helpful in negotiating these last provisions with Union Bank. In 1991, Union Bank recommitted itself to its community lending goals in the area of small-business and minority-business lending.

Bank of America

Bank of America, through a series of discussions with representatives of the California Reinvestment Committee, the Greenlining Coalition, as well as through its own internal efforts to develop an institutionwide community lending program, has emerged with a varied, wide-ranging set of commitments and activities. The bank's 1990 Community Reinvestment Act (CRA) statement provides a summary of CRA-related lending for 1988 and 1989. These results are presented in Table 8.4.

It is worth noting that the vast majority of the $354 million commitment made in 1989 ($310 million) and the $250 million commitment made in 1988 ($222 million) was in single-family home mortgages originated in low-income census tracts.

The Bank of America has specifically committed itself to a goal of $50 million per year for loans on multifamily housing affordable to persons at or below 80 percent of the area median income. The bank will give preference to projects developed by nonprofit sponsors and to projects providing housing at or below 60 percent of the area median income. In preparing for a meeting with representatives of CRC in 1990, the bank listed a number of program delivery problems which bear repeating here. They fairly represent concerns in the development of affordable housing statewide in California.

211

David Paul Rosen

TABLE 8.4
BANK OF AMERICA SUMMARY OF CRA-RELATED LENDING, 1989 AND 1988 ($ MIL)

AFFIRMATIVE AND SPECIAL PROGRAMS	1989	1988
SMALL BUSINESS AND FARM		
Small Business Administration (7A and 504 programs)	25.3	23.0
Farmers Home Admin. (family-size farms)	4.9	4.1
City Improvement Restoration Program (commercial)	1.1	0.9
Center for Southeast Asian Refugee Resettlement	0.1	N/A
Earthquake relief–small business	0.3	N/A
Business Consortium Fund	*	N/A
California Export Finance Program	0.4	N/A
TOTAL	32.1	28.0
HOUSING		
Low-income housing finance (construction, bridge, take-out)	27.8	29.6
FHA and VA home mortgages	32.8	23.1
City Improvement and Restoration Program (housing rehab.)	1.6	1.5
B.A.S.I.C. home improvement and mobilehome	3.0	N/A
Rudolfi Low-Income Housing Program*	4.1	2.2
California Community Reinvestment Corporation (17.5% participation)	*	N/A
Earthquake relief home improvement loans	8.7	N/A
Home mortgages originated in low-income census tracts	231.7	165.2
TOTAL	309.7	221.6
CONSUMER LOANS		
B.A.S.I.C.- Personal, Auto, Home Equity	12.3	N/A
TOTAL AFFIRMATIVE AND SPECIAL PROGRAMS	354.1	249.6

Source: Bank of America, 1990 Community Reinvestment Act Statement, San Francisco, Calif.
*Court stipulated settlement program.

• Limited number of experienced nonprofit developers in the Southern California area.
• For-profit developer projects generally only include 10 percent to 40 percent affordable units.
• Southern California cities (excluding Los Angeles) are just beginning to become players in affordable housing.

- Very few self-help/Farmer's Home Administration builders in Southern California.
- Lead time in development has either been too short or too long.
- Many 1990 projects are in need of state bond financing allocations or tax credit allocations, the availability of which may be problematic.
- Some self-help projects are very small (six to ten units) making it hard for us to compete given our costs. Bank of America State Bank may be able to pick up this area.
- The competition has been very stiff.
- Deal sizes half or less what the Bank saw two years ago.
- Our bond rating just recently became "investor grade" so we were unable to express an interest in projects in need of credit enhancement.

(Bank of America 1990c)

The bank provides a low-cost, limited checking account. Bank of America also provides a "Neighborhood Advantage Program" for consumer and home mortgage debt which uses higher than customary debt-to-income and loan-to-value ratios to encourage loans in selected zip codes. There is no qualifying income level for the Neighborhood Advantage Program. In the summer of 1991, the bank announced a targeted, $20 million Neighborhood Advantage loan program for Los Angeles, Long Beach, and Oakland minority communities. The bank also provides a consumer loan program with low minimum balances for consumers at or below 80 percent of the area median income. This program is similar to Wells Fargo's Low Income Finance Terms (LIFT) program and Union Bank's Low Income Consumer Loan Finance Program.

Bank of America is the only bank in California to have adopted an Office of the Controller of the Currency-approved bank community development corporation. The Bank of America State Bank is a wholly owned subsidiary of Bank of America and participates in California's guaranteed loan program to small businesses through the Cal Regional loan centers. The State Bank may also consider micro-loan pools and other innovative economic development finance programs. Commitments to the State Bank to date have been relatively modest.

Bank of America was a charter investor in the 1990 Oakland Housing Partnership Associates, the first city-corporate housing partnership west of St. Louis. Bank of America also invested in the California Equity Fund that year. Both funds place corporate equity investments in low-income housing in exchange for federal and state tax credits.

In 1991, Bank of America announced a ten-year, $5 billion community lending commitment. This decade-long community lending commitment extends the main areas of community lending in which the bank is already active: affordable housing, single-family home mortgages, small-business lending and related credit programs. This program was announced following discussions with the Greenlining Coalition. Details of the bank's plans for implementing this commitment, the largest in the nation to date, have yet to be released at this writing.

Security Pacific

In 1990, Security Pacific announced a goal of $2.4 billion in community lending over the next ten years. Neither the Community Reinvestment Committee nor the Greenlining Coalition, however, have been able to get Security Pacific to specify how this community lending commitment will be realized. Up until this point, Security Pacific had proven resistant to making any community lending commitments to either CRC, ACORN, or other reinvestment advocates.

The former chairman of Security Pacific played a key role in the formation of the California Community Reinvestment Corporation, and Security Pacific, along with many other California Banks, has pledged a commitment to CRC's overall loan fund of $100 million.

Nevertheless, as the second largest bank in California, Security Pacific's commitments fall short of those made by other similarly sized institutions. The bank has indicated it will provide loans for the construction and rehabilitation of affordable housing. However, the dollar goal and affordability targets for this program have not yet been set at this writing. In the area of permanent loans, Security Pacific will provide $10 million a year in loans to nonprofit developers of housing affordable to persons at or below 60 percent of the area median income. Loans will be for a term of fifteen years, amortized over a thirty-year period at a fixed rate of 6 percent, according to Consumer Union, an active coordinator of CRC activities. Security Pacific, like Bank of America, Wells Fargo, Citicorp, First Nationwide Bank, and a number of other institutions, will make home loans to low- and moderate-income home buyers using flexible qualifying and underwriting criteria. In all cases, most lender's single-family home mortgage purchase programs of this kind are made possible by secondary market purchase commitments and underwriting standards established by the Federal National Mortgage Association (Fannie Mae) and the Federal Home Loan Mortgage Corporation (Freddie Mac).

Perhaps the sternest test for statewide reinvestment advocacy efforts will occur in CRC's and the Greenlining Coalition's response to Bank of America's proposed acquisition of Security Pacific Bank, announced in August of 1991. The Bank of America/Security Pacific merger is the largest bank merger in U.S. banking history, creating a bank second only to Citicorp in size, with total assets of approximately $190 billion and a network of approximately 2,400 branches throughout California and the western United States.

Tom Hanley, a bank analyst with Salomon Brothers, predicts that the new Bank of America earnings could top $2 billion by 1993 and reach $2.35 billion by 1994 (*San Francisco Chronicle*, Aug. 14, 1991). Such earnings would double Bank of America's record 1990 earnings of $1.1 billion. The Bank of America/Security Pacific merger raises enormous questions concerning bank competitiveness, customer service, consumer protection, and responsiveness to community credit needs and community reinvestment commitments. The two banks have adopted starkly different styles in response to statewide advocacy efforts, with Bank of America proving more responsive than Security Pacific executives to working with the reinvestment advocacy community in local communities and statewide.

THE RESURGENCE OF LOCAL GOVERNMENT AND INDUSTRY EFFORTS

One result of the success of the California Reinvestment Committee negotiations, even when such negotiations do not result in a written commitment to specific, measurable community lending goals, is a heightened awareness of community credit needs and the importance of

David Paul Rosen

substantive responses to these needs by local and state government and banks alike. As in Boston, Detroit, Milwaukee, and many other cities, public officials are beginning to take a more assertive stance on lending issues, and lenders are responding.

California Community Reinvestment Corporation

The California Community Reinvestment Corporation (CCRC) was formed in 1989 as a nonprofit mortgage banking corporation to pool $100 million in long-term loan funds for affordable housing developments throughout California. CCRC loans are funded by selling collateral trust notes to member institutions. These loans will eventually be sold in the secondary mortgage market to pension funds and institutions such as Fannie Mae. Participation in CCRC contributes to a bank's record of performance under the Community Reinvestment Act.

The San Francisco Development Fund originally based CCRC on the success of similar consortiums in New York and Chicago, which offer member banks significant advantages as community lenders. As John Trauth, the executive director of the San Francisco Development Fund, explains:

> Three key features of CCRC are specialized lending, risk pooling and sale of loans to the secondary market. Most banks involved in this type of community lending have concentrated in making construction loans, due to the interest rate risk of longer term loans. Previously, only the largest banks were able to provide the resources to underwrite and fund these projects. Through CCRC, the medium sized and smaller banks can participate together with the larger banks to provide this special type of permanent financing. With further exposure, banks may decide to individually underwrite and finance these types of projects.
> (California Community Reinvestment Corporation, 1989)

The CCRC offers permanent, fixed rate loans at ten-, fifteen-, and thirty-year maturities with thirty-year amortization. The interest rate for immediate funding loans is 150 basis points (1.5 percent) over U.S. Treasury bonds for comparable maturities and 175 basis points (1.75 percent) for forward commitment loans. Fees and charges by CCRC are equiv-

216

alent to 2 percent of the loan amount plus an application fee of $1,000. Each development to be funded must maintain affordability for the life of the loan at the following income standards, based on the appropriate metropolitan area designated by HUD.

• 15 percent or more of the units for households earning 80 percent or below area median income, adjusted for family size.
• 40 percent or more of the units for households earning 60 percent or below area median income, adjusted for family size.
• 20 percent or more of the units for households earning 50 percent or below area median income, adjusted for family size.

As Dan Lopez, CCRC's first president, explains, CCRC "is unique in that we offer a loan product that is competitively priced and aimed at making low income housing affordable over the long run. Our goal is not only to expand the supply of low income housing but to make these projects financially successful. It is through this combination of flexible, long term financing and technical assistance that CRC intends to address the housing needs of low income households" (Lopez 1991).

Once loan applications are received, the CCRC staff reviews them and provides the initial screening. The staff also provides technical guidance to developers whose proposals do not initially meet CCRC's underwriting guidelines. After screening, the loan applications that meet underwriting criteria are then submitted to the loan committee, which must give final approval.

The CCRC had fifty-five members as of January 1991 and has a goal of one hundred member banks. Its loan committee has approved $73.4 million in loans with about $20 million committed by April 1, 1991. About two-thirds of its loans have been to nonprofit corporations. Loan amounts to nonprofits are typically significantly less than for-profit corporations, and about two-thirds of funds approved would be lent to for-profit developers. Currently, membership banks participate in loans on a statewide basis. In October 1991, CCRC plans to fund loans on a regional basis. Its members would then participate in deals in their local area, rather than statewide.

Local Government Responses

Very much in response to the visibility of the negotiated agreements and successes achieved by the California Reinvestment Committee and the

David Paul Rosen

Greenlining Coalition, several California cities have begun concerted efforts to assert local community reinvestment policy. In Los Angeles, the city commissioned a major study of lender residential, economic development and consumer loan performance, as well as branch opening and closing trends. The results of that study confirmed industrywide trends of discriminatory mortgage lending practices which have been found in other cities, such as Detroit, Chicago, Denver, Washington, D.C., and New York. The report found

> compelling evidence of widespread, de facto racial redlining in the City of Los Angeles. . . . From 1981–1989, at least twice as many loans were made per building in low minority areas than in minority areas whose residents have comparable incomes. Nearly $5 was loaned per building in low minority communities for every $1 loaned in minority communities with comparable median incomes.
>
> These findings are deeply troubling in light of the City's housing crisis. They imply that neighborhoods with many African American and Latino residents, regardless of those residents' average incomes, are being shut out of the financial market for home purchase and home improvement loans.
>
> (Dymski, Veitch, and White 1991: 9–10)

Additionally, the city convened a Community Reinvestment Committee at the request of Mayor Tom Bradley and City Council President John Ferraro, to develop a blueprint for capital investment requirements in South Central Los Angeles (Watts). A preliminary report from this committee detailed a variety of home lending, small-business, consumer lending, business, and other technical assistance activities aimed at revitalizing the severely disinvested community of South Central Los Angeles, home to nearly 600,000 residents. At this writing, Los Angeles city staff are preparing responses to the lender discrimination study and the South Central Community Reinvestment Committee report.

Four hundred miles to the north, the city of Oakland has taken a slightly different tack. Rather than start by evaluating lender performance, the city's Office of Community Development and Office of Economic Development and Employment commissioned a community credit needs assessment which quantified credit needs in the areas of affordable housing, local economic development and unreinforced masonry seismic safety retrofit construction lending. Over the course of two years, the city succeeded in quantifying, in quite specific categories, the volume of housing and local economic development lending needed throughout Oakland's low-income and minority communities and small business, women- and minority-owned business communities.

The assessment's estimation methodology applied small-business gross receipts reported to the City of Oakland's Business Tax Division by industry category to standard debt-to-asset and debt-to-sales (both short-term and long-term) ratios published by Robert Morris and Associates (RMA). RMA represents the leading bank industry standard for underwriting commercial loans to businesses by industry category and specific enterprise classifications. Thus, the Oakland methodology applies standard, accepted bank underwriting debt ratios to reported sales of Oakland businesses to arrive at the estimates of small-business commercial credit needs. Further, the methodology used minority-business census data from 1984 and 1987 to estimate short-term and long-term debt requirements of black-owned and women-owned small businesses.

Table 8.5 summarizes both short-term and long-term debt requirements for small businesses within Oakland with annual sales between $50,000 and $5 million. This study may represent the first time a metropolitan community has effectively quantified its local economic development credit needs within the small-business community.

The study was further able to specify short- and long-term credit needs for black-owned and women-owned businesses, using a similar methodology. Standard banking industry loan-to-asset ratios, according to RMA and several banking industry standards, were employed to derive these credit needs. The total, $358 million short-term and long-term small-business credit need in Oakland, probably understates actual demand by 25 percent to 40 percent. Further, it does not include an estimate for nonprofit enterprise lending. Additionally, the credit study quantified annual affordable housing credit needs for Oakland. These are summarized in Table 8.6.

In response to the community credit needs assessment, which also found widespread and disturbing evidence of discriminatory lending practices, the Oakland City Council directed staff to prepare ordinances es-

TABLE 8.5

SALES, ASSETS, SHORT-TERM, LONG-TERM, AND TOTAL DEBT REQUIREMENTS:
OAKLAND WHOLESALERS, MANUFACTURERS, RETAILERS, AND SERVICE FIRMS
WITH ANNUAL SALES BETWEEN $50,000 AND $5,000,000 ($ MIL)

INDUSTRY/SALES	ACCOUNTS	SALES[a]	ASSETS	SHORT-TERM DEBT	LONG-TERM DEBT	TOTAL DEBT
WHOLESALERS						
.5–1	250	89	35	5.3	5.7	11.0
1–3	82	148	50	6.4	6.7	13.1
3–5	23	91	30	3.8	3.1	6.9
TOTAL	355	328	115	15.5	15.5	31.0
MANUFACTURERS						
.5–1	354	109	52	5.3	11.3	16.6
1–3	74	123	54	5.7	8.6	14.2
3–5	20	75	31	3.2	5.0	8.2
TOTAL	448	307	137	14.2	24.9	39.0
RETAILERS						
.5–1	1,908	431	187	22.4	37.7	60.1
1–3	293	437	156	19.3	25.6	44.9
3–5	46	180	67	8.1	8.3	16.4
TOTAL	2,247	1,048	410	49.8	71.6	121.4
SERVICE FIRMS						
.5–1	2,732	606	275	30.6	75.6	106.1
1–3	203	334	139	13.4	27.8	41.2
3–5	42	160	64	7.5	12.0	19.5
TOTAL	2,977	1,100	478	51.5	115.4	166.8
ALL CATEGORIES	6,027	2,783	1,140	131.0	227.3	358.2

Source: David Paul Rosen, "Oakland Community Credit Needs: Commercial, Affordable Housing, and Seismic Safety," April 8, 1991, p. ES–3. Study commissioned by the City of Oakland.

[a]Sales are equated with the business tax base of each industry classification, as determined by the Oakland Business Tax Ordinance.

TABLE 8.6
SUMMARY OF OAKLAND'S ANNUAL AFFORDABLE HOUSING CREDIT NEEDS

LOAN TYPE	HOUSING UNITS	LOAN SIZE (AVERAGE)	TOTAL NEED ($ MIL)
Single-family 1–4 unit mortgage purchase loans in 7 CD districts	1,000/year	$90,000	90/year
Home improvement loans	967 (12% of 8,058 units in need)	$20,000	19.3/year
Rental rehabilitation loans	570 occupied (12% of 4,751 in need)	$25,000	14.2/year
	93 vacant (25% of 374 in need)	$35,000	3.2/year
Rental housing construction ($112,000/unit development cost) FY 1991	103 affordable below 80% median income	Construction loand @40% development cost; permanent loans @30% and 50% development cost for very low and low-income units respectively	4.6/year 4.5/year
Bridge loans	1989 Oakland Housing Partnership		2.5–16
Acquisition/ rehabilitation of at-risk federally subsidized projects	1,231	Acquisition	10–20
Rehabilitation of earthquake damage SRO units	1,100 @$50,000/ unit rehabilitation cost	Construction loans @40% rehabilitation cost; permanent loans @30% rehabilitation cost	$22 $16.5
TOTAL			186.8–210.3

Source: David Paul Rosen, "Oakland Community Credit Needs: Commercial, Affordable Housing, and Seismic Safety," April 8, 1991, p. ES–3. Study commissioned by the City of Oakland.

tablishing a Community Reinvestment Commission and a linked deposit ordinance similar to the efforts in Boston, Pittsburgh, Milwaukee, and many other cities. The commission was envisioned as a forum where lenders, credit users, community reinvestment advocates, and city officials could identify and resolve problems in meeting the city's defined community credit needs.

The linked deposit proposal was predicated on a fair share standard of community lending. This standard links a lending institution's "fair share" of the city's specified community lending needs to that institution's asset size or total lending volume. Another feature of Oakland's proposed linked deposit ordinance was a set of comprehensive commercial loan disclosure requirements. City council action on the Reinvestment Commission and linked deposit ordinances is pending at this writing.

LESSONS FOR THE 1990s AND BEYOND

After more than twelve years of diverse community reinvestment efforts resulting in ever larger lending commitments and programs, the 1990s hold promise for consolidating and institutionalizing the practice of community reinvestment lending statewide. The degree to which this promise is realized may be measured against a set of principles which frame a comprehensive community reinvestment agenda for the state. This agenda should specify and quantify by loan product the community credit needs of disinvested, low-income, minority, and rurally isolated neighborhoods and regions throughout California.

Principles of Reinvestment

The central tenet of community reinvestment is simply stated: financial institutions and the capital assets which they control serve dual purposes. First, they must preserve the fiscal integrity of their operations, and the financial interests of their investors, depositors, and customers, by pursuing profitable enterprise while prudently observing "safe and sound" operations. Second, they must serve the credit needs of the communities in which they are chartered to operate and where their depositors live. This second obligation derives not only from the requirements of a democratic economy, one where the general welfare of the citizenry is assured as a matter of public trust, but also from the obligation created by significant public subsidies and privileges provided by the government to the private sector financial community. These include deposit insurance, public loan guarantees, special borrowing privileges, charters to do business, federally chartered secondary markets for residential and commercial loans, large scale, tax-exempt financing made available for private purposes, and the deposits of huge sums of public funds.

Finally, the obligation to reinvest financial institution assets in low-income and distressed communities derives from the self-interests of these institutions in assuring stable economic growth for all communities. This not only creates stable markets for the consumption of credit, insurance and other financial services, but also preserves the community investments made by the financial institutions.

Several premises underline the discussion of reinvestment principles and policy. First, the financial institutions' dual responsibility to engage in profitable enterprise while simultaneously following safe investment practices requires that investments be creditworthy and profitable. Thus, reinvestment commitments must be concentrated in the provision of credit for low-income community economic development projects and services capable of servicing the loan capital which is extended.

Another premise requires that community reinvestment by financial institutions directly benefit low-income neighborhoods and their residents. Former Senator William Proxmire, Carl Holman of the National Urban Coalition, and others concerned with reinvestment policy and practice, note the disturbing tendency of neighborhood reinvestment to precipitate displacement of long-time, low-income residents and to aid gentrification.

Based on these premises, several principles for community reinvestment may be articulated. Adherence to these principles by community advocates, policy makers, regulators and private sector financial institutions will help realize the benefits reinvestment can provide in meeting long-term, comprehensive credit needs of distressed communities. This in turn can help democratize the distribution of the nation's wealth, assuring the integration of disadvantaged citizens and communities in the fabric of our economy and society. These principles include the following.

PROGRESSIVENESS. The benefits of reinvestment activity—housing, community economic development, consumer credit—must measurably accrue to low-income communities and their residents. At a minimum,

David Paul Rosen

these benefits must include affordable, safe, and decent housing, and the creation of equity, wealth, income, and employment in stable occupations with reasonable wages and advancement opportunities.

ACCOUNTABILITY. Mechanisms at the federal, state, and local levels must exist to help articulate the reinvestment agenda, assess the progress of reinvestment commitments in achieving the goals for equitable community reinvestment, and hold private financial institutions publicly accountable for articulating and carrying out equitable and adequate reinvestment commitments.

COMPREHENSIVENESS. Reinvestment commitments of private sector financial institutions must meet two measures of comprehensiveness. First, the scale of their commitment must be sufficiently large to meet the housing and community economic development credit needs of low-income communities. Second, the scope of their commitment must be sufficiently diverse to serve the range of needed housing and community economic development activities. Housing credit needs include new construction; rehabilitation; and ownership of single-family, rental, cooperative, single-room occupancy and temporary shelter. Community economic development needs include small business, credit unions, industrial, and venture development, among others.

INSTITUTIONALIZATION. Marketing, personnel hiring, promotion and training, underwriting, and loan production activities needed for a comprehensive program of community reinvestment must all become business enterprises as highly valued as corporate and public finance, consumer credit or market rate commercial and real estate investment. Token programs of philanthropic giving or concessionary lending operated by small divisions with discrete personnel will never achieve the scale and scope necessary to comprehensively meet low-income community economic development credit needs.

CREDITWORTHINESS. It is not in the interest of reinvestment advocates to propose community loans which likely will fall into default. Conversely, it is not adequate for lenders to simply to conduct business as usual, without examining underwriting standards. For example, reinvestment advocates and affordable housing practitioners helped educate Cali-

224

fornia lenders to understand that affordable housing loans may be underwritten at debt coverage ratios much lower than those for conventional, market-rate projects. This is largely because the demand for affordable housing is extraordinary, and vacancy represents a nominal risk at best to affordable housing projects. While simultaneously promoting the principle of equity, all community reinvestment lending—as any other lending—must remain creditworthy.

Defining and Meeting Community Credit Needs

Before community credit needs can be said to have been met, they must first be defined. The definition of community credit needs must embrace the range of affordable housing and local economic development lending requirements of low-income and minority neighborhoods, their residents, and business people. The categories of community credit need established in the Oakland studies represent a sound start in establishing a common definition. Specialized community lending needs may vary in communities with widely differing needs. For example, seismic safety retrofit construction lending is a critical need in California. Financing for toxic cleanup and environmental mitigation efforts may be defined by some communities as an important credit need. In rural communities, family farm lending may represent an equally critical credit need. Thus, the definition of community credit needs must be responsive to the market areas served by financial institutions, and at a minimum, must provide for the affordable housing and local economic development credit requirements of a region. Without such a common definition, it will remain impossible to evaluate objectively the performance of lenders against defined community credit needs.

The last five years in California exemplify the progress community reinvestment advocates (and local government officials and industry executives) have made in fulfilling the promise of community reinvestment. Nevertheless, much remains to be done. Widespread discriminatory practices are found to exist in every lender performance evaluation done in any U.S. metropolitan community. Fulfilling this promise will require renewed and more vigorous public policy efforts at federal, state, and local levels of government to assure that discriminatory practices are finally stopped, to achieve consensus on the definition of community credit needs, and to provide effective enforcement of fair and affirmative reinvestment lending and investment. Building the capacity for assist-

David Paul Rosen

ance of community development organizations; nonprofit institutions and intermediaries; small, minority-owned, and women-owned businesses; and technical assistance organizations serving the needs of these groups, also represents a vital element of any effort to realize the community reinvestment promise.

Finally, the capacity of lenders to assist these groups must addressed. No longer will it prove adequate for lenders to hire one or two "community loan officers." Rather, the practice of affirmative reinvestment lending, responsive to defined and mutually agreed-upon community credit needs, must be institutionalized throughout the very fabric of the financial industry from the board rooms to the daily business functions of banks and thrifts. Only then can the promising efforts of the last few years in California be said to have truly given rise to an age when low-income and minority communities, their residents, and businesses have the equal access to credit and investment opportunities they need to thrive.

NOTE

1. Research assistance was provided by Elizabeth Seifel, Principal, Elizabeth Seifel and Associates in San Francisco, an economic consulting firm.

REFERENCES

Bank of America. 1990a. *1990 Annual Report.* San Francisco, Calif.
Bank of America. 1990b. *1990 Community Reinvestment Act Statement.* San Francisco, Calif.
Bank of America. 1990c. Staff Memo, Community Development. San Francisco, Calif.
Bradford, Ellis. 1986. Citicorp Bank letter of response to the Board of Governors of the Federal Reserve System regarding the Legal Aid Society of Alameda County and California Reinvestment Committee complaint of Citicorp's acquisition of Great Western Bank. August 8.
California Community Reinvestment Corporation. 1989. *Annual Report.* Burbank, Calif.
Citicorp Savings. 1988. *Community Investment Program.* Oakland, Calif.
Citicorp Savings. 1989. *Community Investment Program.* Oakland, Calif.
City of Oakland. 1989. Office of Finance, Business Tax Data. Oakland, Calif.
Dun and Bradstreet. 1990. *Industry Norms and Key Business Ratios 1990.* New York, N.Y.
Dymski, Gary, John Veitch, and Michelle White. 1991. *Taking It to the Bank: Poverty, Race and Credit in Los Angeles.* June. Los Angeles, Calif.
Federal Reserve Board. 1982. Hearing, Citicorp testimony in the matter of the acquisition of Fidelity Savings.
Legal Aid Society of Alameda County. 1978a. Administrative complaint before the Assistant Secretary for Equal Opportunity, U.S. Department of Housing and Urban Develop-

ment, regarding United Neighbors in Action et al. v. American Savings and Loan Association. June 9. Oakland, Calif.

———. 1978b. Administrative complaint before the United States District Court, Northern District of California, regarding United Neighbors in Action et al. v. American Savings and Loan. August 9. Oakland, Calif.

———. 1980. Administrative complaint before the Department of Savings and Loan, State of California, regarding the Oakland Community for Community Reinvestment et al. v. Fidelity Savings and Loan Association. August. Oakland, Calif.

———. 1986. Complaint to the Board of Governors of the Federal Reserve System protesting Citicorp's acquisition of Great Western Bank. July 3. Oakland, Calif.

Lopez, Daniel. 1991. Interview with Daniel Lopez, California Community Reinvestment Corporation, January. Burbank, Calif.

Morris, Robert, and Associates. 1990. The Annual Statement Studies, 1990. Philadelphia, Pa.

Ronfeldt, Stephen. 1990. Interview with Stephen Ronfeldt, Legal Aid Society of Almeda County, December. Oakland, Calif.

Rosen, David. 1989a. 1989 Community Credit Needs Assessment. Oakland, Calif.

———. 1989b. Public Capital: Revitalizing America's Communities. Washington, D.C.: National Center for Policy Alternatives.

———. 1991. 1991 Community Credit Needs Assessment. Oakland, Calif.Savings Association Mortgage Company. 1989. Annual Report, 1989. Menlo Park, Calif.

Sweet, Clifford. 1986. Memo from Legal Aid Society of Almeda County regarding Citicorp Bank's acquisition of Great Western Bank and home lending deficiencies in the San Francisco–Oakland SMSA. July 16.

Troy, Leo. 1990. Almanac of Business and Industrial Financial Ratios, 1990. Englewood Cliffs, N.J.: Prentice-Hall.

Union Bank. 1990. Community Service Action Plan. Aug. 31. San Francisco, Calif.

Wells Fargo Bank. 1986–1990a. Commercial Banking Group, Total CRA Commitments. Unpublished memoranda. San Francisco, Calif.

———. 1986–1990b. Real Estate Industry's Group Affordable Housing Real Estate Lending. Unpublished memoranda. San Francisco, Calif.

———. 1990a. 1990 Annual Report. San Francisco, Calif.

———. 1990b. 1990 Community Reinvestment Act Report.

Calvin Bradford
Gale Cincotta

Chapter 9

THE LEGACY, THE PROMISE, AND THE UNFINISHED AGENDA

OVER THE LAST TWO DECADES a quiet revolution has taken place (Bradford 1989). The old anti-redlining movement has grown into a new community development movement. The uniting of the "people power" of community-based action groups, the technical skills of community-based developers, funding from government and foundation grants and programs, and the capital and credit resources of the private financial markets has created new experiments and models for housing and community economic development partnerships. A powerful coalition of community action groups, community-based housing and economic development groups, civil rights groups, legal assistance organizations, and technical assistance providers has emerged.

The seven stories chronicled in the previous chapters reflect the overall lessons of the history of reinvestment and provide a context to assess its future. A principal lesson has been learned: strong, community-based organizing for community reinvestment is essential. Such organizing has been the key to past victories. Given the changes occurring today in the financial industries and financial regulatory agencies, community-based action will prove even more essential in the future.

THE COMMUNITY REINVESTMENT ACT AND THE LACK OF A DOMESTIC DEVELOPMENT POLICY FOR BANKING

For residents of redlined, disinvested, and declining communities the hundreds of billions of dollars that will eventually be spent bailing out the savings and loans and commercial banks is a double penalty. These lenders, referred to here generically as bankers, pursed development in

228

other nations whose cultures, politics, and economies they did not understand—and the loans have failed. Banks followed the lure of huge
profits in high growth industries, in new real estate development, energy
loans, and junk bonds—and the loans failed. While the bankers invested
in foreign economies, suburban and sunbelt growth, and corporate
mergers our existing small towns, inner cities, and minority communities
have continued to decline—starved for private capital and dependent on
the dwindling resources of government welfare programs. For residents of
these communities, the federal government has borrowed against the future of their children to rescue the bankers who already abandoned these
communities in their time of need. The reinvestment movement has
focused on the failure of bankers to pay enough attention to the needs of
existing communities.

National foreign policy defines the need for access to capital and
credit as an essential resource for Third World economic development.
Yet, in domestic policy, the government economists in the Federal Reserve System and most economists used by the banking industry consider
reinvestment in communities with economic distress as a violation of
market forces. Policymakers define high growth areas as in need of credit
and areas with depressed economies as having a capital surplus. The efficient market should transfer funds from areas of surplus and feed them to
areas needing credit. In this view, one of the results of interstate banking
and consolidation is a more efficient system in which funds from deposits
in declining economic areas are moved to high growth areas. Residents
of the urban and rural communities that are in need of economic development call this redlining and disinvestment; but from the view of many
neoclassical economists, this is market efficiency. The life blood for economic development in the Third World is a virus infecting the free market in the United States.

The Community Reinvestment Act (CRA) is the only law that
recognizes an obligation on the part of the banking industries to serve
the needs of American communities. This act was created by the people
that the lenders failed to serve. The bill to create the CRA was opposed
by the banking lobby and by the federal agencies that regulate banks and
savings institutions. Community reinvestment has worked because of the
efforts of community people to overcome not only the economic problems of their communities but also the continued opposition and intran-
sigence of the banking industry and the regulators.

229

Calvin Bradford and Gale Cincotta

THE POLITICAL VALUES OF THE REINVESTMENT MOVEMENT

The values of the reinvestment movement are best expressed in the response from one of the leaders of the reinvestment movement—Anne Devenney from the Northwest Bronx—when she was asked what she was. She responded, "I am a radical, conservative American." The movement's values are radical in that they embody the courage to confront the people and institutions that stand in the way of reinvestment and that participate in disinvestment and contribute to community decline. The movement is conservative both in its opposition to big government and its reliance on the private sector. It is American in its fundamental support for the free enterprise system with its focus on the engine of private capital. It values saving money to invest in the future. Banks collect the myriad little caches of individual savings and provide capital, in the form of loans, to the thousands of families, businesses, and institutions that comprise the local communities in which people live and upon which people depend for security, shelter, livelihood, education, and enjoyment.

Urban development and poverty programs failed to embrace these values. Urban renewal—often tagged as "Negro Removal"—did not address the needs of minorities and inner-city residents. It sought to replace them with higher income, white residents. Even though the Great Society and the War on Poverty programs focused on the needs of the people who had been targeted for removal under the urban renewal programs; they did little to rebuild the communities within which most minorities and poor people were forced to live. Indeed, the War on Poverty tended to replace the private economy of capital investment with a government economy that was based on direct support for subsistence maintenance. That is, the vitality and regenerative processes of the private economy were replaced by the maintenance economy of government welfare systems where the only dynamic was the management of the community into eventual abandonment (Bradford et al. 1979).

Reinvestment organizers learned the value of the selective role of the government as a limited but critical participant in their lives and communities; but they rejected approaches that turn people into clients of government programs rather than economic citizens. Organizing within the War on Poverty program too often focused on getting people their "entitlement" to government funds and programs rather than to the resources to free themselves from dependency on government programs. Power was defined by controlling and running these programs and services. The end result was not the improvement of the communities in which the vast majority of poor and moderate-income minorities lived. Rather, people often found themselves waiting to be rescued, by Congress, by a president, by social workers, and by bureaucrats.

In many ways, the reinvestment movement was a place-centered reaction to the War on Poverty program. Its focus was on economic renewal—but this time, not the renewal of the place by removing the existing people, but the renewal of the place *and* the people through policies that assured access to capital and credit, along with selected and targeted government investment and resources, so that the local economies and communities could be rebuilt for the benefit of those who lived there. The forces that forged reinvestment into a national movement emerged from the reaction to the exploitation of racial change by members of the real estate industries and the disinvestment in these communities by the private sector as minorities moved into previously white communities. The banking community was both the symbolic and the financial leader of this disinvestment. The disinvestment process was based on income and the age of the community, and so it impoverished small towns and rural areas as well as inner cities. Yet it was based primarily on race, as Gregory D. Squires ably recounts in the introductory chapter. As communities changed racially, the private economy was replaced with a government economy, symbolized most dramatically for the reinvestment movement in the replacement of private home lending by Federal Housing Administration (FHA) and Veterans Administration (VA) lending. This resulted in massive blight as realtors and mortgage lenders engaged in blockbusting and fraud to exploit racial fears and destroy the communities into which minorities were moving (Metropolitan Area Housing Alliance and National Training and Information Center 1975; National Commission on Neighborhoods 1979; Naparstek and Cincotta 1976).

THE LEGACY OF THE DUAL HOUSING FINANCE SYSTEM

Properly regulated and carefully prescribed, the FHA programs of the Department of Housing and Urban Development (HUD) and the programs of the Veteran's Administration are powerful drugs for housing ills; but

231

unregulated and overprescribed, they are extremely toxic and lethal to entire communities. The abuse of these programs—combined with lax regulation by HUD and the VA, and the innate higher risk of these government loans in their own right—condemn these minority and transitional neighborhoods to a future of abandonment and blight (Bradford 1979).

This market of FHA/VA loans and conventional loans is separated on racial lines. It is separated between private depository institutions (conventional lenders) and government insured and guaranteed FHA and VA lending through mortgage companies. (See, for example, Shlay 1987b; Bradford and Marino 1977; Bradford 1991; Feins 1976; Northwest Community Housing Association 1973; Home Ownership Development Program 1973; National Commission on Neighborhoods 1979; and Peterman and Sanshi 1991.) The government's domination in the mortgage and lending market in minority and transitional communities results in massive destruction to the markets where it is concentrated in older, existing cities. It results in high concentrations of abandonment and foreclosure; but it is so lucrative to the real estate agents and government lenders involved that it can drive out the conventional lenders even when they want to reinvest. Moreover, the specter of government influence in the mortgage and lending market is so terrifying that its introduction into a new community can destroy a once healthy market and eliminate the chance for racial and social integration to succeed.

This process of neighborhood destruction contributes to the false belief in the traditional white banking community that racial change undermines a healthy community. Fear of racial change, often expressed by conventional lenders when racial transition is anticipated, creates an incentive for reaping huge profits from the process of rapid racial resegregation. Real estate agents, using racial steering and subtle forms of panic peddling, are the first agents of transition. As conventional lenders withdraw, an army of mortgage companies equipped with a seemingly endless and unregulated flow of FHA/VA supported loans moves into the void and creates a blaze of sales (Bradford 1984). Whites flee to the areas financed by conventional lenders and minorities are steered into each changing neighborhood with the promise of FHA and VA loans. The exploitation of racial fears to encourage white flight and reap the profits from a huge volume of sales and loans becomes a wildfire continually spreading through the healthy communities in its path.

Without the strength and stability of conventional lenders in these communities, mortgage bankers and brokers, working with a cadre of real estate agents, reap profits from massive and rapid racial resegregation. Lax monitoring and bad property management practices by HUD and the VA have resulted in high levels of abuse—leading to extensive abandonment and blight in the communities undergoing change. Unwary homebuyers are often sold defective homes or homes they cannot afford—and the firestorm of FHA and VA lending leaves behind a scorched earth of abandonment and blight.

Even without these abuses and scandals, the concentration of FHA lending in communities with lower incomes and older housing ensured higher foreclosure rates among new and unwary homebuyers. Prior to the late 1960s, FHA was used primarily for new construction and in newer areas. The FHA's very low down payments and liberal credit underwriting policies, made it possible for many homebuyers to acquire a house with limited financial resources. In newer homes this was not a critical problem. In the initial years, all of the systems of the home were new and did not need major repairs. Over time, the rapidly increasing property values provided new equity against which one could borrow for major expenses. One could always sell the home for enough to pay off the loan, if necessary.

However, in older areas where the homes often needed major repairs soon after they were purchased, the liberal financing left homeowners without the resources to meet these needs. Property values did not rise rapidly in these areas and there was no new equity against which to borrow. Without prepurchase counseling, or default counseling after people got into financial trouble, thousands found themselves in foreclosure. This was compounded by the practices of the mortgage companies that filed for foreclosure as soon as possible in order to avoid servicing costs and to claim the insurance proceeds.

The National People's Action (NPA) was born in 1972 in a coming together of communities all over the country that were suffering from the harm done by many different HUD programs. The first national demonstration of NPA was against HUD Secretary George Romney. Yet the movement also was fused together by the belief that communities had been redlined by private investors. The first institutions to be clearly identified were the hazard insurance companies that canceled homeowner policies in white communities as minority transition approached.

233

Then the focus moved to the banking industry—the heart of the nation's economic system. It was the reinvestment campaign of the NPA that drew national attention to the redlining issues and the need to bring private financial institutions back into disinvested communities.

The early and powerful focus on housing—and single-family housing in particular—tended to obscure the larger concerns of the reinvestment movement. For instance, the Home Mortgage Disclosure Act (HMDA) of 1975 is recognized as the first national victory of the movement against the banking industry. The information was to make public where lenders did and did not make loans. In its original form, the bill was called the Financial Institutions Reporting Act and it had included provisions for the disclosure of deposits and commercial lending as well. The movement's interest in the fuller array of business development loans and banking services has reemerged in recent years.

CRITICAL ELEMENTS OF THE REINVESTMENT MOVEMENT

Reinvestment began as both an economic and a civil rights issue. The reinvestment movement does not deal with these issues as abstract philosophies but as basic survival issues for those in the affected communities. That is why direct participation by the community in the reinvestment process has always been so important. Consequently, community organizing around reinvestment—people power—has been at the core of the reinvestment movement. It is the organizing that provides the vehicle for identifying disinvestment and reinvestment issues and defining public accountability for the programs that are developed.

At the beginning of the movement, communities demanded recognition as legitimate participants in lending-policy decisions. They needed the resources to organize, and resources to assess the records of lenders, and the power to intervene in lending policies and programs. Two major pieces of national legislation were key. The HMDA provided the necessary data for reinvestment organizing and the CRA officially recognized the legal obligation of lenders to serve all the residents and needs of their communities. In particular, the CRA provided clear standing for representatives of the community to challenge the right of lending institutions to secure charters, branches, relocations of facilities, mergers, and acquisitions.

A defining quality of reinvestment approaches has been their ability to establish new partnerships. These are not only partnerships between the community and lending institutions or the government but also partnerships among various community groups, coalitions, and organizations. The partnerships have made it possible for programs and agreements to respond to different and diverse local needs, situations, and locations. Yet, the collaborations had to grow out of all of the community work that preceded them. Thus, organizing, the right and the resources to intervene, community economic development capacity, civil rights, response to community needs, partnerships, and accountability are the eight factors that define the reinvestment movement. The union of these factors makes the reinvestment movement unique.

Organizing

Community organizing has been the driving force of the reinvestment movement from the beginning. Often, the reinvestment movement has been seen as confrontational, involving demonstrations—direct actions against lenders, government agencies, or anyone who refused to deal with the community concerns. Shel Trapp is staff director of the National Training and Information Center (NTIC), and its chief organizer for more than twenty years. This is the training, organizing, and research organization for the NPA. Trapp responds to claims that such organizing is no longer needed in his book, *Blessed Be the Fighters*:

> "That was good for the '60s, but it isn't the way to do things [today]." That is a comment often heard in reaction to a demonstration sponsored by a community organization. People making that comment do not realize five things.
> 1. Demonstrations result when all other avenues have been blocked.
> 2. Demonstrations are the result of injustice.
> 3. Demonstrations are the result of concern at injustice.
> 4. Demonstrations show power.
> 5. Most importantly, demonstrations work.
> (Trapp 1986:35)

> "Confrontation was good for the '60s, but this is the . . . age of partnerships." That really sounds great, but the basis of partnership is equality and respect. My experi-

235

Calvin Bradford and Gale Cincotta

ence in the '60s, '70s, and '80s has been that while we
are willing to form partnerships with anyone who is willing to come to the table and seriously discuss the issues, I
have not seen too many of our opponents come to the
table willingly. . . . Partnerships are great as long as
there is mutual respect. Community organizations usually
have to fight to get that respect. It reminds me of the
story of the farmer who was asked why he hit his mule
over the head with a two-by-four. His response was,
"That is just to get his attention." In all the partnerships
we formed, we first had to get the attention of our opponents. Translated, that means we've had to confront
them.

(Trapp 1986:13–14)

The organizing that emerged from the reinvestment movement
was unique in many ways. It was unique in that the organizing did not
take the typical role of opposing an institution and trying to block its
activities in the community. Rather, the organization was aimed at insuring that the institution would carry out its activities in the local communities organized around the issue.

The redlining movement was particularly unique in its interracial
structure. As Gregory D. Squires notes in Chapter 1 of this volume, the
Kerner Commission defined two communities—one black, one white—
separate and unequal. When community groups began to organize
around FHA abuses (blockbusting and redlining in Chicago), students of
Saul Alinsky told the organizers that this was a mistake. They said that
banking issues were too complex and distant from the people's daily lives
to mobilize organizing efforts. Moreover, they argued, racially changing
communities were not organizable. The tensions between working-class
whites who remained in their old communities as more affluent whites
escaped to the suburbs and blacks moving into these same communities
as they aspired to improve their lives was nothing but a time bomb waiting to explode in racial violence. There was no lack of this violence in
the country—and some groups did try to organize around FHA issues as a
means of blocking minorities from buying homes in white areas. Despite
this racist climate, the National People's Action was an organization of
white, minority, and racially changing communities. It became the lead-

ing force in reinvestment policy and programs and still retains this position after more that twenty years.

The secrets of this dramatic organizing success were outlined by Gale Cincotta in her tenth annual address to the NPA before over three thousand participants at the national conference in Baltimore (Cincotta 1981). There were two key points. First, Cincotta said, "I will bet that nobody expects to be rescued by a knight in shining armor, by any politician, by big business . . . by Paul Volker of the Federal Reserve System, or anyone. We know that the only way that we survive is ourselves— ourselves and organizing." Second, "we have found the enemy and it isn't us!" The enemy was not each other—it was a system that discriminated against minorities and older communities—something they all shared in common. Finally, NPA was an organization that gave people courage and power because they were not fighting to change the American system, but to make it work in their communities.

Members of NPA were outraged that the bankers had taken their savings and instead of investing it back into their communities, as they all believed was the role and obligation of these institutions, had given it to other communities—suburban and white communities that grew as these older, minority, inner-city, and rural communities were starved for lack of money to maintain themselves and rebuild their economies. The outrage that both blacks and whites felt was the deep and sincere outrage of people who believed in the traditional values of their society. It was a movement to confront the institutions that had betrayed them—institutions they had believed in and supported with their life's savings.

Direct community participation provided direct accountability to the people affected by the disinvestment and the reinvestment. While there are examples in the previous chapters where public interest groups seem to have been an effective substitute for direct neighborhood participation, such as in California, in general where the community base and ability for community action have withered away, reinvestment has suffered.

The seven case studies report varying degrees of success. These levels of success and the comprehensiveness of the programs are directly related to the strength of the community organizing involved in reinvestment campaigns. Strong community coalitions were organized in Chicago and Pittsburgh. A series of organizations participated in the agreements in Milwaukee, sometimes combining their power in coalitions and

Calvin Bradford and Gale Cincotta

sometimes using their independent power. Some groups engaged in direct action and demonstrations to bring the lenders to the negotiating table.

In Atlanta, where the organizing was weakest, the least effective and least comprehensive programs were developed. Indeed, the banks' response to the sudden attack in the local media was to create a poorly thought-out program that produced some significant loan failures. These failures have been highly publicized through the publications of the local Federal Reserve Bank (Zimmerman 1990) and have encouraged bankers' concerns about the wisdom of reinvestment for low-income people. In spite of some notable successes in California, the lack of a powerful state-wide base contributed to the inability to reach written agreements with some lenders or any agreements at all with others.

In Detroit and Boston huge, but generally vague, commitments were made by lending institutions thus putting pressure on later processes to define the programs more clearly. In Boston, formal mechanisms were developed to continue the refinement—but along paths that separated the community coalition into different processes—splitting the unity and power of the coalition. This left the groups working on home loans, for example, isolated in dealing with the least productive segment of the agreements. In Detroit, the community participants in the reinvestment programs were drawn together late in the process, and the focus was more on certain personalities than real grass-roots organizations. It took years for the community-based and church-based development groups— and other community organizations—to develop a real monitoring and planning structure and direct relationships with the banks involved. As the case study recognizes, the lack of early organizing and the lack of assistance from more experienced organizations contributed to a situation where the commitments were controlled by the lenders and where the commitments lacked real targeting and detail.

In Chicago, Pittsburgh, Boston, and Milwaukee strong coalitions and active individual organizations have produced a range of agreements and programs that address many different needs. In Pittsburgh and Chicago, especially, a strong base of community action and community development groups has produced a broad range of programs designed to meet both general needs and specialized niches not served by other programs or lenders. In Boston, there had been a long history of reinvestment—with the Massachusetts Urban Reinvestment Advisory Group (MURAG) negotiating sixteen agreements in the Boston area before 1988

238

and assisting some of the groups involved in the later agreements. Here, the disadvantages of a new and inexperienced set of coalition partners was not as devastating as it was in Atlanta, where there was no reinvestment tradition. This attests to the effectiveness and power of strong community organizations and the ability to develop a community capacity for housing and economic development.

Almost all of the agreements involved some contact and assistance from some regional or national community or technical assistance group. The National People's Action, the largest association of community organizations, and its technical assistance arm, NTIC, have assisted in eighty-one agreements, including work with the groups in Milwaukee, Boston, Pittsburgh and Atlanta. The largest regional assistance provider is MURAG, which has negotiated or assisted in over twenty agreements. The Association of Community Organizations for Reform Now (ACORN) the largest national membership organization with local chapters across the country in low-income and minority communities, has negotiated twenty-five CRA agreements. The Center for Community Change in Washington, D.C. has assisted in about twenty-five agreements, including some of the agreements in California. The Woodstock Institute in Chicago has provided reports on mortgage lending in Chicago for many groups and it has participated in several agreements as well.

In the past, and at present, a variety of groups have contributed expertise. For instance, in the last five years, legal assistance groups have joined in the CRA process. Their activities have been concentrated in the Southeast, where they have participated in negotiating eleven agreements, but they have also played a role in agreements in Indianapolis, Philadelphia, and California. Some of the local chapters of national civil rights groups—such as the National Association for the Advancement of Colored People (NAACP) and the Urban League—and several fair housing groups have joined in negotiations for agreements in several places, including Toledo, Orlando, Baltimore, Dallas, Gary (Indiana), and Akron. Often several groups form a coalition, as we see in the cases of Milwaukee, Chicago, Pittsburgh, California, and Boston. This is true in many other places as well, as evidenced by the Duluth Reinvestment Coalition, the Maryland Alliance for Responsible Investment, the Charlotte Reinvestment Alliance, and the Indianapolis Reinvestment Alliance. Some coalitions or groups have multiple agreements with different lending institutions, such as the five agreements for the ACORN chapter in St. Louis, three agreements for the San Antonio Reinvestment Alliance, the sixteen agreements for the Massachusetts Urban Reinvestment Advisory Group, or the fourteen agreements with various chapters of Iowa Concerned Citizens for Improvement (ICCI).

Organizing is a critical ingredient in reinvestment efforts. Though divers groups have been involved in various cities, leadership and participation by members of impacted communities have proven to be essential.

The Resources to Intervene

In order to intervene, community groups have acquired the tools to research lending patterns, the organizational capacity to engage the lending institution in negotiations, and the ability to define needs and solutions. The key resource that was the driving force around which the national reinvestment movement first developed its campaign was disclosure information about the lending patterns of financial institutions. Where community groups were able to collect information on lending patterns from legal records of homes sales and property liens, these studies showed that the claims of disinvestment were true. These studies became powerful resources in the hearings that led to the Home Mortgage Disclosure Act (HMDA) (Committee on Banking, Housing and Urban Affairs 1975). There are many types of data used now by community organizations to review the lending records, profitability, capacity, services, and policies of lending institutions, but HMDA remains the one, virtually universal, information resource. All of the case studies in this book incorporated analyses of lending patterns using HMDA data. Since HMDA was passed, surveys done for NTIC (Bradford and Przybylski 1979, and Bradford and Schersten 1985) have recorded over 350 uses of HMDA by community-based organizations in over 125 cities—with over 7,800 annual uses of HMDA by lenders, regulatory agencies, government agencies, and community groups combined.

In addition to information resources, groups need financial resources. In each of the seven case studies herein, there was some need at some point for organizing and confrontation. For community and issues organizing, financial support is critical. Yet, most foundations are uncomfortable with this and have gravitated away from community organizing, making the false claim that this type of activity is no longer needed in the age of partnership.

Adding to this problem is the number of lenders and board members of lending institutions who are also directors or board members of foundations that control financial resources. In the past few years, CRA activities funded by one major foundation were achieving significant results through several groups around the country. During a recent funding cycle, pressure was exerted on the foundation by board members claiming that CRA activities were a form of blackmail against lending institutions. The foundation initiated a special report that showed the positive outcomes of its funding efforts. Nonetheless, shortly thereafter the foundation told CRA grant recipients that it would no longer define a category of CRA activities for funding. Thus, the power of the financial institutions can be brought to bear on the financial resources that communities need to organize around the issue.

The rhetoric about the value of partnerships and the desire of both community groups and funders to become involved in the technical part of "making deals" for development projects has undermined the need for support for issues and community organizing. In some cases, community action groups evolve into community development organizations, sometimes losing their ability to deal with real organizing needs and to work with community organizers and organizations (Przybylski, Gardner, and Shurna 1981; Kolodny 1985). The most successful coalitions dealing with reinvestment have overcome the tensions between the organizing and development groups. Most development groups involved in reinvestment see the need for action groups that have the independence to hold lenders accountable and that can organize around reinvestment issues both locally and nationally to change policy and develop new programs that can be used by the development groups. Many agreements, especially those patterned after the agreements in Chicago, have provided for various forms of funding for community development and community issues groups.

The Right to Intervene

The CRA has been the primary tool of intervention and HMDA has provided data on lending (presently restricted to housing lending). In all of the cases studied herein some part of the campaign revolved around applications covered by the CRA and an analysis of HMDA lending data. The CRA campaigns have resulted in over two hundred reinvestment agreements of some kind. Interstate banking activities, and the activity of lenders engaged in regional consolidation to strengthen their positions in the face of national competition and interstate banking, have provided a massive increase in the opportunities for groups to use the CRA to review

Calvin Bradford and Gale Cincotta

lending records and raise reinvestment issues. Over 80 percent of the existing agreements have been negotiated since the advent of interstate banking in 1984. These agreements involve over three-hundred different community-based groups in over seventy metropolitan areas and rural communities (Bradford 1992).

Community-Based Development Capacity

Like the anti-redlining movement of community action groups, the focus of community-based development corporations has been on the economic needs of the existing residents of a community. Yet the community development movement and the reinvestment movement grew along separate, though sometimes parallel, tracks. While the Ford Foundation made large investments, beginning in the 1960s, in a limited number of Community Development Corporations (CDCs) that engaged in a wide range of economic development and business development activities, government support for these corporations soon followed with funding through the Community Services Administration. President Reagan's efforts to remove all the remnants of the War on Poverty programs finally eliminated this funding. During the 1970s, the number of CDCs nationally never rose to many more than two hundred. In spite of the withdrawal of government funding, CDCs not only survived, but they have prospered to become a significant force in the economic future of severely depressed communities. Today it is estimated that there are more than 2,000 community-based development corporations in the country (National Congress for Community Economic Development 1989).

The majority of CDCs historically have concentrated on low- and moderate-income housing projects, with government financing and private foundation grants as the major capital resources. Where the banking industry was involved, it was typically on construction financing and mortgage financing when huge government grants and foundation subsidies could reduce the risks to terms acceptable to very conservative lenders. Foundation and government funds also have represented a major capital resource in economic development activities. In addition, there have been a number of efforts to create special capital pools in order to provide services such as revolving loan pools and socially responsible equity investment programs. Generally, in all of these activities to tap capital markets for the work of the CDCs, there had been little common work with the community action groups.

Events in the past few years have conspired to present opportunities for the coming together of the reinvestment movement and CDC activities. Both groups now recognize that a much more comprehensive and sophisticated set of vehicles is needed to draw on private capital resources and to get these funds out into successful community development activities. As the federal government has withdrawn resources from housing programs, low-income housing has become even more of a local organizing issue. With little success at securing funding from Washington, many community organizations have tried developing their own CDCs for housing. While community-based direct action might produce reinvestment in single-family mortgages, the production of low- and moderate-income housing projects and the purchase and rehabilitation of both single-family and multifamily housing in areas where the housing stock has suffered deterioration require some development entity to carry out community revitalization—even if loans were available.

Thus, in retrospect, community action efforts came to define problems that could be solved only if there were capable entities that could carry out housing development at the community level and in the interest of the community members. Getting commitments from lenders was possible by the traditional organizing process, but getting the funds out, and even defining a real demand for the loans, required the development of, or support of, housing development corporations, and the related training and equity investment programs.

On the economic development side, job development and business development have become one of the most powerful driving forces in community organizing. Fifteen years ago, organizers could confine most of their activities to seeking benefits from government programs in order to get their share of the economic pie. Today, economic development issues are important to almost every organization, but business and job development have not been so amenable to the traditional organizing and action processes. They require additional capacity and development skills. While getting access to business credit from banks has become the most important new aspect of bank reinvestment activity, it has also been the least successful in terms of being able to get these loans out into the community.

For community development corporations, the reduction in federal funding and changes in the tax laws affecting housing, in particular, have created obstacles to their continued growth and development.

243

Moreover, just as the community organizers must respond to increased job-creation and economic development issues, so too must CDCs move beyond housing and into the larger economic development world. The problems this creates for CDCs are enormous. Business development is much more sophisticated and complex than housing development. Business development requires more complex financing. Without high levels of government subsidy and without real estate as the major source of collateral, the problems of seeking capital in the private markets are severe. New business development, unlike many forms of housing development, is seen by the private sector as a very high risk proposition. Even more than in housing projects, sound management and marketing skills are required—as are skills in product development and innovation.

In addition, the need to engage in economic development has raised questions about the role and impact of CDCs whose central focus always had been to start their own businesses. With very few exceptions, both the existing and potential level of job creation by such corporations amounts to only a small fraction of the local economies in which they are located. Many CDCs have responded by changing their focus, and many new CDCs have been developed to provide support and packaging resources to existing business and to entrepreneurs wishing to start new businesses or locate new or existing business in the community.

This new role of being the packager, marketer, and advocate for business within the community, rather than actually being the business itself, provides some real opportunities to overcome the impact and scale limitations of CDCs that simply develop their own businesses. It is this new role that provides the most incentive for cooperation with the community action groups. As advocates for existing and new businesses, these CDCs must respond to the financial requirements of the conventional business world. They must deal with the need for business lending by the banking industry as a major area of concern. In almost all of the reinvestment agreements and programs designed today for meeting low- and moderate-income housing needs and for commercial, industrial, and business development, the agreements include specific roles or loan pools for CDCs.

The Chicago case shows how the CDCs were integrated into the negotiations by the coalition of action groups to provide capacity and credibility to the community demands and goals. In the original process of community accountability, two city-wide but community-based development corporations—one for housing and one for commercial and industrial development—were defined as the conduit for the program loans. A special role was defined for community-based developers in some of the Milwaukee agreements as well. In Pittsburgh the coalition was comprised largely of development groups—with a focus in both housing and business development. In Boston, the role of the community development organizations was defined both in the structure of the reinvestment challenges and negotiations and in the implementation of the programs.

Typically, community-based development organizations are important in defining credit needs and in providing a capacity to generate loan applications. In heavily disinvested communities where private developers are not inclined to get involved, it is the community-based development organizations that provide the capacity to package projects and loans and manage the development once it is financed (Bradford 1990). In reinvestment campaigns, these organizations provide guidance in defining the specific products and services that are needed to reach critical and particular community needs. Even in Atlanta where no community agreements were reached, the involvement of community-based developers was essential in defining a program for reinvestment. Their involvement provides legitimacy for the demands of the community, as was clearly the case in Chicago and Pittsburgh. In turn, the agreements and programs often include additional resources to build the community's capacity to grow economically as a critical element in reaching targeted lending goals. Where lending agreements have failed to produce loans, it is often related to the lack of involvement or lack of capacity of community-based development groups to implement the programs.

Civil Rights

The reinvestment movement, with its original focus on redlining, was born in the tension of racial change. It has always been a movement for civil rights in its opposition to the racially discriminatory behavior of financial institutions. Its unique and powerful contribution to the civil rights movement is that it emerged from working-class white and upwardly mobile black communities. These communities were potential cites of racial violence because whites were determined not to let racial change destroy their communities and blacks were determined to take advantage of the opportunities to move into more desirable communities.

Calvin Bradford and Gale Cincotta

The redlining issue provided both groups with a vehicle to understand that both groups were victims.

Interracial cooperation came not from psychological soul searching or moral invocations for understanding. It came from the respect that each group found for the other as they applied their skills to dealing with the outside forces that they identified as destroying the communities that they now shared. This was a classic case of groups unifying to fight a common enemy. Organizers had found a source of common goals and strength in a situation that had been defined by experts as a source of violence and divisiveness. As Gale Cincotta put it when referring to these so-called experts, "I think they suffered from too much education. They never knew how much community people cared" (Cincotta 1981). While racial divisions exist in reinvestment struggles, as demonstrated in the early Milwaukee efforts, the very act of organizing and taking collective action forge a bond that often overcomes the forces of racism.

The first CRA challenge was filed in Toledo by the Fair Housing Center. But, in general, the traditional civil rights and fair housing groups did not become part of the reinvestment movement until recently. Perhaps there was too much suspicion of the white-working class participants in reinvestment efforts because they were not like the well-educated liberal whites who had become involved in the civil rights movement (Berry 1979). Perhaps it was that much of the activity of the civil rights groups had been on developing ways that people could escape from inner-city communities, while the reinvestment movement wanted to transform these communities. For the fair housing groups, their activities had always been concentrated in white, typically suburban communities and focused on trying to gain access for minorities. The reinvestment movement was concentrated in inner-city areas, often already minority areas and frequently areas of severe economic decline. In the past several years, some fair housing groups have discovered that the communities where they once created opportunities for minorities have been victimized by the disinvestment process that used the initial access for minorities to exploit racial fears and profit from full-scale resegregation. Communities that were once targets for fair housing have now become targets for reinvestment.

Realizing that, the civil rights community is being drawn into the reinvestment movement with the recognition that unless fair lending is part of fair housing, the process of disinvestment will plague the opportunities they create for integration. Fair housing groups are now becoming actively involved in lending issues. For example, the major studies of redlining and lending issues as well as the effort to develop testing programs for discrimination in lending in Chicago in the last few years have been undertaken by the Chicago Area Fair Housing Alliance (Orfield 1988; Cloud 1991). The Milwaukee case describes how the national attention to lending discrimination that was created by the *Atlanta Journal/ Constitution* resulted in fair housing activities there, with the development of the Fair Lending Project as the most recent coalition involved in community reinvestment activity. At the national level, the National Fair Housing Alliance has made lending issues one of its central concerns for research, education, and litigation.

Response to Local Needs

The early agreements tended to concentrate on single-family mortgages and home improvement lending. While the first written agreement in Chicago was signed in 1974, the first oral agreement resulted from the reinvestment campaign in Chicago in 1971, with Security National Bank. It is instructive to note that it included equal commitments of $4 million for housing and business loans. More recent agreements tend to include lending for multifamily rental or cooperative housing to provide affordable housing for low- and moderate-income groups. In the last five years, agreements also often include allocations for commercial and industrial or small business lending and grants from the lenders to build the development capacity of the neighborhood action and development groups involved in the programs. The case study in California reveals how the assessment of business lending needs is becoming central to the reinvestment movement.

The vast majority of all agreements involve changes in the terms and underwriting standards for the loans. Many programs provide reduced application or processing fees, and some waive these costs altogether. Many programs provide lower interest rates for certain home and business loans in order to make them more affordable. Some programs alter underwriting standards that tended to discriminate against lower-income homebuyers, minority neighborhoods, or small businesses. Some programs concentrate on hiring practices while others concentrate on fair housing initiatives. Some programs concentrate on providing basic banking services (check cashing and deposit services) and on the opening and

247

closing of branches and other offices. Many programs are patterned after the diverse elements of the Neighborhood Lending Programs in Chicago, but with additions and deletions reflecting local concerns and needs.

There is great variation in these agreements and programs, expressing the diversity of local needs and concerns. In California, the primary concern in housing lending is for affordable housing. As the California and Boston cases illustrate, in areas of high housing cost, an absolute priority is placed on producing housing for low-income people. In places like Chicago, while lower-income housing is a priority, some communities are so depressed that they see their needs being met by efforts that also bring in higher income residents. The mechanism of providing for community endorsement of loans and the approval of all loans counted in the programs by the review boards provides a means for communities to set standards appropriate to their needs.

It is within communities where there are diverse needs that it is hardest to maintain the coalitions and to develop comprehensive programs. In Boston, community-based participants had differing priorities among small business, multi-family, or single-family needs. This created a struggle within the fragile and shifting coalition as well as struggles between the community groups and the lenders. These are tensions and issues that can be resolved and forged into multipurpose agreements with good organizing—as in Chicago and Pittsburgh—or that can result in mutually respected independent efforts, such as in Milwaukee.

Partnership

As a form of partnership, reinvestment predates the rhetoric and programs that began to emerge during the Carter administration. Most partnership models tend to exclude the actual citizens who are supposed to benefit (Bradford 1983; Squires 1989). Reinvestment creates partnerships that are not two-sided partnerships between the government and the private sector, but three-sided—with a direct role for the community. Reinvestment represents a partnership at the most expansive economic levels in this country including major capital institutions and local communities, poor people's organizations and minority organizations. It creates accountability in the most participatory way—reflecting understandings of economic development and direct networks of producers and consumers.

These are the most difficult of partnerships because they bring together people with very different goals and interests, rather than depending upon people with an initial shared vision. In this process, confrontation is often the context of the initial meeting. The reinvestment process is inaugurated through processes that develop mutual respect out of this initial confrontation. Interestingly, the conversion experiences of lenders have been a common element of the reinvestment process leading to successful partnerships and programs. One lender in Texas, who later appeared on a television program to advocate reinvestment, began his initial meeting with the local reinvestment group by noting, "It looks like a good day for a hanging."

Research shows that commitment is key to reinvestment. The difference between lenders who invest in declining, inner-city, lower-income, or minority communities and others is not a product of a bank's size, capacity, or sophistication but its attitude (Boggs, Bradford, and Duncan 1986 and Boggs, Sorenson, and Isserman 1988). In Minneapolis and St. Paul, for example, the combined assets of the two largest banks (Norwest and First Bank) are over $22 billion (*Thompson Bank Directory*, 1991), yet the lender with the best reputation for community lending (including an award from the state) is Western State Bank, which has somewhat more than $100 million in assets. Reinvestment is designed to change attitudes. That is why the organizing, and even confrontation, are so often necessary and effective. It can take a major jolt to move a lending institution to change its attitude about its loan policies and its views of particular neighborhoods and groups of people.

The case studies describe the tactics and negotiation processes used by community groups to get lenders' attention and to gain recognition and respect. The development capacity of groups in Pittsburgh and Boston was critical to gaining respect, but in Chicago, that respect did not develop until the lenders were taken on tours to see the communities and to see the results of the community development efforts. These are partnerships that were built as bridges over troubled waters—not partnerships that flowed together out of common streams. In many cases, the agreements involve the use of government and other special development programs, such as in Pittsburgh, Boston, Chicago, and California. Indeed, nearly all of the multifamily housing projects achieved affordable rents through one or more government programs or subsidies. In some cases, as in Chicago and Pittsburgh, special programs were developed by state or local agencies just to work with the reinvestment programs. The role of leveraging private funds rather than replacing private funds brings the government into an investment role in addition to its role in enforcing fair housing and reinvestment laws. Here, the government becomes part of the partnership. This defines a reinvestment role for the government as a limited investment partner in the local economy, not as the institutions that replaces the private economy.

Once the partnerships are formed with the lending institutions, it is possible for the community and lending institutions to act together to change the policies and practices of other key factors in the reinvestment process. In Chicago, for example, after five years of operating the Neighborhood Lending Programs, it was clear that the real missing partner was not the community or the bank, but the federal government. Secretary of HUD Jack Kemp was brought to Chicago by NTIC and the participants in the Neighborhood Lending Programs to be shown what they had done and what was left to do. They were able to define collectively what they could do for future reinvestment and exactly how much government funding was needed to bring the federal government into the partnership to achieve the reinvestment goals. Community groups and lenders who had once been at odds now worked together on policy and program initiatives to complete a mutually supported development agenda.

Accountability

The HMDA and the CRA provide a national legal framework for developing effective and accountable reinvestment efforts, but more specific measures are essential at the local level if reinvestment programs are to succeed. However positive the relationships between lenders and community partners, the best programs contain formal processes for accountability. One of the problems of moving forward in California is that the relationships with the lenders depend largely on good will alone. Without even written agreements in most cases, there are few means by which the community can hold lenders accountable if the attitude or priority— or particular officers—in the lending institutions change. This can be compared to the formal and individualized review boards in Chicago and Pittsburgh that had participants from community groups and lender institutions. These processes produce a review of all loans, routine reporting on lending activity, and a forum for identifying problems and developing solutions and new initiatives. They also provide for constant contact between community groups and lenders, giving each personal access to the other. It is through these constant contacts that other lending programs and other policy initiatives often develop (Bradford 1990).

In Detroit and Boston, the agreements were vague and provided for little or no formal accountability. Yet in Boston, the organizations set up to plan and review each of the four areas of concentration do provide a means of review and accountability that has been used to move the programs along, identify problems, and even provide some groups with the context in which to negotiate some specific agreements. Simply the obligation to meet and review progress has wrestled some specificity and community control out of a process that was based on good will and the unilateral definitions of goals by the lending institutions alone. In Detroit, with only some initial reporting commitments, it has taken much longer to establish a community-based monitoring and review structure.

These forms of accountability are familiar to community organizers, but not to corporate managers. In a purely economic sense, they allow consumers direct access to suppliers and they provide for the development of products and services directly responsive to the needs of a set of consumers, but they do so at the cost of total freedom on the part of the suppliers—the lenders. This direct accountability is a creative, but new, model in the American business world. The various forms of accountability that are developed in these reinvestment agreements represent unique and fascinating experiments in the tensions between a free market economy and a democratic political system that provides for the protection of the rights and needs of the minority as well as the majority.

Despite the victories that have been won and the important lessons learned about the essential elements of successful reinvestment programs, powerful barriers to future gains remain. Many of the problems noted by Squires continue or have resurfaced in slightly different forms— and new barriers have been erected. Federal enforcement efforts, industry restructuring, and direct attacks on the CRA threaten the future of reinvestment.

THE FAILURE OF THE FEDERAL REGULATORS

In addition to playing a role as a partner in reinvestment programs, the main function of the government in reinvestment is to enforce the reinvestment laws and regulations. While the Financial Institutions Reform, Recovery, and Enforcement Act (FIRREA) expanded disclosure and strengthened CRA related requirements, many of the gains made in the last two decades by community organizations through legislation, negotiation of reinvestment agreements, and litigation have been undermined by the enforcement practices of the federal agencies that regulate depository institutions. The agencies are the Federal Reserve Board (Fed), the Office of the Comptroller of the Currency (OCC), the Federal Deposit Insurance Corporation (FDIC) and the Office of Thrift Supervision (OTS) (previously the Federal Home Loan Bank Board [FHLBB]. In spite of the best intentions and legislative efforts of Congress, the policies and practices of these agencies—and of HUD and the VA (Veterans Administration)—have actually encouraged the disinvestment and redlining of inner-city and minority communities and encouraged speculative investments in white areas.

As Squires points out, the Community Reinvestment Act imposes an "affirmative" requirement on lenders to serve the needs of all the people and neighborhoods in the communities they serve. The Fair Housing Act requires that they not discriminate. Thus far, case law has maintained the position that policies that discriminate "in effect" violate the law. Taken together, this imposes an affirmative requirement on lenders to serve the needs of minority communities and to insure that no policies, intentionally or in effect, fail to take full advantage of opportunities to serve minorities. Nonetheless, these agencies have not only failed to apply an affirmative standard, they have defended this dual market and actually aided and abetted in the wholesale disinvestment of minority communities by the institutions they regulate.

In addition to the studies and reviews of lending cited in the case studies (Squires and Velez 1987; Shlay 1987b; Finn 1989; Bradbury, Case, and Dunham 1989; Everett, Gallagher, and Blossom 1988; Dedman 1988) scores of community-based analyses (Bradford and Schersten 1985; Bradford and Przybylski 1979) and a host of formal studies in such places as Cleveland (Quereau and Obermanns 1989), Philadelphia (Goldstein 1986), New York City (Williams 1988), Washington, D.C. (Shlay 1985), and Baltimore (Shlay 1987a) all confirm the consistency and pervasiveness of conventional lenders withdrawing services from inner-city, minority, and transitional neighborhoods. When asked to respond to such studies, the regulatory agencies respond with an argument that reminds one of the outlawed "separate but equal" ideology for racial segregation.

The regulatory agencies invariably declare that these studies ignore the government-supported FHA/VA market and the lending of mortgage bankers and mortgage brokers—who originate three-fourths of these government loans. In hearings before the Senate Subcommittee on Consumer and Regulatory Affairs, John LaWare, of the Federal Reserve System Board of Governors, responded to precisely these studies and commented that these patterns could be explained by factors other than discrimination, factors such as the "traditionally high level of activity by mortgage bankers and finance companies" (LaWare 1990:5).

In response to Senate Banking Committee Chairman Senator William Proxmire's call for an explanation for the racial patterns revealed in the Atlanta Journal/Constitution articles (Dedman 1988), all of the regulatory agencies filed reports in August of 1988. Three of these four agencies specifically pointed to the role of mortgage bankers and FHA/VA lending as an excuse for the patterns (Federal Reserve Board 1988; Clarke 1988; Seidman 1988) The fourth agency, the FHLBB, admitted that its own loan-log data revealed much higher rates of rejections for blacks than whites but claimed that it was too busy with safety and soundness problems to do complete examinations and that the review it did make in Atlanta "does not suggest intentional discrimination" (Wall 1988, emphasis added). The concentration on "intentional" discrimination is particularly problematic in lending where much of the discrimination results from general underwriting policies which may appear to be neutral, but which have a discriminatory effect. A 1989 study of lending in the Boston market was originated by a member of the Boston Fed research staff. Like scores of other studies, this analysis found a relationship between race and levels of lending that could not be explained by income, wealth, housing value, or other similar factors. However, the authors of this study addressed both the intentional discrimination issue and the obligations of lenders under the CRA by pointing out that "unlike other lenders, commercial banks and thrifts have an affirmative obligation under the Community Reinvestment Act of 1977 to help meet the credit needs of their entire community. Thus, even if the disparities in the mortgage market activity were not the fault of lenders, banks and thrifts would be expected to help correct the situation" (Bradbury, Case, and Dunham 1989).

Ironically, just prior to the time this study was begun the Fed made a decision about a CRA challenge that demonstrates the regulatory agency does not share this understanding of its enforcement role. The case involves the 1987 application to the Fed by SunTrust, parent of

Trust Company Banks in Atlanta, to buy another bank. A challenge by community groups pointed out that Trust Company had only one mortgage product and that it was not attractive to most minorities. The challenge also pointed out that the bank had closed several offices in communities after they became minority communities—even though the deposit base in at least one community increased significantly. The bank responded in a letter to the Fed that it understood that it had consciously decided to offer only one type of mortgage and that it realized this type of mortgage would not serve the markets in older, stable communities (Dickinson 1987:3). The letter specifically indicated that the bank understood the effect of this was not to serve minority communities and then asked the Fed not to apply the effects test. Such an admission of the clear understanding of the effects of the policy would seem to move the issue from an effects test question to a question of intentional discrimination. Yet, the Fed granted the application with no response to this admission of discrimination.

This challenge became the focus of one set of articles in the *Atlanta Journal/Constitution* series. In 1989, another challenge was filed against Trust Company, pointing out that it had continued to close branches in minority communities. In March of 1990 the Fed granted this application as well. When the Senate Subcommittee on Consumer and Regulatory Affairs held fair lending hearings in October 1989, the representative of the Fed twice defended the overall fair housing record of his agency by indicating that it had found no "deliberate discrimination" in its reviews of lender behavior (LaWare 1990: 4–5).

One of the casualties of deregulation, along with the monumental costs of the savings and loan debacle, has been the enforcement of fair housing and equal credit opportunity laws. In the spirit of deregulation and because they were occupied with mounting S & L and bank failures, the federal financial regulatory agencies reduced their fair housing and CRA compliance efforts. For example, during the height of the failures of savings and loans the FHLBB, which regulated S & Ls, all but abandoned these "consumer" examinations altogether. As late as 1990, the OTS (which replaced the FHLBB in regulating savings and loans) was still promising the Subcommittee on Consumer and Regulatory Affairs of the Senate Banking Committee that it was finally prepared to engage in active fair housing and consumer compliance enforcement again (Kluckman 1990).

An unfortunate reality is that almost no applications are ever denied by the regulatory agencies on CRA, fair housing, or any other grounds. The four financial regulatory agencies reported in hearings before the Senate Banking Committee in 1988 that in the past ten years they had denied only eight of 40,000 applications covered by the CRA (Proxmire 1988: 7–8). As Squires recounts in his introductory chapter, at Senate hearings on fair housing enforcement held by Senator Alan J. Dixon in October 1989, all four financial regulatory agencies reported that in the past ten years none of them had been able to identify a single case of discrimination to refer to the Department of Justice. This record seemed even more astonishing since representatives of the Toledo Fair Housing Center testified that they had successfully brought suit against several lenders for discrimination in lending in that one small city (Dane 1990; Smith 1990).

Ironically, the Fed denied an application by Continental Bank in Chicago in 1989 and forced Harris Bank in Chicago to withdraw an application in 1990—and eventually gave Harris a failing CRA rating. These measures were taken under claims of poor CRA performance. While it is clear that any lender might do more in fair housing, both of these banks are involved in major community reinvestment and lending programs—programs that have been extremely effective at guiding conventional funds back into minority communities in Chicago for both single-family and multifamily housing. Reviews of public ratings by the authors of this chapter and NTIC staff indicate that other lenders, all across the country, who have no record of affirmative programs for reinvestment and fair housing—and some who are cited by the regulators for Fair Housing Act violations—have routinely been given high CRA ratings and been granted applications even in the face of continual challenges by community groups. It appears from these actions that not only do the regulators endorse the dual housing market, but they are willing to penalize those institutions that take aggressive steps to overcome conventional lending discrimination and act affirmatively on fair housing.

With lax enforcement by the regulatory agencies, lenders have been allowed to continue to allocate their resources toward high growth areas, speculative investments and the building and maintenance of white communities while withholding their credit from inner-city, minority, and transitional communities. Lacking access to conventional lending, minority and transitional communities are left to be served by the federally insured and guaranteed markets of the FHA and VA lending programs. Community groups, civil rights organizations, and fair housing groups have had to carry the burden of CRA and fair housing enforcement in the absence of responsible intervention by the financial regulatory agencies.

When regulators were cited by Congress for failing to enforce fair housing and reinvestment as prescribed by the law, they literally blamed community groups for not forcing them to do their jobs. In the July 1989, CRA hearings before the Senate Banking Committee's Subcommittee on Consumer and Regulatory Affairs, the Federal Reserve Board responded to a question about how often it had granted applications to institutions with poor CRA records by stating that "the Board approved about 70 applications where the CRA rating was less than satisfactory— and very few of these involved CRA protests" (Federal Reserve Board 1990: 126).

Yet, even when the community has filed a challenge and the regulatory agency has placed some obligations on the lender, the regulatory agencies fail to enforce compliance with their own directives. For example, in commenting on regulators' practice of giving "conditional approvals" to applications with reinvestment obligations imposed by the agencies, Gale Cincotta reported to a Senate committee: "Several lenders that got conditional approvals in the early years of the CRA actually made less loans afterwards, and became the subject of a second CRA protest. Bank of Indiana was one such repeat offender. In 1980, the OCC approved their merger application based on the conditions that they develop a CRA compliance plan. Over the next six years, the bank failed to make a single mortgage loan in the City of Gary" (Cincotta 1988: 37). It was only after community groups negotiated a $50 million reinvestment program that the bank suddenly began making many loans in communities where the regulator claimed there was a "lack of demand." Negotiated reinvestment agreements have now placed billions of dollars in communities where the lenders and regulators claimed there was no demand.

Looking back over the activities of the regulators, Cincotta testified, "We though we were going to have a partnership with the regulators doing more than they have been, and that it would be . . . the unusual cases that the community would have to go out and deal with the financial institutions (Cincotta 1988: 33). The community had anticipated having a role in enforcement only rarely, but in reality community participation has become the norm.

DENYING PUBLIC ACCESS TO INFORMATION

Not only have the regulatory agencies failed to play an aggressive role in enforcing the CRA and Fair Housing Act, but also they have obstructed efforts to provide for disclosure of lending patterns so that the public can make its own decisions about the records of financial institutions. When the Fair Housing Act was first passed, the financial regulatory agencies considered keeping data on race, but failed to implement the plans. A 1971 survey by the Federal Home Loan Bank Board received only seventy-four responses—but 30 percent of the respondents indicated that they did not make loans in minority and lower-income communities (Federal Home Loan Bank Board 1972). A 1973 HUD questionnaire to all regulated financial institutions reported a 97 percent response rate (U.S. Department of Housing and Urban Development 1974). Data for the fifty cities with the largest minority populations indicated that 18 percent of the lenders admitted discrimination against minority communities. Still no data on race were collected. In 1974, the four banking regulatory agencies participated in a one-time pilot survey program on all home loan applications (Federal Home Loan Bank Board 1975; Federal Reserve Board and the Federal Deposit Insurance Corporation 1975; Comptroller of the Currency 1975). In reviewing the results before the Senate Banking Committee, Massachusetts Institute of Technology economist Lester Thurow indicated that there was virtually "a zero probability" that the consistent patterns of higher loan denials for minorities could have occurred without a pattern of race discrimination (Thurow 1976).

In 1975, the Home Mortgage Disclosure Act was passed. In an early draft it included individual loan data on race and income. The final form, however, only provided for aggregate loan disclosure by census tract. As Squires discussed in his introduction, a lawsuit filed by thirteen civil rights groups in 1976 (Urban League, et al. 1976) resulted in three of the regulatory agencies (the FDIC, the FHLBB, and the OCC) adopting loan-log registers with data on race and income. Two of the agencies (the FDIC and the OCC) dropped the logs when the settlement terms expired in the early 1980s. The third agency, the FHLBB, failed to use the data from its logs in examinations.

When the summary data from these logs was secured by the *Atlanta Journal/Constitution* through a Freedom of Information Act request, the data revealed huge differences between white and minority rejection rates in metropolitan areas all across the country (Dedman 1989b). Because the data listed disparities in loan rejection rates for whites and minorities for the fifty largest metropolitan areas in the country, stories appeared in many local newspapers such as in Baltimore, Boston, Cleveland, Milwaukee, and Minneapolis. Dedman's analysis revealed that the disparities in lending over the years had actually increased. This precipitated amendments to HMDA in 1989 that required lenders—this time including mortgage banking companies—to disclose loan application data by race, sex, and income.

Many people thought that a twenty-year battle for racial recordkeeping and disclosure had been won. Now that Congress had amended the HMDA to require disclosure by all significant lenders and to require disclosure of data on the race, sex, and income of the buyer, along with data on applications and rejections, the public would have more access to better data to track the dual market all across the nation. Yet when the Fed developed the regulations for this disclosure, it postponed release of the HMDA data from March of each year until at least October—even though the Fed required the lending institutions to file copies of the data with the regulatory agencies earlier than ever before. Technically, the amendments that provided for disclosure of data on race, gender, and income were *in addition to* the existing HMDA requirements to provide data on the locations of loans. Nonetheless, the Fed used the requirements of the amendments to postpone any disclosure of any HMDA data to the public.

Civil rights groups were particularly concerned about overall patterns of adverse treatment of individual minority borrowers compared to whites. Community groups were more concerned about discrimination against neighborhoods with substantial minority populations. Those with experience in research and community reinvestment universally agreed that the disclosure regulations needed to provide the public with data on the race of applicants and loan recipients by census tract. When the Fed released the format for public disclosure, however, there was no provision for disclosing lending activity by race and census tract together.

There were ten sets of disclosure tables produced for each lender. For the whole nation, the Fed pointed out that the stack of disclosure reports was taller than the Washington Monument. Throughout this paper trail, the Fed had refused to release racial lending patterns by census tract. The Fed refused to release to the public, at the lending institution or at the regional depositories, the individual loan logs that lenders supplied to regulators in compliance with the new HMDA requirements. These data would be available only to those with sophisticated computer equipment who could purchase and analyze computer tapes from the Fed (tapes that would not become available until months after the October release of the HMDA tables). Since the critical intervention in the dual market is to identify the small areas on the edge of change and to compare lending in one neighborhood versus another, the omission of these data from public disclosure is a devastating blow to the community groups who have been the major enforcers of the CRA. To release these data only to those with the sophistication and economic resources to use computers is a form of discrimination in effect.

While the Fed denied the public access to the racial lending data, its own economists at the Fed in Washington and in Boston ran their own analysis of the data. On October 21, 1991, the Fed released the Washington Fed study results of the national data (Canner and Smith 1991). The results show huge disparities between loan rejection rates for whites and minorities. Nationally, whites were rejected about 14 percent of the time while Hispanics were rejected 21 percent of the time and African-Americans were rejected almost 34 percent of the time. The Fed tried to explain the differences by noting that minorities often have more employment instability and less net worth than whites; but these disparities were not eliminated when one controlled for income. Indeed, the data in the Fed study revealed that high income African-Americans were rejected at rates higher than low-income whites. Moreover, an earlier study by the Mortgage Insurance Companies of America had revealed that when it reviewed the performance of its loans by income, across all categories of loans, lower-income borrowers had lower default rates than higher-income borrowers (Carlton 1988: 356–57).

At the time of the press conference to release these data, John LaWare said that he was concerned and that these problems would be investigated. Ironically, just the month before, the Board of Governors of the Federal Reserve System, including LaWare, had unanimously re-

259

jected a proposal to engage in a program to test lenders for discrimination in lending. Even in the face of massive evidence of a problem in discrimination, the Fed refused to engage in practices to increase its enforcement efforts.

INDUSTRY RESTRUCTURING, THE CHANGING REGULATORY CLIMATE, AND THE IMPLICATIONS for REINVESTMENT

There are four dominant trends in the traditional banking industry and one overall trend in financial industries as a whole that are critical to reinvestment issues. One trend is toward increasing standardization in loan and service products. The second trend is toward increasing consolidation and concentration. The third trend is toward cost accounting for specific products, services, and functions. The fourth trend is the integration of local and financial institutions into international financial markets. Each poses challenges to the reinvestment movement.

The initial deregulation of the savings and loan industries in the 1970s allowed these institutions to start paying higher interest rates on their deposit accounts. As lenders competed for deposits, they often found themselves paying more on deposits than they collected on the inventory of housing loans in their portfolios. The crisis this created caused the industry to introduce measures to protect itself from these problems in the future. One measure was the use of floating interest-rate loans, so that interest rates on loans kept pace with interest rates paid on deposits. Another was to sell loans in the secondary market. This allowed lenders to treat their loans as liquid assets, so that they could change their portfolio of loans to avoid a squeeze of profits between the interest paid for accounts and the interest gained from loans.

Commercial banks participated in these measures as well. Small commercial banks had to raise interest rates on loans as they raised interest rates on deposits in order to compete with larger institutions. Loans with floating rates became the norm for commercial lending. Large commercial banks had to seek new investments as corporations increasingly turned to stocks and bonds—instead of bank loans—as a means of raising capital. Large losses in particular industrial sectors (such as energy), regional losses in real estate markets, and losses in foreign investments all put additional pressures on lenders to find new, high-return markets to cover losses and provide the necessary profits for growth. Higher costs for

260

funds placed a squeeze on profit margins. Competition with other financial service providers forced depository institutions to reduce consumer costs and fees in the most competitive areas—reducing profit margins. Lenders sought to reduce overhead and develop products that were the most cost efficient.

Standardization

One major result of the increased competition is the trend toward standardized deposit and loan products. Standardized products have lower overhead and need less processing—as well as less skill—to implement. This is true throughout the financial services industries. For example, as lenders seek to find markets to sell their loans, there has been a phenomenal growth in secondary markets, especially in home mortgage lending. Home mortgage lending is a simple industry with relatively few loan products and very basic underwriting procedures. The Federal National Mortgage Association (FNMA, or Fannie Mae) is the largest secondary mortgage market institution. It purchased or securitized over $120 billion in mortgages in 1990. The second largest secondary institution is another quasi-government entity—the Federal Home Loan Mortgage Corporation (FHLMC, or Freddie Mac). It purchased or securitized about $70 billion in mortgages in 1990. These secondary market institutions specialize in standardized types of mortgages—what Fannie Mae calls "plain vanilla mortgages." Efforts to create secondary markets for special kinds of development loans have not been as successful as the development of markets for simple, standard, loan products.

Consolidation and Concentration

When the reinvestment movement began in the early 1970s, there were almost 20,000 banks and savings institutions. By 1990, there were only 16,000 left (Bureau of the Census 1973; *The U.S. Savings Institutions Directory* 1990; and *Thompson Bank Directory* 1991). The greatest part of this decline has come in the savings and loan industry, whose number declined by 40 percent during this time. More recently, the number of commercial banks has been declining by several hundred each year. There are two major reasons for these declines. First, massive financial failures in the savings and loan industry—with a growing incidence of failures among commercial banks—have been primarily responsible for the decline in the number of institutions. Second, with the advent of interstate banking, banks have been able to compete on a regional level—and in some cases on a national level—for the banking business in each state. Prior to the efforts of states in the 1980s to change their laws and allow for interstate banking, depository institutions used a myriad of "nonbank" institutions to move across state lines and establish a base of deposits and loans. Nonbanks are institutions that serve limited roles, such as taking deposits or servicing loans, but are not technically defined as banks. The proliferation of interstate banking laws in the 1980s has allowed regional banks to spread into adjoining states, and sometimes to hopscotch across the country, in order to open full-service institutions. The result has been consolidation in local and regional markets and the emergence of several new regional banks, adding to existing banks that already operate on a national and international scale.

Now, there is a new wave of growth. In addition to continuing past trends of consolidation of local and regional institutions, the new growth results from the mergers of some of the regional giants, such as the mergers of Manufacturers Hanover Trust and Chemical Bank or Bank of America and Security Pacific (long-time giants), or the merger of North Carolina National Bank (NCNB) and C & S/Sovran (two winners of the regional growth wars).

The financial crisis in the savings and loan and commercial banking industries has produced government responses that support additional concentration. As institutions fail, the assets of failing institutions are folded into existing institutions in "regulatory" mergers or "forced" mergers and acquisitions. Whatever changes take place at the federal levels will surely encourage these consolidations—in addition to expanding the range of new businesses that will be permitted under the banking laws. The move toward national branching will support more acquisitions and mergers. Congress is consciously and deliberately developing policies aimed at producing what it believes to be a banking system with fewer, but stronger, institutions. This will be a banking system with less focus on lending and more focus on other financial services. This is supposed to give us a banking system that is financially sound nationally and more competitive internationally.

Unit Pricing and Accounting

The third trend that emerges from the past financial problems of the banking industry is the move toward cost accounting by the individual services, products, and functions within a lending institution. In the past, there were some functions, such as check processing, where lenders tended to monitor the costs with some precision; but in general, profitability was measured over entire divisions of an institution, for entire product lines, or even over the entire institution as a whole. Today, lenders attempt to define the costs associated with each activity and with each specific product and service. This has led to unit pricing for some services, such as business checking accounts with a basic charge for an account and then specific unit charges for each check cashed and each deposit made. In a larger sense, this has focused attention on the profitability of each operating unit and each function of the lending institution as a cost center in itself. This forces each unit to defend its profitability within the lending institution. This also places an emphasis on short-term profits over front-end investments that may not yield profits for some time—investments like reinvestment programs and economic development activities.

Globalization and Total Market Competition

Added to these three trends in the domestic banking industry is the integration of local and national financial institutions into international financial markets and industries creating a total competition for all credit products and services. Here investments in loans of any kind compete with investment in all other forms of financial services and products— and in a world-wide market. In light of the traditional, commodification approach to housing discussed by Squires, this next "higher" stage of industry restructuring portends reduced levels of capital for housing for this nation's disinvested communities.

All of these trends have important implications for affordable housing production and the economic development goals that are part of community reinvestment. Reinvestment often involves developing fairly complex programs, building specialized capacities, or working with financing packages that involve many investors, grants, subsidies, and loans together. Reinvestment often involves relatively small loans with a need for careful underwriting and monitoring. This means a higher transaction cost than a lender could get on larger loans with more standard and routine underwriting requirements. The performance of reinvestment loans has generally been quite good—with some of the major reinvestment programs reporting losses that are much lower than their regular portfolios (Bradford 1990). Aside from the requirements of the CRA, reinvestment has no regular role in the banking industry, and the needs of reinvestment stand at odds with some of the trends in the banking industry.

The present need for mortgage credit in the housing markets is fed by the growth of the secondary mortgage markets. These markets have prospered on the basis of standardized loan products. Lenders have responded by seeking borrowers that meet the "plain vanilla" parameters of the secondary markets. For people in inner-city areas with older homes needing major repairs, for lower-income people, for people in areas where there is a wide variation in housing construction types and a mix of land uses, and for people in minority communities the increasing standardization leaves them out of the market. The desire to minimize underwriting costs works against lower-income buyers, older homes, and communities where more complex lending and rehabilitation programs are needed. Small loan sizes and more complex loans make the loans less profitable at origination though frequently more secure in the long run. Where there are seriously decayed multifamily buildings, the programs necessary to rehabilitate these units require loan products that are some-times extremely complex. With the increased centralization of bank management at central offices, lending authority and flexibility in lend-ing are often removed from the local branches and offices. This results in less responsiveness to community needs.

For business lending, the consolidation of the banking system cre-ates larger banks with more sophistication. But this sophistication is not focused on the needs of depressed communities. Rather this sophistica-tion is aimed at the development of new products and services for the upscale, large corporate, or international markets. Retail lending services are also subject to standardization in the business area. For example, a study in New England found that while the recent period of deregulation and bank concentration had not eclipsed credit in rural areas, borrowers reported the greatest difficulty in getting loans from the larger institu-tions and lenders that were affiliated with large holding companies (Markley 1990).

Access to banking services is another problem exacerbated by these trends. In testimony before the House Banking Committee, finan-cial researcher Jonathan Brown (1991) pointed out that the largest insti-tutions do not provide the most complete services or services at the most competitive rates. In New York, for example, Brown cites a study by the New York City Department of Consumer Affairs that reviewed the "value of their checking accounts to low-balance and medium balance depositors." Citibank, the largest bank in the nation, ranked forty-seventh out of the forty-nine banks in the survey. Brown cites a New York state agency study of lending rates for New York City that found the largest banks among those with the highest interest rates. In general, Brown notes that numerous studies of concentration and its effects on product pricing show consistently that costs for the customers increased with increased concentration of the markets in fewer, but larger, institutions.

In many areas, two or three lending institutions already control the vast majority of deposits. The control of the market is concentrated at levels that would normally be defined as monopolies—but in the banking industries, the federal goal is actually to increase this concentration. As acquisitions and mergers have taken place, some patterns have emerged. As lenders expand, they acquire institutions with locations in high growth areas—sometimes closing branches and offices in low-growth or depressed communities. For many inner-city communities, the location of branches and the hours of operation and services are major concerns—and the subject of CRA challenges. As lenders seek to reduce all costs for each unit of activity, facilities in inner-city and rural areas are at a disadvantage compared to high-growth areas. Where older communities have an advantage for the lenders it is in providing deposits that can be used to finance loans in newer and higher-income communities. As concentration increases, there are fewer lenders to serve local communities.

But there is evidence that lenders are likely to withdraw their services altogether from lower-income and minority communities. In Milwaukee, people first organized around a closing of a financial institution and the loss of deposit and lending services. As a result of that campaign, the institution remained in the community. In Illinois where the community reinvestment movement had resulted in the governor establishing the first state commission on redlining, one of the key background studies traced the branching and relocation patterns of savings and loans in Chicago, revealing that between 1960 and 1974 these institutions had leapfrogged from the south, to the west, and then to the north as the minority populations moved into the areas they originally served (Feins, Grothaus, and Bradford 1975). A major study in New York City examined the record of branch openings and closings from 1978 through 1988, finding similar patterns of disinvestment in lower-income and minority communities (Leichter 1989).

As Squires observed in the introduction, one consequence of the concentration and globalization of financial institutions is that housing investment must increasingly compete with virtually all other types of investment. For the larger banks with international markets, any form of domestic lending has to be competitive with alternative foreign investments. Seen in this light, the inner-cities and rural areas of America are competing directly with development lending in the Third World and business investments in all the industrialized and post-industrialized nations.

Where lenders engage in community lending, the regulatory agencies have shown a tendency to consider these loans as automatically having higher risks. The National People's Action met with representatives of the Comptroller of the Currency and with the chairman of the Federal Reserve in the summer of 1991 to express their concern at reports from lenders that regulators were forcing them to classify community loans as "nonperforming" loans even though the payments have always been made on time and in full. Some proposals for changing the deposit insurance system would link rates to the risk of the loan portfolio for a lender. If the regulatory agencies fail to understand the soundness of community loans, this could force community lenders to pay higher insurance premiums. Banks pay no deposit insurance at all on foreign deposits, even though the government fully covers these deposits in case of bank failure. Thus, lenders are encouraged to seek foreign deposits while they are discouraged from making investments in older, rural, inner-city, lower-income, or minority communities here at home.

Perhaps the most serious implication of industry restructuring and changes in the regulatory climate is the growing direct attack on the CRA. When Congress engaged in debate on the banking reform legislation proposed during 1991, several direct proposals were made to eliminate the power of the CRA. William Seidman, retiring head of the FDIC said that he thought that the CRA was no longer needed. Small institutions claimed that the CRA created massive reporting burdens and that small lenders naturally served their communities anyway. Larger institutions claimed that if they had a passing rating on their CRA examinations by the regulators (ratings that have been made public since July 1990), then they should be exempt from any future CRA challenges at least for several years.

In both the House and Senate, amendments to the banking bills proposed creating exemptions from the CRA (and even the HMDA and other banking and fair housing regulations) for small institutions (generally those with less than $100 million). Amendments in both houses also created "safe harbor" provisions for institutions with passing CRA ratings—exempting them from reviews and challenges for certain activities and certain periods of time. The proposed exemption of institutions with assets under $100 million dollars would exempt about 85 percent of all institutions from coverage by the CRA. Lax regulation has always produced only a few lenders that do not get passing CRA ratings. One national review of the first full year of public ratings (CRA/HMDA Update 1991:8) revealed that 86 percent of all institutions received passing ratings. The combination of exemptions for size and safe harbor would exclude all but a tiny number of lenders from any CRA requirements at all.

In responding to claims that CRA creates a huge burden, community groups pointed out that the only requirements of the CRA are that the lender develop a statement of the community it will serve (with a map) and define the types of credit it will make available to this community. Such statements are often only two or three pages long and hardly change from year to year. In addition, a lender must keep a public file with the CRA statement, the public rating, and any comments filed with the lender on CRA issues. Finally, the lender must post a standardized public notice informing the public about the CRA, the statement, and file. These are the only formal requirements. Community people maintain that if a lender actually makes community loans and provides banking services, those records leave their own trail in the banker's files.

Research suggests that small lenders do not necessarily serve their communities better than large institutions, in spite of the high interest rates and costly banking services found among many of the largest lenders. In addition, some areas of the country are dependent upon small lenders. A Ford Foundation study of banks in West Virginia showed that the majority of all bank assets in the state were in banks with less than $100 million in assets (Boggs, Sorenson, and Isserman 1988). Compared to the country as a whole, these were among the most well capitalized, most profitable banks in the nation. Yet these banks, on average, had one of the lowest loan-to-deposit ratios of the banks in any state. Their overall loan to deposit ratio was just 58 percent—compared to 76 percent for the nation. Their commercial loan-to-deposit ratio was only 10 percent—compared to 25 percent for the nation. In Iowa, where ICCI reviewed the records of the small lenders that dominate many communities in that state, they found similar problems in 1991, with some lenders having loan to deposit ratios of less than 25 percent. In reviewing the lists of CRA ratings, the authors found that small lenders actually have higher levels of noncompliance ratings with the CRA than large lenders.

At the same time, the public CRA ratings seem to be inconsistent and in many cases fail to reflect serious CRA problems. In Chicago, the Harris Bank and First National Bank both developed similar neighborhood lending agreements, yet the Comptroller of the Currency gave First National Bank an outstanding rating while the Fed failed Harris. Several ratings reviewed by the authors mention numerous and continual violations of the Fair Housing laws, yet those lenders were given passing, and even outstanding, ratings. One lender was given an outstanding rating with a major emphasis on the lender's participation in developing a city business loan program, when, in fact, the lender was not eligible to participate in the program. The Harris Bank in Chicago has been a major supporter of multifamily loans for affordable rental housing—the most serious need for low-income people. It was failed by the Fed while the Fed gave outstanding ratings in New York to both Manufacturers Hanover and Chemical Bank. Together these two banks have more than $100 billion in assets to serve the city with the largest multifamily housing problems and needs in the nation. Yet, between them, these two lenders made only one multifamily loan in 1990. These developments illustrate the problems with relying on public ratings for creating safe harbor for lending institutions.

BACK TO THE FUTURE: COMMUNITY ORGANIZING AS THE KEY TO REINVESTMENT

Today, it is evident that what has been achieved in terms of the right to intervene, the obligations of lenders, and the resources to intervene cannot be taken for granted. When HMDA was first passed, it had a five-year sunset provision. Community groups had to mount a national effort to save HMDA and then to make it a permanent law. This required organizing a national campaign, year after year, for several years until the goal was reached. The lessons of the summer of 1991 show that even permanent laws like CRA and HMDA cannot be taken for granted—and efforts to strengthen them also open up opportunities to gut them. The only protection is a strong base of constituents who will fight for the protection of these laws.

This will require the cooperative efforts of community action groups, community development organizations, civil rights and fair housing groups, and all of the local cities and agencies that recognize the need for private reinvestment to meet area housing and community development needs. While this effort will require organizing at the national level, these attempts to create national coalitions will fail if they do not recognize the primacy of strong local groups. In opposing the effort in 1991 to gut the CRA, there were several national coalitions and organizations at work in Washington. Nevertheless, a review of the successful efforts to ward off these attacks reveals that the real strength of the opposition was based in the power of local groups. Senators and congressmen knew that these issues were of concern to local groups in their districts because these groups made that clear. In at least two cases in the House, the pressure of local groups—even actions at the home of one legislator (Nawrocki 1991)—convinced them that people cared about this legislation, and they changed their previous votes and defeated the efforts to gut the CRA. In the Senate, one opposition senator was so impressed with the concern his constituents showed that he even helped convince one of the sponsors of the legislation to gut the CRA to give up on his attempts to do so.

Keeping a primary focus on building and maintaining the strength of local groups is vital for another reason. Once the laws are in place, reinvestment needs to take place at the local level, where programs and policies can be tailored to the differing needs of each community. Programs have to be held accountable to the local community. The source of both the development of programs and the community accountability is a strong local base of community organizing complemented by activities that build the capacity of local communities to engage in development activities themselves. All of the other facets of reinvestment hinge upon the driving force of strong community organization.

269

Calvin Bradford and Gale Cincotta

Government agencies and officials have often played a critical role in reinvestment policy and programs. Legislators like William Prox-mire (past chairman of the Senate Banking Committee) or Henry Gon-zalez (chairman of the House Banking Committee) have played essential roles in introducing and passing legislation. State and local government are defining all kinds of programs to use public funds and public powers to leverage banking funds for reinvestment (Peters, Stumberg, and Ward 1988; Stumberg 1990; and Flax-Hatch 1991). Many states have reinvest-ment requirements in their state banking laws, some with clear state-level CRA provisions. All of these programs, laws, and regulations can be of great benefit for reinvestment programs.

Yet, the public cannot depend upon the good will or good inten-tions of legislators or agency officials to monitor reinvestment. The first disclosure regulations to produce data on race and income were devel-oped in California in 1976 by a reform-minded regulator in the Califor-nia Department of Savings and Loan; but these regulations came before the development of a powerful statewide base of support for their use. Eventually, once the regulator left, the regulations were lost.

The Detroit case demonstrated how critical the state banking commissioner was in securing reinvestment agreements. If he had not delayed Comerica's application under that state's CRA, the agreements would never have been developed and the community might never have been able to gain a seat at the table for negotiations and monitoring. Still, this commissioner's job depended upon the governor who ap-pointed him. That governor failed to campaign in Detroit, taking the minority vote for granted. Ignored by the governor, many minorities did not vote and he lost his reelection bid. Now the governor and the bank-ing commissioner are gone.

These types of patterns repeat themselves at the local, state, and national levels. The lessons are that the organizing power of the commu-nity base is the only resource that can be depended upon to preserve reinvestment victories. At any given point, a legislator, an agency offi-cial, or some government agency can play an important part in an issue or policy; but over the long haul, community reinvestment remains a movement determined by people power.

The media frequently provides another valuable resource for rein-vestment by serving to make the issues known to the public. The Pulitzer Prize–winning articles published in the Atlanta Journal/Constitution (Ded-

270

man 1988), and the articles published in the *Detroit Free Press* (Everett, Gallagher, and Blossom 1988) which were nominated for a Pulitzer Prize, were major forces in gaining public recognition that redlining and discrimination in lending had not disappeared after the initial fight in the 1970s. The rash of redlining studies that appeared in newspapers across the country after these stories raised national awareness and contributed to an environment in which there was a window of opportunity to advance fair housing and reinvestment initiatives. The *Atlanta Journal/Constitution* articles on black and white rejection rates across the country (Dedman 1989a, 1989b) were directly tied to the legislation that amended HMDA to require disclosure of the race, gender, and income of loan applicants, and to the public disclosure of the CRA ratings for lenders. Efforts which had been frustrated for years were suddenly the focus of national attention that produced swift results.

But the participation of the media is a two-edged sword. When the media takes up the cause, it can be taken away from the community. In Atlanta, where the media coverage resulted in dramatic changes in legislation at the national level, the community never got a single CRA agreement. The community had hired an experienced consultant and devised a sound plan with the technical support and safeguards to enable lenders to make loans to low-income people who would normally not be eligible to own a home. Caught up in the media attack, the lenders made a sudden lending commitment that failed to have the sound provisions originally proposed by the community coalition. When the loans began to fail, this story spread in the lending and regulatory communities in the country and raised questions about the risks of community lending in general. In the name of reform, the lenders finally revised the program— adopting safeguards originally proposed by the community groups who had been cut out of the program.

Moreover, the media is influenced not only by the community perspective but also by the perspective of the lenders and regulators. A 1987 article in the *Wall Street Journal* (Schmitt 1987) surveyed banker's views of reinvestment agreements and found they saw them as "pure blackmail." Although citizens were exercising rights granted to them under federal law, this article became a rallying cry for lenders trying to resist the CRA challenges that accompanied interstate acquisitions and regional mergers. This article prompted the board members of one major foundation to reconsider its funding for CRA activities. Even after the

Calvin Bradford and Gale Cincotta

nationwide coverage of the redlining issues in 1988 and after the release of the HMDA data by the Fed in 1991, community groups involved in reinvestment activities—especially when there is the threat of filing a challenge to a bank's activities—are still portrayed in derogatory terms (*Business Week* 1988). In describing the creation, activities, and accomplishments of the new Fair Lending Project in Milwaukee, for example, *Business Journal* (Cooper 1991:1) described the group as a "pit bull" that used "confrontation" and "antagonism to motivate lenders." The media, like the politicians and government officials who often come to the aid of reinvestment, is no substitute for a strong community power base.

The waves of growth in interstate banking that gave rise to the vast majority of the reinvestment campaigns and agreements have revealed the centrality of strong community organizing in confronting the increased complexity of this interstate and megabank merger and branching activity. When the CRA was first passed, most community groups were generally concerned about single-family, and maybe multifamily, housing needs in their local communities. Their local lenders might engage in applications for relocation of an office or branch, but they routinely negotiated with the same lenders and so they developed a familiarity with the lending policies and even the lending officers of each institution.

With the advent of interstate banking this has changed. Now, groups are often faced with a new lender coming into a community from another state. An ACORN chapter in Phoenix, for example, found itself facing applications from banks in New York, Minnesota, and California. In order to evaluate the performance of a bank, they need information about the bank's local lending patterns in a location sometimes several thousand miles away. They need to know if this bank, one with whom they have never dealt and in some cases of whom they have never even heard, serves its local communities well. There may or may not be community groups back in the lender's home state that can respond to this question.

Even if they are able to assess the record of this incoming lender, they may have to deal with a regulatory agency in another region of the country. For instance, when Chase Manhattan applied to buy a bank in Phoenix, the application was to the Fed in New York, not to the local Fed in San Francisco which covers Arizona. In the case of Chemical Bank in New York acquiring Texas Commerce Bank, groups in Dallas

272

and San Antonio became involved in the application, again to the Fed in New York. This required not only contacting community groups in New York but also cooperating with community groups' efforts in Dallas and San Antonio.

In other cases the acquisition of a holding company is accompanied by applications to consolidate the banks of the holding company being purchased with the existing banks of the holding company making the acquisition. For example, when Norwest bank holding company, from Minnesota, buys a holding company in Cedar Rapids, Iowa, it applies to the Minneapolis Fed, but then it wants to merge this Cedar Rapids bank with its own Norwest bank in Iowa, which it owns from previous interstate activity. So, Norwest applies to the Comptroller of the Currency in Kansas City for this merger. Iowa Citizens for Community Improvement have been trying to work with Norwest on farm lending issues and because they have been rebuffed by the holding company, they want to file a challenge to this acquisition and merger. They now have to deal with two regulatory agencies, one in Minneapolis and one in Kansas City (each with the different regional districts and each with different time periods and processes for challenges and extensions of the review and comment period).

Add to this the concerns of two groups in Minnesota, the Duluth Reinvestment Coalition and Minnesota Community Organizations Acting for Change Together (COACT, which operates largely in the rural areas of Minnesota's farming region). These groups have been trying to deal with Norwest on its applications to consolidate twenty-three of its Minnesota banks into nine regional banks. This already involved filing challenges to the Comptroller of the Currency on five of these applications for mergers of Norwest's own banks. When these Minnesota groups discover Norwest's application to make the acquisition and merger in Iowa, they must file another challenge in Minnesota as well as begin to work with the groups in Iowa—not only to coordinate their efforts but also to see what kinds of agreements are made and to insure that agreements in one place do not get the lender off the hook on making agreements in another place.

The merger applications of some of the megabanks are so complex as to prohibit coordinated challenges from all of the concerned community groups across many states and cities. The merger of NCNB and C & S/ Sovran, for example, covers communities in nine states and almost forty metropolitan areas. In such cases it is clearly impossible to obtain the necessary information about the lending records of the institutions involved within the short period for making comments or filing a challenge to an application. Comment periods can be as short as ten days for a branch application or as long as thirty days for some mergers and acquisitions. The amount of disclosure data that may be reviewed has increased tenfold and will continue to increase if efforts to add commercial loan disclosure data prove successful.

Community groups need increasingly rapid and efficient communications as well as researchers and organizers who can focus on each application in order to effectively organize the concerned organizations. The problem of maintaining coalition solidarity in the face of banks' divisive strategies is a significant one even in one city—as in the Atlanta, Boston, and Milwaukee cases. The problem is magnified many times when challenges involve groups in several different states and many different cities when the groups have never worked with each other before. For instance, in the megamerger applications of NCNB and C & S/Sovran, and Manufacturers Hanover and Chemical, one organization—ACORN—made side deals with the lenders involved and left the many other organizations involved in the challenges negotiating with regulators willing to accept these small commitments as sufficient to resolve all the issues involved in multiple challenges. In a situation where groups cannot form working coalitions, they should not allow individual group negotiations and agreements to undermine their efforts to work with the lending institutions. This will be one of the major challenges for reinvestment organizing in the coming years.

Even when there is no challenge, it is important to develop sophisticated means of implementing agreements. This involves either developing a capacity within groups already dealing with the bank, or finding some outside resource to do the development work or to work with the local businesses to insure that the money moves into the community. Increasingly, we find that groups must contend both with the implementation issues of complex housing and economic development agreements and with multiple challenge or negotiation groups and even multiple regulatory agencies.

Trends in the banking industry and the continued evolution of policies for deregulating financial industries will require powerful and continual organizing to insure that strong community reinvestment provisions and obligations are maintained and nurtured. Current trends provide the wrong incentives to lenders for both community lending and community banking services. Full access to banking facilities and services (deposit services as well as loans) and strong community lending obligations are the major policy issues for the coming years. Reinvestment requires strong legislation to insure that increased concentration and deregulation are not used to justify abandoning local communities and sacrificing the progress that has been made.

There will be increased attention on the community side to branching patterns and to challenging lenders that do not provide services and accounts to all members of their communities. As concentration produces more and more virtual monopolies among the lenders that serve both urban and rural areas, basic banking services will grow as an issue, particularly if the larger institutions close more branches and increase the rates for basic banking services.

The major focus of most reinvestment programs has been on residential lending and this is where the greatest gains have been made. Many government housing programs now incorporate the reinvestment approach. The Financial Institutions Reform, Recovery, and Enforcement Act of 1989 (FIRREA) created an obligation on the part of lenders borrowing from the Federal Home Loan Bank system to pass a test for "community support." In addition to this requirement, FIRREA mandated the Federal Home Loan Bank system to create an Affordable Housing Program that would provide funds from the system to lenders engaged in producing low-income housing. In 1990, the passage of the Affordable Housing Act placed an obligation on jurisdictions receiving federal dollars to leverage the public funds provided by the act with matching funds. Private lenders should be the main source of these matching funds. If lending institutions do not respond to these programs, then more public funds will have to be appropriated by Congress. This provides an incentive for both liberals and conservatives to support these reinvestment programs or face larger budget expenditures for housing.

For reinvestment groups organizing must take place both around creating public funds for housing and around leveraging those funds through reinvestment programs. Three-way partnerships between the public, private, and community sectors that are now required by the Affordable Housing Act provide an incentive for bringing local and state governments into reinvestment programs, where they have been conspicuously absent in most communities. As the affordable housing crisis worsens, this may help create a wider coalition for reinvestment.

It has taken almost fifteen years for community organizing to restructure the support industries for residential lending, especially single-family lending. When the private mortgage insurance companies and the secondary mortgage market institutions, especially Fannie Mae and Freddie Mac, failed to restructure their own practices to eliminate redlining and discrimination against older communities and lower-income borrowers, the National People's Action led the campaigns to bring them to the negotiating table. Then the National Training and Information Center developed a series of experimental and pilot programs involving both the private mortgage insurance and secondary market institutions. These have been expanded into commitments for billions of dollars in loans and are moving toward changing the basic underwriting standards throughout the industries.

Attention has now turned to ensuring access at the lowest income levels, especially through multifamily investments in rental properties. These efforts have focused on voluntary partnership programs. Yet even with this progress, the records of Fannie Mae and Freddie Mac in serving low-income communities are quite limited. This has finally resulted in legislation that will require specific allocations of the investments by Fannie Mae and Freddie Mac to reach lower-income households and minority communities.

A major unfinished agenda is business lending. The large commercial banks that will be the main beneficiaries of expanded banking powers and interstate branching are commercial lenders, not housing lenders. Commercial lending is the real driving force of the local economy, especially for small and medium-sized firms that cannot raise money on their own through issuing stocks and bonds in the capital markets. Most CRA agreements, as the cases in this book illustrate, now contain business lending provisions. Some creative efforts are being made, as in Oakland, to define business needs and lending goals. But the business lending programs are often the least effective. There is no public information on business lending. There are no records like the property transfer and mortgage lien records for property loans that could provide some indication of the roles of financial institutions in serving the local needs for business lending. Even if the needs are identified, there is no way to tell who is or is not serving those needs.

In Chicago, there has been a limited form of commercial loan disclosure since 1974 for lenders that receive deposits from the City of Chicago. These records still need to be improved, but they can be collected without an unreasonable burden on the lending institutions (Flax-Hatch 1987). The Neighborhood Lending Programs that Chicago Reinvestment Alliance negotiated with three major downtown banks contained major business lending programs that set a standard used in many later agreements. These lending programs were based on needs defined in the community and a review of the poor lending records of these financial institutions in commercial lending in the neighborhoods (Bradford 1990). The success of this approach suggests that commercial loan disclosure must have a high priority in order to realize the wider economic development goals of reinvestment and to make the public aware of the problems.

Within the broader context of the restructuring of the financial industries, the changing regulatory climate, and the need for resources that serve to develop strong community-based organizing, a number of research questions are raised. There is both academic research and action research that advances the reinvestment agenda. This discussion concentrates on the latter. The difference is not in the quality of the research, though one of the authors of this chapter discovered in doing a survey of HMDA uses and reinvestment agreements that there was an *inverse relationship* between the sophistication of the research and the size and quality of the reinvestment programs achieved.

As an experienced organizer in reinvestment, Shel Trapp describes the role of research in moving the issues this way:

> At NTIC, we put a lot of effort into research, but we
> know that without organizing, that research is useless.
> One organization used computers and projections to do a
> very sophisticated piece of reinvestment research in a
> certain city. They charged a hefty fee and are negotiating
> for a similar contract in another city, but to date, not
> one dollar of reinvestment has been generated. In con-
> trast, NTIC did a one-day research/organizing training ses-
> sion in a different city six months ago which resulted in
> a $1,250,000 reinvestment program for the community.
> Expecting research without organizing to accomplish

something is like expecting a eunuch to become a father.
It just doesn't work.

(Trapp 1986: 14–15).

This is not to say that community research is less concerned with
accuracy and correctness than academic research. One could argue quite
the contrary. If an academic is wrong about some point, nothing is
harmed but the reputation of the researcher. If research about community conditions, needs, or issues is wrong, the entire community will
suffer. Therefore, while community groups do not have the resources for
massive academic studies applying complex methodologies—or have the
time to engage in projects that take many months or even years to complete—the community is concerned about the research being as sound as
possible within the constraints of time and budget that political reality
imposes.

In general, research providing information that can be used by a
wide range of groups in different contexts is better than very intensive
studies of particular problems or narrowly focused research questions. In
policy development through organizing, information is a tool for interaction and change. People learn by experience and in the process of intervention. Research that provides an initial point of intervention or that
provides groups with material to raise an issue is most important. In the
process of interaction and negotiation, more detailed information, cor-
rections, and revisions are incorporated into the process of organizing
and policy development as issues are fine-tuned and developed. Given
this perspective, some of the key research issues for the future are the
following:

• There is a need to review the ratings given by regulators against
community evaluations of those lenders' records to show the problems
with the rating process. This would be valuable in hearings about the
ratings and CRA enforcement by the regulators. This would focus
attention on the problems of using ratings for creating safe harbor,
and it would help encourage better evaluations.
• There is a need to evaluate the outcomes of reinvestment programs.
We have several programs that have been in existence for several
years, but only one formal, detailed evaluation of the reinvestment

programs in Chicago and some occasional reports and anecdotal information about other programs. This would help in the development of more effective programs and it would provide more systematic data about what does and does not work—as well as providing data about the real risks and losses in these efforts.

- There is a need to study the patterns of branching, acquisition, and merger to see which institutions are most active and what effects these activities have on which communities are served and which communities are not served. These efforts should also investigate the levels of concentration (share of deposits and monopolies) that result from these activities.

- There is a need to investigate the new HMDA data on race, gender, income, and home lending to assess levels of discrimination and to develop techniques for identifying institutions for complaints, challenges, testing, and litigation. The results of these studies should compare the analysis of HMDA data with the public ratings given to the lenders by their regulators. This can provide material for oversight hearings on fair lending enforcement.

- In the general area of HMDA analysis, community groups need support systems that can serve as clearinghouses for access to HMDA data and for assistance in analyzing the HMDA data, especially under the deadlines of the comment periods for possible challenges. Very few groups have the computer capacity to use these data effectively, and most groups do not need to develop such a capacity for their normal operations.

- There is a general need for clearinghouse functions for HMDA data, CRA agreements, and other sources of information on banking institutions and community reinvestment programs. These types of information can be valuable in challenges, in legislative campaigns, in program development, in negotiating agreements, and in monitoring programs. The body of information is now quite large and beyond the practical means of most organizations involved in reinvestment.

As is the case with supportive public officials and media, professional research support can be ephemeral. But where the research effort is grounded in a strong community-based organizing effort, it can be a powerful tool for reinvestment.

Calvin Bradford and Gale Cincotta

THE QUID PRO QUO FOR DEREGULATION
AND EXPANDED BANKING POWERS

When the CRA was passed, there was a powerful debate between the community interests and the regulators over the format for implementing the law. The regulators decided to reject any form of specific targeting or allocation of credit in favor of leaving the means of meeting the objectives of the Act up to each lender and the community. This has provided much more flexibility and freedom in designing unique local programs and policies. But it has failed to establish reinvestment as a serious goal in most lending institutions. In spite of all the visible progress documented in this book, the majority of needs are still unmet. Just as the reluctance of Fannie Mae and Freddie Mac to take seriously their commitments to serve low-income groups and minority individuals and communities has finally resulted in direct legislative allocations of their funds to meet these goals, there is a growing sentiment among many community interests and concerned legislators to move in that direction with banking institutions.

In 1977, the first national conference on bank reinvestment was held in Chicago. Conference participants included community leaders and representatives of many different financial services industries, from banks to pension funds. In one session, participants familiar with community development needs estimated how much funding it would take to address the majority of these needs. Those familiar with the assets of the financial industries calculated that these needs could be met for about 5 percent of the total assets of the financial industries. The participants who had first been impressed with the size of the need were suddenly struck with the minute level of all financial resources that the need represented. For all of the effort that has gone into reinvestment agreements, they still represent only a tiny fraction of this 5 percent.

The notion of introducing some direct allocation of credit for the expansion of banking privileges has been growing over the years. In the interstate banking law passed in Minnesota in 1986, the state defined a set of development lending categories and outlined a process whereby the state commissioner of commerce would negotiate with a bank entering the state to establish specific targets in these categories based on the bank's size and resources (Stumberg 1990). This has become a model for other state reinvestment legislation. In the federal legislation to provide

280

for national interstate branching, Representative Joseph Kennedy of Massachusetts proposed that institutions branching across state lines be required to make specific lending commitments as a condition for receiving those branching rights.

In the broadest sense, the banking industry is asking American taxpayers to provide the resources and insurance to bankroll the efforts of the largest American banks to compete with the largest foreign banks. They are asking to be permitted to engage in a whole new range of financial services, when it is evident that the expansion of any business into new areas creates an increased risk of failure. They want to move into the insurance industries and into stocks and bonds. This will not create more or better stocks or bonds for the public, nor will it create more or better insurance. It will only allow banks to take some of the business away from the institutions that already serve those markets. Research suggests that as these banks grow, their consumer products will become even more expensive to their clients (Brown 1991). The main markets that large banks want to serve in their lending are foreign markets, which will most likely take away American jobs.

Meanwhile they have already incurred such huge losses in their existing investments that the United States is in debt for hundreds of billions of dollars to bail them out. Local housing and economic development programs cannot be advanced in part because the national debt is so great. As if all of this is not enough to provoke the American people, the industry seeks to gut the CRA so that the banking system will have no legal obligation to serve the communities of America. Meanwhile, the reinvestment movement has been seeking only a small fraction of the total banking resources and has made a tremendous effort to organize and build its own development capacity to use these funds effectively to build a private economy in our American communities. Consequently, the numbers of reinvestment organizations and the range of allies is growing.

From the perspective of the banking industry, the battles to save the CRA which emerged in 1991 may seem like an indication of the vulnerability of the CRA. However, from the viewpoint of an organizer who sees strength in public outrage, the efforts of the banking industry to gut the CRA represent an offense that will result in a growth of the reinvestment movement. This time the movement may not be so patient with voluntary programs and agreements. The banking institutions have an opportunity to display their commitment and the creativity of the free market system—or they will confront the specter of reinvestment credit allocation as the quid pro quo for their new powers and rights.

References

Berry, Brian J. L. 1979. *The Open Housing Question: Race and Housing in Chicago, 1966–1976.* Cambridge, Mass.: Ballinger.

Boggs, Bruce S., Calvin Bradford, and William Duncan. 1986. "Commercial Credit and Rural Economic Development." Paper presented at the Symposium of the Rural Economic Policy Program (a collaborative program of the Aspen Institute for Humanistic Studies, the Ford Foundation, and the Wye Institute), May 7. Wye Island, Md.

Boggs, Bruce S., David J. Sorenson, and Andrew Isserman. 1988. *Commercial Bank Lending Patterns and Economic Development in West Virginia.* Berea, Ky.: Mountain Association for Community Economic Development and Regional Research Institute, West Virginia University.

Bradbury, Katharine L., Karl E. Case, and Constance Dunham. 1989. "Geographic Patterns of Mortgage Lending in Boston, 1982–1987." *New England Economic Review* (Sept./Oct.), 3–30.

Bradford, Calvin. 1979. "Financing Home Ownership: The Federal Role in Neighborhood Decline." *Urban Affairs Quarterly* 14 (3): 313–35.

———. 1983. "City Venture Corporation: A Case Study of the Politics of Public–Private Partnerships." *Journal of the American Planning Association* 49 (3): 326–35.

———. 1984. "Report on the Role of the Veterans Administration in Causing Rapid and Massive Racial Resegregation." Submitted to the Court by the plaintiffs in the case of *Jorman et al. v. Veterans Administration et al.* C.A. No. 77 C 581: Northern District of Illinois (May 18).

———. 1989. "Reinvestment: The Quiet Revolution," *Neighborhood Works* 12 (4): 1, 22–26.

———. 1990. *Partnerships for Reinvestment: An Evaluation of the Chicago Neighborhood Lending Programs.* Chicago: National Training and Information Center.

———. 1991. "Never Call Retreat: The Fight against Lending Discrimination." In *Credit by Color: Mortgage Market Discrimination in Chicagoland*, ed. Catherine Cloud. Chicago: Chicago Area Fair Housing Alliance.

———. 1992. *Community Reinvestment Agreement Library.* Des Plaines, Ill.: Community Reinvestment Associates.

Bradford, Calvin, Leon Finney, Stanley J. Hallett, and John L. McKnight. 1979. *Structural Disinvestment: A Problem in Search of a Policy.* Evanston, Ill.: Center for Urban Affairs, Northwestern University.

Bradford, Calvin, and Dennis Marino. 1977. *Redlining and Disinvestment as a Discriminatory Practice in Residential Mortgage Loans.* U.S. Department of Housing and Urban Development. Washington, D.C.: U.S. Government Printing Office.

Bradford, Calvin, Leonard Rubinowitz, and Darel Grothaus, eds. 1975. *The Role of Mortgage Lending Practices in Older Urban Neighborhoods: Institutional Lenders, Regulatory Agencies and Their Community Impacts.* Evanston, Ill.: Center for Urban Affairs, Northwestern University.

Bradford, Calvin, and Michael Przybylski. 1979. *A Guidebook: Home Mortgage Disclosure Act and Reinvestment Strategies.* U.S. Department of Housing and Urban Development. Washington, D.C.: U.S. Government Printing Office.

Bradford, Calvin, and Paul Schersten. 1985. *A Tool for Community Capital: Home Mortgage Disclosure Act 1985 National Survey.* Minneapolis, Minn.: Hubert Humphrey Institute of Public Affairs, University of Minnesota.

Brown, Jonathon. 1991. Statement before the Committee on Banking, Finance, and Urban Affairs of the U.S. House of Representatives, Sept. 26.

Bureau of the Census, U.S. Department of Commerce. 1973. *Statistical Abstract of the United States 1973: National Data Book and Guide to Sources.* Washington, D.C.: U.S. Government Printing Office.

Business Week. 1988. "The 'Blackmail' Making Banks Better Neighbors." Aug. 15.

Canner, Glenn, B. and Dolores S. Smith. 1991. "Home Mortgage Disclosure Act: Expanded Data on Residential Lending." *Federal Reserve Bulletin* (Nov.): 859–81.

Carlton, J. Edward, Jr. 1988. Statement before the Committee on Banking, Housing, and Urban Affairs of the U.S. Senate, in hearings on the Community Reinvestment Act, March 22–23. Washington, D.C.: U.S. Government Printing Office.

Cincotta, Gale. 1981. Address delivered at the Tenth Annual National People's Action Convention, March 15. Baltimore, Md.

———. 1988. Statement before the Committee on Banking, Housing, and Urban Affairs of the U.S. Senate, in hearings on the Community Reinvestment Act, March 22–23. Washington, D.C.: U.S. Government Printing Office.

Clarke, Robert L. 1988. Letter (and attachments with analysis of the Atlanta situation) to Senator William Proxmire, Aug. 16. Washington, D.C.: Comptroller of the Currency.

Cloud, Catherine, ed. 1991. *Credit by Color: Mortgage Market Discrimination in Chicagoland.* Chicago: Chicago Area Fair Housing Alliance.

Committee on Banking, Housing, and Urban Affairs, U.S. Senate. 1975. *The Home Mortgage Disclosure Act of 1975: To Improve Public Understanding of the Role of Depository Institutions in Home Financing,* hearings May 5–8. Washington, D.C.: U.S. Government Printing Office.

Comptroller of the Currency. 1975. *Fair Housing Lending Practices Pilot Project: Form C Approach,* July 14. Washington, D.C.: Comptroller of the Currency.

Cooper, Geoff. 1991. "A Pit Bull for Milwaukee's Central City." *Business Journal* (Sept. 23–29).

CRA/HMDA Update. 1991. "First Year of 'Public' CRA Ratings," September. Washington, D.C.: Financial World Publications, 6–8.

Dane, Stephen. 1990. Statement before the Subcommittee on Consumer and Regulatory Affairs of the Committee on Banking, Housing, and Urban Affairs of the U.S. Senate, in hearings on discrimination in home mortgage lending, Oct. 5, 1989. Washington, D.C.: U.S. Government Printing Office.

Dedman, Bill. 1988. "The Color of Money." *Atlanta Journal/Constitution,* May 1–4.

———. 1989a. "Blacks Turned Down for Home Loans From S & Ls Twice as Often as Whites." *Atlanta Journal/Constitution,* Jan. 22.

———. 1989b. "Racial Lending Gap Less in South Than in Midwest." *Atlanta Journal/ Constitution,* Jan. 22.

Dickinson, Georgett B. 1987. Letter from Georgett B. Dickinson, Assistant General Counsel, Trust Company Bank to William B. Estes III, Examining Office, Federal Reserve Bank of Atlanta, October 22.

Everett, David, John Gallagher, and Teresa Blossom. 1988. "The Race for Money." *Detroit Free Press,* July 24–27.

Federal Home Loan Bank Board. 1972. *1971 Urban Lending Survey.* Washington, D.C.: Office of Housing and Urban Affairs, Federal Home Loan Bank Board.

———. 1975. *Fair Housing Information Survey: Form A Approach,* Aug. 18. Washington, D.C.: Federal Home Loan Bank Board.

Federal Reserve Board. 1988. "Federal Reserve Board Staff Analysis of *Atlanta Constitution* Study," with a cover letter to Senator William Proxmire from Alan Greenspan, Chairman of the Board of Governors of the Federal Reserve System, Aug. 8. Washington, D.C.: Federal Reserve Board.

———. 1989. Response to questions to the Federal Reserve Board by Senator Alan J. Dixon, in Subcommittee on Consumer and Regulatory Affairs of the Committee on Banking, Housing, and Urban Affairs of the U.S. Senate, hearings on enforcement of the Community Reinvestment Act, July 31. Washington, D.C.: U.S. Government Printing Office.

———. 1990. Reply to questions in the Subcommittee on Consumer and Regulatory Affairs of the Committee on Banking, Housing, and Urban Affairs of the U.S. Senate hearings on enforcement of the Community Reinvestment Act, July 31, 1989. Washington, D.C.: U.S. Government Printing Office.

Federal Reserve Board and the Federal Deposit Insurance Corporation. 1975. *Fair Housing Survey: Form B Approach,* May 2. Washington, D.C.: Federal Reserve Board and the Federal Deposit Insurance Corporation.

Feins, Judith D. 1976. "Urban Housing Disinvestment and Neighborhood Decline: A Case Study of Public Policy Outcomes." Ph.D. diss., Department of Political Science, University of Chicago.

Feins, Judith, Darel E. Grothaus, and Calvin Bradford. 1975. "An Analysis of Relocations, Mergers, Branching, and Establishment of Facilities by Chicago Area Savings and Loan Associations." In *The Role of Mortgage Lending Practices in Older Urban Neighborhoods: Institutional Lenders, Regulatory Agencies, and Their Community Impacts,* ed. Calvin Bradford, Leonard Rubinowitz, and Darel E. Grothaus. Evanston, Ill.: Center for Urban Affairs, Northwestern University.

Finn, Charles. 1989. *Mortgage Lending in Boston's Neighborhoods, 1981–1987: A Study of Bank Credit and Boston's Housing.* Boston Redevelopment Authority.

Flax-Hatch, David. 1991. *Banking in the Public's Interest: Promoting Community Development with the Public Deposits of Cities and States.* Chicago: Woodstock Institute.

———. 1987. *Tracking Chicago's Business Bucks: Commercial Lending and the Chicago Municipal Depository Ordinance.* Chicago: Woodstock Institute.

Goldstein, Ira. 1986. "The Impact of Racial Composition on the Distribution of Conventional Mortgages in the Philadelphia SMSA: A Case Study." Philadelphia: Working paper, Institute for Public Policy Studies, Temple University.

Home Ownership Development Program, City of Baltimore. 1973. "Home Ownership and the Baltimore Mortgage Market. In Committee on Banking, Housing, and Urban Affairs 1975.

Kluckman, Jerauld C. 1990. Statement before the Subcommittee on Consumer and Regulatory Affairs of the Committee on Banking, Housing, and Urban Affairs of the U.S. Senate, in hearings on mortgage discrimination, May 16. Washington, D.C.: U.S. Government Printing Office.

Kolodny, Robert. 1985. *Organizing for Neighborhood Development: A Handbook for Citizen Groups.* Washington, D.C.: Center for Community Change.

LaWare, John. 1990. Statement before the Subcommittee on Consumer and Regulatory Affairs of the Committee on Banking, Housing, and Urban Affairs of the U.S. Senate, in hearings on discrimination in home mortgage lending, October 5, 1989. Washington, D.C.: U.S. Government Printing Office.

Leichter, Franz S. 1989. *Banking on the Rich: Commercial Bank Branch Closings and Openings in the New York Metropolitan Area, 1978–1988.* New York: Franz S. Leichter.

Markley, Deborah. 1990. *The Impact of Deregulation on Rural Commercial Credit Availability in Four New England States: Final Report to the Ford Foundation.* Amherst, Mass.: Department of Resource Economics, University of Massachusetts at Amherst.

Metropolitan Area Housing Alliance and National Training and Information Center. 1975. "Redlining and FHA: New Research Proves Dual Home Financing in Chicago Neighborhoods." In Committee on Banking, Housing, and Urban Affairs 1975.

Naparstek, Arthur J., and Gale Cincotta. 1976. *Urban Disinvestment: New Implications for Community Organization, Research, and Public Policy.* Washington, D.C.: National Center for Urban Ethnic Affairs and National Training and Information Center.

National Commission on Neighborhoods. 1979. "Neighborhood Reinvestment." In *People*

Building Neighborhoods: Final Report to the President and Congress of the United States, 65–127. Washington, D.C.: U.S. Government Printing Office.

National Congress for Community Economic Development. 1989. *Against All Odds: The Achievement of Community-Based Development Organizations.* Washington, D.C.: National Congress for Community Economic Development.

Nawrocki, Rochelle. 1991. "Iowa cci Wins Key Victory For cra!" *Disclosure* 124 (Sept.-Oct.), 1.)

Northwest Community Housing Association. 1973. "Mortgage Disinvestment in Northwest Philadelphia." In Committee on Banking, Housing, and Urban Affairs 1975.

Orfield, Gary, ed. 1988. *Fair Housing in Metropolitan Chicago: Perspectives after Two Decades.* Chicago: Chicago Area Fair Housing Alliance.

Peterman, William, and Qi Sanshi. 1991. "Lending Discrimination in Metropolitan Chicago: Continuing Connection Between Race, Racial Change and Mortgage Credit." In *Credit by Color: Mortgage Market Discrimination in Chicagoland,* ed. Catherine Cloud. Chicago: Chicago Area Fair Housing Alliance.

Peters, Farley, Robert Stumberg, and Roxanne Ward. 1988. *Legislative Sourcebook on Financial Deregulation.* Washington, D.C.: National Center for Policy Alternatives.

Proxmire, William. 1988. Comments of Senator William Proxmire before the Committee on Banking, Housing, and Urban Affairs of the U.S. Senate, in hearings on the Community Reinvestment Act, March 22–23. Washington, D.C.: U.S. Government Printing Office.

Przybylski, Michael, Joseph Gardner, and Edward Shurna. 1981. *Controlling Neighborhood Development: A Manual for Community Organizations.* Chicago: National Training and Information Center.

Quereau, Gay D., and Richard Obermanns. 1989. *Race and Mortgage Lending in Cleveland, 1987.* Cleveland: Cuyahoga Plan.

Schmitt, Richard B. 1987. "Public Service or Blackmail? Banks Pressed to Finance Local Projects." *Wall Street Journal,* Sept. 10.

Seidman, L. William. 1988. "Analysis of Housing Credit by State Nonmember Banks in Atlanta," with a cover letter to Senator William Proxmire, Aug. 22. Washington, D.C.: Federal Deposit Insurance Corporation.

Shlay, Anne B. 1985. *Where the Money Flows: Lending Patterns in the Washington, D.C. Maryland-Virginia smsa.* Chicago: Woodstock Institute.

———. 1987a. *Maintaining the Divided City: Residential Lending Patterns in the Baltimore smsa.* Baltimore: Maryland Alliance for Responsible Investment.

———. 1987b. *Credit on Color: The Impact of Segregation and Racial Transition on Housing Credit Flows in the Chicago smsa from 1980–1983.* Chicago: Chicago Fair Housing Alliance.

Smith, Shanna. 1990. Statement before the Subcommittee on Consumer and Regulatory Affairs of the Committee on Banking, Housing, and Urban Affairs of the U.S. Senate, in hearings on discrimination in home mortgage lending, Oct. 5, 1989. Washington, D.C.: U.S. Government Printing Office.

Squires, Gregory D., ed. 1989. *Unequal Partnerships: The Political Economy of Urban Redevelopment in Postwar America.* New Brunswick, N.J.: Rutgers University Press.

Squires, Gregory D., and William Velez. 1987. "Neighborhood Racial Composition and Mortgage Lending: City and Suburban Differences." *Journal of Urban Affairs* 9 (3): 217–32.

Stumberg, Robert. 1990. *Banking on the States: The Next Generation of Reinvestment Standards—Report to the Ford Foundation.* Washington, D.C.: Center for Policy Alternatives.

Thompson Bank Directory. 1991. New York: Thompson Financial Publishing.

Thurow, Lester, 1976. Statement before U.S. Senate Committee on Banking, Housing, and Urban Affairs, hearings on equal opportunity in lending and oversight of equal opportunity in lending enforcement by the bank regulatory agencies, March 11–12. Washington, D.C.: U.S. Government Printing Office.

Trapp, Shel. 1986. *Blessed Be the Fighters*. Chicago: National Training and Information Center.

Urban League et al. v. Comptroller of the Currency et al. 1976. C.A. No. 76–0718: Federal District Court, District of Columbia (April 26).

U.S. Department of Housing and Urban Development. 1974. *Private Lending Institutions Questionnaire: Initial Report on Returns*. Washington, D.C.: U.S. Department of Housing and Urban Development, Office of Fair Housing and Equal Opportunity. In Committee on Banking, Housing, and Urban Affairs, U.S. Senate, hearings on equal opportunity in lending and oversight on equal opportunity in lending enforcement by the bank regulatory agencies, March 11–12, 1976. Washington, D.C.: U.S. Government Printing Office.

U.S. Savings Institutions Directory. 1990. New York: Rand McNally.

Wall, M. Danny. 1988. Letter to Senator William Proxmire, August 19. Washington, D.C.: Federal Home Loan Bank Board.

Williams, Peter M. 1988. *Race and Mortgage Lending in New York City: A Study on Redlining*. New York: Center for Law and Social Justice, Medgar Evers College.

Zimmerman, Ronald N. 1990. "Lessons Learned from the Atlanta Mortgage Consortium." Atlanta: Federal Reserve Bank of Atlanta.

About the Contributors

CALVIN BRADFORD is president of Community Reinvestment Associates, a consulting firm specializing in housing and reinvestment. He has contributed to research and policy development in these areas for twenty years. Recent publications include *Partnerships for Reinvestment* (1990), "Never Call Retreat: The Fight against Lending Discrimination" (1991), and "Reinvestment: The Quiet Revolution" (1989).

LYNN M. BRAZEN was involved in the formation of the Atlanta Community Reinvestment Alliance and its subsequent CRA negotiations with Atlanta lenders. She serves on the Atlanta Mortgage Consortium advisory board and is president of the board of Southeastern Reinvestment Ventures, a community loan fund. Since 1990, she has been employed as Affordable Housing Specialist with the Federal Home Loan Bank of Atlanta.

JAMES T. CAMPEN is Associate Professor of Economics at the University of Massachusetts/Boston. His publications include *Benefit, Cost, and Beyond: The Political Economy of Benefit-Cost Analysis* (1986).

GALE CINCOTTA is a founder and present chairperson of the National People's Action and executive director of the National Training and Information Center. She was a member of the President's National Commission on Neighborhoods in 1978, received a Rockefeller award for distinguished citizenship, and was named a "Woman of the Year" by *Ms.* magazine.

DAVID EVERETT, Washington, D.C. business correspondent for the *Detroit Free Press*, has been a newspaper reporter and editor since 1974. His reporting has won local, state, and national awards and has taken him to twenty-seven states and eight foreign countries. Everett graduated from the University of Tennessee and taught journalism at Wayne State University.

STAN F. FITTERMAN received his master's degree in city planning from the Georgia Institute of Technology in 1988. He is currently the director of the Division of Housing Services for Citrus County, Florida.

About the Contributors

MICHAEL L. GLABERE is a veteran community organizer in Milwaukee. He is currently pursuing a doctoral degree in urban studies at the University of Wisconsin–Milwaukee.

LARRY E. KEATING is an associate professor in the Graduate Program in City Planning at the Georgia Institute of Technology. He is a cofounder and currently vice president and treasurer of the Community Design Center of Atlanta.

JOHN T. METZGER is a President's Fellow in the Ph.D. program in Urban Planning at Columbia University, and a research associate with the Real Estate Development Research Center. He has coauthored articles, book chapters, and reports on community reinvestment, local economic development, and urban planning. He was coordinator of the Pittsburgh Community Reinvestment Group, 1989–1990.

JEAN POGGE is vice president and manager of development at South Shore Bank, a community development bank in Chicago. Prior to joining the bank she was president of Woodstock Institute, a non-profit organization that explores and promotes forms of investment in disadvantaged communities. She has coauthored a number of Woodstock Institute publications, including *Tools for Lenders: A Guide to Successful Community Reinvestment* (1989), *Banking Services for the Poor: Community Development Credit Unions* (1991), and *The Business of Self-Sufficiency: Microcredit in the United States* (1991).

DAVID PAUL ROSEN is principal and founder of David Paul Rosen and Associates, a public interest consulting firm in Oakland, California, specializing in capital formation strategies for low-income and minority neighborhoods in the fields of affordable housing, economic development, and school finance. His most recent books include *Public Capital: Revitalizing America's Communities* (1990) and *Housing Trust Funds* (1989).

GREGORY D. SQUIRES is Professor of Sociology and member of the Urban Studies Program Faculty at the University of Wisconsin–Milwaukee. He is coauthor of *Chicago: Race, Class and the Response to Urban Decline* (1987) and editor of *Unequal Partnerships: The Political Economy of Urban Redevelopment in Postwar America* (1989).